The Experience of Language Teaching

CAMBRIDGE LANGUAGE TEACHING LIBRARY

A series covering central issues in language teaching and learning, by authors who have expert knowledge in their field.

In this series:

The Experience of
Language Teaching

Rose M. Senior

CAMBRIDGE UNIVERSITY PRESS
Cambridge, New York, Melbourne, Madrid, Cape Town, Singapore, São Paulo

Cambridge University Press
The Edinburgh Building, Cambridge CB2 2RU, UK

www.cambridge.org
Information on this title: www.cambridge.org/9780521612319

First published 2006

Printed in the United Kingdom at the University Press, Cambridge

Typeface 9/11pt Sabon   *System* QuarkXPress™

A catalogue record for this book is available from the British Library

Library of Congress Cataloging-in-Publication Data

Senior, Rose M.
The experience of language teaching / Rose M. Senior.– 1st ed.
    p. cm. – (Cambridge language teaching library)
Includes bibliographical references and index.
ISBN 0-521-61231-4 – ISBN 0-521-84760-5
1. Language and languages–Study and teaching.   I. Title.   II. Series.

P51.S42 2006
418.0071–dc22

                                                    2005033655

ISBN–13   978-0-521-84760-5 hardback
ISBN–10   0-521-84760-5 hardback
ISBN–13   978-0-521-61231-9 paperback
ISBN–10   0-521-61231-4 paperback

To language teachers everywhere

Contents

Contents

List of figures

Acknowledgements

This book would not have been possible without the input and support of a number of people. First and foremost, I would like to express my sincere thanks to all the teachers who provided data for this book. In particular I would like to thank the teachers who participated in the second phase of the research, and who allowed me not only to interview them on a regular basis, but also to observe them teaching their lessons. I would also like to thank my colleagues at Curtin University who have surrounded and supported me over the years.

Certain individuals have been instrumental in helping me to refine my understanding of communicative language teaching. These include Zhichang Xu, with whom I spent many happy hours comparing and contrasting teaching approaches in Australia and China, and Paul Mercieca, who provided invaluable feedback on Chapters 2, 3 and 11. Vera Irurita cast her experienced eye over Chapter 1 and checked that I had provided an accurate representation of grounded theory development procedures, while Tony Marshall was kind enough to discuss the biological images in Chapter 12.

My most heartfelt thanks go to two people, without whom this book would not have come into being. The first is Michael Breen, who has unfailingly encouraged and supported me in my research. My work has benefitted greatly from Mike's critical input, always given with great generosity and sensitivity. The second person who has helped me to achieve my goal of writing this book is my husband Clive, who has supported me steadfastly in so many ways and with considerable patience and endurance. I could not have written this book without his good-humoured scepticism and consummate editorial skills.

Preface

Why I've written this book

I've written this book for a number of reasons. I've always wanted to share with others the wealth of insights that I've collected over the years through interviewing language teachers about their work. As my data-base has grown, so the pressure to share its contents with others has also built. Writing this book has given me the opportunity to synthesise and present the insights of language teachers in what I hope is an interesting and readable format.

Writing this book is also a way of expressing my sincere gratitude to all those teachers who have been so generous with their time, allowing me to interview them in depth. I feel I owe it to them to bring into the public domain their thoughts, feelings, practices and concerns – even though their identities remain hidden. I've found language teachers to be a dedicated, principled and articulate group of people – and I believe that their voices need to be more strongly heard.

I've enjoyed writing this book. Although the process of writing and rewriting text is enormously laborious and time-consuming, it can also be intensely satisfying and rewarding. This is particularly true when words can be found to express new concepts, when chapters begin to take shape, when sections fall into place – and when a coherent picture eventually starts to emerge.

I hope this book will make a useful contribution to the associated fields of classroom language teaching and classroom-based research. Living in the most isolated city in the world has, in a strange kind of way, been something of an advantage. Although in this electronic age physical distance is illusory rather than real, my physical isolation has enabled me to observe and to reflect upon current trends and debates in language teaching from a distance. This book marks the end of that isolation. I hope that the teacher insights presented here will contribute to current discussion and debate, and perhaps increase our understanding of what it means to be a language teacher.

Rose Senior
Perth, Western Australia

Introduction

What this book is about

This book is about what it is like to be a language teacher today. It describes the thoughts, feelings, beliefs, behaviours and daily practices of language teachers working in a range of teaching situations in English-speaking countries. The majority of the teachers teach English on intensive courses to adults, while a smaller number are involved in teaching languages to young people in schools. All the teachers interviewed or observed for the book are engaged in communicative language teaching, incorporating interactive speaking activities into their lessons on a regular basis.

> Carter and Nunan define communicative language teaching (CLT) as: 'an approach to the teaching of language which emphasises the uses of language by the learner in a range of contexts and for a range of purposes; CLT emphasises speaking and listening in real settings and does not only prioritise the development of reading and writing skills; methodologies for CLT tend to encourage active learner involvement in a wide range of activities and tasks and strategies for communication.' (2001: 219)

The book provides a frank and honest account of teachers' classroom practices from the perspective of those best able to provide it: the teachers themselves. It describes not only the way things should happen in language classrooms, but also the way things happen in practice. It describes the highs and lows of language teaching: the rewards and frustrations, the successes and failures, times when lessons flow smoothly and times when they do not. It describes how language teachers manage their classes and cope with the myriad events that are part and parcel of being a classroom language teacher.

The book presents a holistic picture of life in communicative language classrooms. It highlights the complexity of classroom life, by identifying the wide range of factors that influence the on-the-spot classroom decision-making of experienced teachers. It draws attention

1

to the many aspects of everyday teaching that are familiar to language teachers but seldom described – either by researchers or by teachers themselves. In particular the book highlights the reciprocal relationship between the behaviour of teachers and that of their classes, and the interrelated nature of teachers' pedagogic and class management practices.

Who this book is for

This book is intended for a wide readership that includes the following:

1. Language teachers who wish to read about classroom life that reflects their own experience. Such teachers may find it illuminating to have the classroom behaviour and practices with which they are familiar described and explicated.
2. Language teachers from around the world who would like to learn more about communicative language teaching as it is practised in western educational contexts.
3. Teacher trainers who wish to raise their trainees' awareness of the complexity of classroom language teaching, and who may be seeking alternative frameworks for teacher-development programs.
4. Diploma students interested in reflecting upon aspects of their current practice.
5. Postgraduate students who wish to identify an aspect of classroom language teaching to investigate in a research project.
6. Academics in the area of classroom-based research who are interested in qualitative research and the kinds of results it can produce.

How the book can be used

The book takes the form of a narrative text with an overall storyline that continues sequentially from chapter to chapter. It may be read in a number of ways depending upon the reader's area of specific interest. The following are some suggestions as to how the book might be used by different categories of readers:

- Those interested in obtaining a global impression of the experience of language teaching in communicative classrooms in English-speaking countries may wish to read the book in a sequential manner.
- Practising teachers who are interested in learning more about specific aspects of language teaching or managing classes of language learners may wish to dip into the book and read selectively. For example, they

may wish to obtain additional ideas on how to manage students in sensitive ways, or learn more about the role of humour in the language classroom.

- Teacher educators may wish to read a number of chapters in the book, selecting from them issues that they believe are important for trainee teachers to think about. They may choose to select real-life examples from within the chapters in order to stimulate discussion amongst either trainees or language teachers participating in professional development workshops.
- Readers with an interest in the application of group dynamics theory to language classrooms will find that many of the chapters, particularly Chapter 9, relate to this topic. Throughout the book they will find descriptions of both teacher and student classroom behaviour that relates to the construct of class cohesiveness.
- Readers who wish to learn more about grounded theory development procedures may find it informative to examine in some detail, and to reflect upon, the contents of Chapters 1, 11 and 12.
- Researchers in the area of teacher cognition research may find that the overall approach of the book (using teachers' impressions as a way of accessing the everyday reality of language classrooms) is of interest – together with the insights and caveats provided in Chapter 11.
- Those who have highlighted the gap between theory and practice, or lamented the lack of theoretical frameworks for understanding complex classroom processes, may find it interesting to consider whether the teacher-generated theory proposed in Chapter 12 may provide a possible way forward.

The purpose of the boxes

Each chapter contains a number of boxes that contain additional information and references designed to expand or illuminate the adjacent subject matter in the following ways:

- by providing references to research findings that reflect, expand upon or refine the insights provided by the teachers interviewed for the book;
- by giving selected quotations from educationalists whose general statements illuminate further the processes and practices described in the book;
- by providing suggestions for further reading.

The purpose of the boxes is: (1) to provide research evidence to support the insights provided by practising teachers; (2) to show where the book is located within the overall direction of classroom-based and teacher cognition research; and (3) to provide future researchers with leads that they may wish to follow up (either for alternative research approaches, or for new subject matter for classroom-based research). The boxes have been kept to a minimum in order not to interfere with the narrative flow of the text. They are not intended to be exhaustive.

The research basis for the book

This book draws on research conducted over a 12-year period (1992–2004). The research took the form of five interlinked studies, all of which were based on extended teacher interviews. A grounded theory approach was used to collect and analyse the data (see Chapter 1). The first of the studies led to the identification of the overall framework for the book, while the subsequent studies refined the insights from the first study and broadened the scope of the research.

A total of 101 teachers were interviewed during the course of the research. All the teachers were native English speakers with a university degree and a language-teaching qualification. However, the ages, educational backgrounds, qualifications and life experiences of the teachers varied considerably. The youngest were in their twenties, while the oldest were nearing retirement age. The majority of the teachers had worked in other fields, or had been engaged in other forms of teaching, prior to becoming language teachers.

A significant number of the teachers whose experiences and views are described in the book had either a certificate or a diploma awarded by Cambridge ESOL – 38 per cent had a Certificate in English Language Teaching to Adults (known as CELTA), while 22 per cent had a Diploma in English Language Teaching to Adults (known as DELTA). A further 4 per cent of the teachers had both CELTA and DELTA qualifications, while 18 per cent had completed, or were in the process of completing, degrees at masters or doctoral levels.

The Certificate in English Language Teaching to Adults (CELTA) is an initial qualification designed for people with little or no previous teaching experience. It can be taken in either full-time (four weeks) or part-time mode (12 weeks). The Diploma in English Language Teaching to Adults (DELTA) is an advanced TESOL/TEFL qualification for practising English-language teachers that can be taken in either full-time (2–3 months) or part-time mode (6–12 months). For further information see the website http://www.cambridgeesol.org/teaching/index.htm.

Those who did not have CELTA or DELTA qualifications (such as the foreign-language teachers interviewed in the fifth study) had obtained language-teaching qualifications that also prioritised the development of speaking skills and group work in the classroom. All the teachers who provided data for the book had therefore been exposed to the central precepts of the communicative approach as it is understood and practised at the present time in countries such as the UK and Australia.

Despite the commonalities in their training experiences, the teachers interviewed for the book were disparate in terms of their language learning and teaching experiences. Many had had the experience of being second-language learners themselves – although the conditions under which they had learnt and the degrees of proficiency they had attained varied greatly. A significant number of the teachers had spent time overseas, many of them working as English-language teachers. Their collective experiences involved teaching in countries as disparate as Malta, China, Japan and Argentina.

Study One

The first study examined the beliefs of 28 experienced teachers engaged in the teaching of English to adults across a range of programs in a single language centre attached to a university in Perth, Western Australia. I gave the teachers open-ended questionnaires in which they jotted down their ideas about good classes and lessons. Then, using their notes as a guide, I audio-recorded a 45-minute interview with each teacher, transcribing and analysing the data as soon as possible after each interview. This process of ongoing data collection and analysis enabled me to ask more probing questions of each subsequent interviewee.

The study set out to answer the following research question: What, in the minds of a sample of experienced language teachers, constitutes a good language class? The results provided clear evidence that, in the minds of teachers, good classes were those that functioned effectively as groups. The notion of class cohesiveness was therefore the central phenomenon, or core category, to which all other categories could be linked.

After reading extensively in the area of social psychology and gaining a broad understanding of how groups develop and function, I identified a framework from the group dynamics literature that could be used to guide the collection and analysis of the data for the subsequent studies.

Study Two

The second study was by far the largest of the five studies in terms of its breadth and the amount of data gathered. In it I documented the social–psychological development over time of eight individual language classes, each one taught by a different teacher. The teachers taught in five different educational institutions and taught classes ranging from beginners to advanced. The classes contained students from a wide range of nationalities and educational backgrounds. I documented the social evolution of each class from the first to the last day of each ten-week course, focusing particularly on individual and group behaviours that appeared to help or hinder the development and maintenance of class cohesion. I gathered data by doing the following:

1. Observing each class for three hours a week, noting down how students behaved individually, in small groups and collectively, and how the teachers taught and managed their classes.
2. Conducting 45-minute interviews with each teacher on a weekly basis, using my own notes and the teachers' weekly teaching programs as a starting point. I encouraged the teachers to talk about how they felt their classes had developed over the previous week, encouraging them to describe events and behaviours that they believed had helped or hindered the social evolution of their class groups. I recorded, transcribed and analysed all the interviews.
3. Interviewing all the students from six of the classes (100 students) for approximately 20 minutes each, using an open-ended 'feelings' questionnaire as a starting point. I was particularly interested in ascertaining the degree to which the students' impressions of their classes did or did not match those of their teachers. I was also interested in how comfortable the students felt in their classes, and how satisfied they were with their learning. I gathered data from the students in the two low-level classes differently. I interviewed the class of 'false beginners' (students with some previous knowledge of English) in small groups, and gave the true beginners the 'feelings' questionnaire translated into their mother tongue.

The objective of the second study was to identify common evolutionary patterns occurring across all the classes. Did each of the classes progress through a series of similar stages? If so, did the stages occur in a particular order, and last for similar lengths of time? The results of this part of the research were disappointing: each of the classes had a unique developmental profile and no common patterns could be detected. It was, however, possible to identify a host of similar kinds of behaviours and processes occurring in all the classes – although how teachers and students reacted to one another to create the unique culture of each class differed widely from class to class.

Large amounts of additional data were collected during the course of the study: data that were not used when the study was written up, since the focus was on the social–psychological aspects of language classrooms (as opposed to pedagogic practices). These data remained in large, untapped categories with headings such as 'flexibility', 'adaptability', 'spontaneity', 'adjustment' and 'balance'. The redundant data from the second study generated a new set of questions, which included the following: Why are teachers so flexible, and why do they so seldom follow their lesson plans? How are teachers able to make so many classroom decisions on the run? What is the basis of their classroom decision-making? What is the role of intuition in language teaching? Why is humour so widely used in language classrooms?

Study Three

The third study took the form of an ongoing series of interviews conducted over several years in which I sought answers to the above questions. I used the same interviewing techniques that I had used in the previous studies, putting teachers at ease by asking them about their present teaching circumstances, and then asking them for their personal insights relating to the above questions. Again, the interviews lasted an average of 45 minutes and were audio-recorded and transcribed. In this study I interviewed a total of 39 additional teachers working in a range of different schools and colleges around Perth. As all teachers do, the teachers brought to the interviews insights gained not only from their experiences of teaching in Perth, but also from their language-teaching experiences in other contexts and cultures, their personal experiences as language learners, and their general life experiences.

The group of teachers in Study Three included seven recently trained language teachers (ranging in age from 21 to 56), three teacher trainers, and several more teachers who had mentored trainee teachers and been observed by them.

The process of adding the data from these interviews to the database enabled me to start to answer 'Why?' questions. I began to understand *why* teachers were so flexible in their lessons, *why* teachers could use the same materials yet teach so differently, *why* humour was such an integral part of the armoury of so many teachers, and so on. Yet again, analysis of the data generated further questions which focused more broadly on the nature of professionalism in language teaching. These questions included the following: Is the fact that teachers behave in unplanned ways in their classrooms related to the level of professionalism that they believe they have obtained? What gives language teachers most professional satisfaction (enabling them to continue to teach under conditions that are often far from ideal)? Conversely, what kinds of conditions and contexts are related to high levels of language-teacher dissatisfaction? How does the classroom decision-making of novice language teachers differ from that of experienced language teachers?

Both Study Four and Study Five were conducted to establish the extent to which the findings were replicated in other contexts. The focus of Study Four was on the professionalism of language teachers, while the focus of Study Five was on teachers' class management practices. Both these studies were smaller, discrete studies that supplemented the data collected from the other, larger, studies.

Study Four

The fourth study took the form of 45-minute interviews with ten experienced language teachers working in three different language-teaching institutions in the UK. The interviews focused on the teachers' teaching practices and perceptions of professionalism in response to the questions outlined above. In other words, the teachers were asked similar questions to those asked during the latter part of Study Three.

The results of this study indicated that there was a high degree of congruity between the insights of the teachers working in Australia and those of their counterparts working in the UK. It was possible to integrate the data into the same categories as those developed for the previous three studies.

Study Five

The fifth study was a supplementary study conducted at the end of the research process. It took the form of 16 interviews conducted with foreign-language teachers working in a range of both primary and high schools in the Perth metropolitan area. The teachers were native speakers of English engaged in teaching a range of foreign languages including French, Italian, Indonesian, Japanese, German and Spanish. As with Study Four, the objective of the study was to ascertain the degree to which the findings from the previous studies were applicable to teachers teaching in other situations.

Study Five focused specifically on class-management practices. Did experienced teachers of foreign languages to children use the same kinds of class-management strategies as those engaged in teaching language to adults? The results of the study indicated that teachers who taught languages successfully in schools, in contexts that were sometimes extremely challenging, used a range of strategies similar to that of their counterparts engaged in teaching language to adults.

Overview of the database

In sum, the database for the book is extremely extensive. It includes data collected over a 12-year period from more than 100 practising teachers who described classes ranging in size from 10 to 25 students. A typical class would contain approximately 15 students. The eight teachers who participated in Study Two were interviewed on ten separate occasions. The database therefore includes data from approximately 130 hours of audio-recorded interviews that were transcribed verbatim, supplemented by data gathered in other ways.

The teachers who participated in the five interconnected studies were all (apart from one teacher from China who supplied supplementary data and insights) native speakers of English who had been trained in the communicative approach (see below) and who based their teaching around it. The ways in which the individual teachers implemented the approach form the basis of the book – while the assumptions that under-pin the approach are identified and discussed in Chapter 11.

From the research a composite picture evolved of what it is like to be a language teacher working in an English-speaking country at the present time. It is this picture that is presented in the pages of this book.

Insights from secondary sources

As each study progressed and patterns in the data began to emerge, I examined secondary sources in whichever research areas appeared to be relevant. Insights from these sources further informed and clarified my interpretations of the teachers' practices and classroom experiences. This background reading confirmed that the research upon which the present book is based is part of an overall research movement that accepts the complexity of human behaviour in naturalistic settings – and seeks to understand it in all its richness and variety.

A note on terminology

'The communicative approach'; 'communicative language teaching' (CLT)

I use the above terms interchangeably to refer to the approach used by the teachers whose practices are described within the pages of this book – an approach that involves providing students with a range opportunities to practise the target language in pairs and small groups within the language classroom. According to Richards and Rodgers (2001: 172), this approach to language teaching quickly assumed the status of ortho-doxy in British language-teaching circles.

'Western educational contexts'; 'western educational settings'; 'western language classrooms'

In writing the book I have found it necessary to highlight the fact that the practices of the teachers described here are context-specific. In order to do this I decided to use the above expressions. While I do not particularly like the term 'western', it provides a convenient means of distinguishing between contexts in which language teachers are relatively free to teach in individualistic ways, and contexts in which teachers find themselves working under tighter educational constraints.

'Experienced language teachers'

Whenever I wished to describe teachers who have more experience than others I have used the term 'experienced language teachers'. In so doing I am using the word 'experienced' to reflect everyday usage (as opposed to the more specific way in which it is used in the technical literature). It should be noted that although many of the teachers in the book considered themselves experienced, or talked about their years of experience, they did not perceive themselves as 'experts' and never described themselves as such. I have therefore avoided using the term 'expert' altogether in this book. Those wishing to examine the debate concerning the nature of expertise and the relationship between being 'experienced' and being 'an expert' will find many references in the current literature. I have, however, referred to studies of expertise in the boxes, since this is the word favoured in the technical literature.

'Trainee language teachers'; 'newly trained teachers'; 'novice teachers'; 'novice language teachers'

In Chapter 2 I have used the words 'trainee language teachers' or 'trainees' to describe language teachers in training, while in Chapter 3 I have used the term 'newly trained teachers' to refer to those who have recently joined the workforce. Where I needed an overarching term to describe both trainee teachers and teachers in their early days of teaching, I have used the terms 'novice teachers' or 'novice language teachers'. 'Novice' is used in the technical literature to describe teachers with little or no teaching experience: either student teachers or teachers in their first years of teaching.

'Language teaching professionals'; 'the language teaching profession'

Debate has continued for many years about how to define the term 'professional' – and about whether or not language teaching (or indeed any kind of teaching) constitutes a profession. In the pages of this book, and particularly in Chapters 3 and 10, I use expressions that include the words 'profession' and 'professional', including 'the language teaching profession', 'language teachers considering themselves as professionals', and 'having opportunities for professional development'. I have used these terms because teachers themselves do so, and also because it seems natural to use the words in a way that reflects their common usage. However, I am aware that in the technical literature the terms 'profession' and 'professional' are used in more narrow and specific ways.

'Adult language learners'; 'students'

Whenever I want to make it clear that I am referring to adults who are learning the target language I use the term 'adult language learners'. However, I refer generally to learners in the classroom (whether adults or children) as 'students', a term that is widely used by teachers.

'The target language'

Although I use the term 'target language' to describe the language that students are learning in their classrooms, in practice this nearly always refers to English. Because many of the insights can be applied to the teaching of other languages, I decided to use the more general term 'target language' whenever I could.

'Language-learning activities'; 'language-learning tasks'

There has been much discussion over the years about the definition of the word 'task' (see Littlewood, 2004, for an overview of different definitions of the word 'task', and for a discussion about the difference between tasks and exercises). Although some researchers and teacher educators distinguish between the terms 'language-learning activities' and 'language-learning tasks', I have chosen to use the terms interchangeably throughout the book. In my view, the term 'task' connotes a language-learning activity that has a purposeful feel to it, whereas the term 'activity' has a slightly more frivolous feel (giving the impression of a classroom activity that keeps students busy, but from which they may not necessarily learn a great deal). However, since the distinction is a fine one, I have tended to use the terms interchangeably.

'Class cohesiveness'; 'class cohesion'

I have chosen to use the above terms interchangeably when referring to the notion of the collective feeling of unity that is present to varying

11

degrees in language classes (see Chapter 9). Although 'cohesiveness' is the term used by social psychologists to describe the quality demonstrated by groups that have progressed to a high level of maturity and productivity, 'cohesion' is a more commonly used term that has the same basic meaning.

'Assumptions'; 'beliefs'

For the sake of clarity and simplicity I use the term 'assumptions' to refer to teachers' beliefs that remain below the threshold of consciousness and are seldom articulated. I use the term 'beliefs' to refer to the personal convictions about language teaching and learning that teachers are able and willing to express. Researchers in the area of teacher cognition use these and a range of additional terms in highly specific ways (see Borg, 2003: 83, for further comments on the terminology used by researchers).

How the book is organised

The book contains 12 chapters. Chapter 1 describes the research procedures that were used to integrate large quantities of unstructured, qualitative data into coherent storylines, and identifies the overall framework of the book.

The lead-in chapters, Chapters 2 and 3, set the scene. Chapter 2 describes the reasons why people go into language teaching, and the experience of learning to teach one's mother tongue on short, intensive courses, while Chapter 3 follows the progress of language teachers as they gradually mature. It outlines the changes that commonly occur in the minds of language teachers as they come to regard themselves as experienced teachers who are committed to ongoing self-improvement.

Chapter 4 focuses on the early days of language classes. It describes the range of techniques that experienced language teachers use to create and maintain the kinds of classroom atmospheres that they believe are suitable environments for communicative language practice. It also draws attention to the dual roles played by experienced language teachers in their classrooms.

Chapters 5 and 6 focus primarily (but not exclusively) on adult learners of English. Chapter 5 shows how students do not leave their personal lives at the classroom door, but bring with them to the class a whole range of personal agendas, needs, wants and concerns. Chapter 6 then describes how experienced language teachers go about managing individual students, showing that they do so in ways that are driven by a desire to maintain a spirit of social equilibrium within their class groups.

Chapters 7 and 8 focus on the flexibility of language teachers as they balance pedagogic and social aspects of their classrooms. Chapter 7 focuses on pedagogic aspects of language classrooms, explaining why language teachers are able to make so many on-the-spot decisions in their classrooms – and why they find it necessary to do so. Chapter 8 focuses on the ways that the behaviour of teachers and students in language classes are mutually dependent. It describes in particular how humour, together with learning tasks that engage the whole person, are powerful ways of vitalising the atmospheres of language classrooms.

Chapter 9 describes the evolution and maintenance of classroom communities – showing that experienced language teachers have an intuitive understanding of group dynamics principles. This chapter draws attention to an important feature of classroom behaviour: that it is frequently both pedagogically and socially driven.

The following two chapters, 10 and 11, stand back from the data to provide a broader perspective. Chapter 10 gives an overview of the contexts within which language teachers find themselves working, describing the aspects of their work that they find the most frustrating and the most rewarding.

Chapter 11 takes a critical stance, suggesting why it is necessary to treat teacher perspectives with caution. It then explores language teachers' assumptions, beliefs and values, seeking to explain the motivational forces that underpin their classroom decision-making. The chapter suggests that language teachers implement the communicative approach in pragmatic ways that are consistent with their individual beliefs and value systems.

The final chapter of the book, Chapter 12, draws together the threads from the earlier chapters, describing the many considerations that experienced language teachers are able to take into account in order to maintain a sense of balance in their classrooms. After proposing a model that encapsulates the integration of pedagogically and socially driven classroom behaviour, the chapter proposes a socio-pedagogic theory of classroom practice.

1 Establishing the framework for the book

This chapter describes the steps that were taken to identify a suitable framework for the book. Section 1.1 describes why a qualitative research approach was selected to examine classroom processes, and why it was decided to conduct the first of the five interlinked studies upon which the book is based as a grounded theory study. Section 1.2 describes the data collection and analysis procedures that are an integral part of grounded theory development, and that must be followed in the prescribed way if a grounded theory is eventually to emerge. Section 1.3 describes the framework that was identified on the completion of the first study. This framework, taken from the discipline of social psychology, enabled a wide range of classroom behaviours to be collected – and their interrelationships explored.

1.1 Selecting the research approach

Which path to follow: qualitative or quantitative?

An important decision faced by any person embarking on any kind of research project is what kind of research approach to adopt. The researcher first needs to decide whether to conduct research that is towards either the qualitative or the quantitative end of the research spectrum: research that aims to describe or explain a particular phenomenon, or research that aims to investigate hypotheses and to present findings in numerical terms. A range of both practical and psychological factors influences the decision of the researcher. Practical considerations include access to suitable locations for the research, availability of willing informants, and time constraints. Psychological factors include the kind of research the investigator considers worthwhile to carry out, and what kind of research the investigator feels comfortable in conducting.

In my case I knew that I was interested in investigating interaction in language classrooms in order to reach a broad understanding of what was occurring. I intuitively felt that qualitative research approaches 'fitted' naturalistic settings such as language classrooms more closely than did quantitative approaches. Language classrooms are not experimental laboratories (places where quantitative research of a scientific nature is traditionally conducted), because in classrooms it is impossible to exclude all the variables that may influence the findings. In controlled environments such as laboratories it is much easier to establish cause–effect relationships, since extraneous variables can be identified beforehand – and then either eliminated or acknowledged to have had a possible effect on the findings. This is virtually impossible to achieve in naturalistic settings.

'In the varied topography of professional practice, there is a high, hard ground overlooking a swamp. On the high ground, manageable problems lend themselves to solution through the application of research-based theory and technique. In the swampy lowland, messy, confusing problems defy technical solution. The irony of this situation is that the problems of the high ground tend to be relatively unimportant to individuals or society at large, however great their technical interest may be, while in the swamp lie the problems of greatest human concern.'   Schön (1987: 1)

I considered that I would feel more comfortable if I acknowledged at the outset what my intuition and experience told me: that the widest possible number of variables are interacting with and influencing one another in any language classroom at any point in time. I therefore felt that I should focus on the interrelationships between a wide number of variables – rather than selecting and investigating in detail a narrowly circumscribed aspect of classroom interaction, and ignoring other variables that might be influencing the findings. Metaphorically speaking, I decided that I wished to observe classroom interaction through a wide-angle lens – rather than putting a preselected aspect of classroom interaction under the microscope.

A further reason why I decided to adopt a qualitative approach was that I enjoyed writing and was happy to present my findings descriptively. It was a challenge to try and present the data in sufficient richness and depth to convince the reader of the validity of the findings. In effect I felt more comfortable about presenting my findings descriptively than I did about presenting them in quantitative form. (It is tempting for quantitative researchers who have gathered data from a relatively small sample of subjects to imply that their findings have general application. However, unless the sample is a large-scale statistical one that has been selected randomly – something that it is extremely difficult to achieve in an educational setting – the findings may only be of limited application.)

15

A key aspect of qualitative research is that its objective is not to produce findings that are capable of general application, but rather to produce results that 'resonate'. By 'resonate' I mean the ability of the research findings to ring true to those who encounter them. I decided that I felt more comfortable using a research approach that would enable me to present my findings in such a way that readers in other settings might say to themselves, 'Yes, that's right. That's how it is!' I wanted the onus to be on the reader to accept the findings because they made sense to them – rather than on myself to 'prove' that the findings were valid.

Focusing on teacher cognition

Having decided to conduct a qualitative research study, I now needed to decide how best to access the significance that the words and behaviour of both teachers and students in language classrooms have for others. Leaders in the field, such as Breen (1986) and Allwright and Bailey (1991), have highlighted the limitations of observational research, which can only document behaviour that can be directly observed. Such research does not enable the researcher to access the things that are going on inside people's heads – or the interpretations that individual class members put on the words and actions of others.

Teacher cognition research – research into the unobservable cognitive dimension of teaching: what teachers know, believe and think – is a burgeoning area in educational research (Borg, 2003). This strand of research is based on the premise that teachers draw on complex, personalised networks of knowledge to make their classroom decisions. I decided that I would use the thoughts, views and impressions of classroom language teachers – not with a view to describing individual teacher belief systems, but as a way of more fully understanding classroom interaction. As outlined in Chapter 11, this approach has its limitations, as does any other research approach. However, I decided that, on balance, interviewing teachers and trying to understand their personal interpretations of classroom events would be a fruitful way of uncovering and more fully understanding the complex pedagogic and social reality of language classrooms.

In sum, at this point I knew that I wished to conduct qualitative research. I also knew that I wished to base my research on interviews with classroom teachers. What I now needed to do was to select from a number of qualitative approaches the one that was most likely to enable me to achieve my research objective: a global understanding of classroom processes.

Why conduct a grounded theory study?

Recent years have witnessed a growth in interest in qualitative research, with increasing numbers of qualitative studies being conducted – certainly in the field of education. Qualitative studies are still eschewed by some people, who consider that they are less 'do-able' within limited timeframes, and produce findings that are often too lengthy to be reported in conventional-length articles in research journals. The perception also persists in some quarters that qualitative research is somehow 'woolly': less rigorous and less 'scientific' than quantitative research, which takes much of its terminology from the hard sciences. However, the quality of research is not related to the approach that is used: there can be both good and bad research of any kind. Many people about to embark upon research find themselves naturally drawn towards conducting qualitative studies. This is particularly so with researchers with a teaching background, who often wish to conduct research that they believe likely to produce results that can have direct relevance for everyday classroom practice.

It is now increasingly recognised that there are a number of well-established qualitative research traditions, each of which has its own particular merits and its set of core precepts and recommended procedures. Many of the understandings and procedures (such as interviewing techniques) are common across the various traditions, albeit with subtle differences and points of emphasis.

In his book, *Qualitative inquiry and research design: Choosing among five traditions* (1998), Creswell provides a useful overview of five well-established traditions of qualitative research: biography, phenomenology, grounded theory, ethnography and case study. Creswell also describes the origins of grounded theory and its somewhat chequered career in terms of the dramatic falling out of Glaser and Strauss, the two sociologists who originally developed and described grounded theory development procedures in 1967.

When I came to embark on the first of the five studies upon which this book is based I decided to conduct a grounded theory study. This decision was partly based on my desire to obtain a holistic view of language classrooms: to try to understand how all the various pieces of the classroom 'jigsaw' fitted together. I was intrigued by the fact that the objective of grounded theory is, as its name suggests, to develop theory that is grounded in the data, and that gradually emerges from the data in an organic way rather than being imposed from outside. I decided that I would like to try my hand at theory building. Little did I realise that, although I was able to develop a localised theory by the end of the first study, it would take me a further ten years to formulate a more generalised theory that might be applicable to a wider range of contexts.

'Grounded theory is a highly systematic research approach for the collection and analysis of qualitative data for the purpose of developing explanatory theory that furthers the understanding of social and psychological phenomena. The objective of grounded theory is the development of theory that explains basic patterns common in social life.'   Chenitz and Swanson (1986: 3)

The other factor that influenced my decision to conduct a grounded theory study was chance. It so happened that the postgraduate department of the faculty of nursing in the university where I worked had a long tradition of supporting grounded theory research. Postgraduate seminars, where researchers were introduced to the key precepts of grounded theory and given opportunities to internalise them within a supportive environment, were regularly run. I joined one of these seminar groups in 1993, and from then on became a committed grounded theory researcher.

Grounded theory is not for everyone, but it has served my purposes admirably. Interestingly, it is an approach that is favoured by researchers in the health sciences who wish to conduct studies into practitioner experiences, such as the experience of working in neo-natal wards or the experience of caring for people with Alzheimer's. The experience of being a language teacher is in some respects similar to that of being a health professional: working at the grass roots level, relating to a variety of individuals under sometimes challenging conditions, routinely having to make on-the-spot decisions, and so on. It seemed that grounded theory was a research approach that might lend itself particularly well to investigating language classrooms.

Comment

Recent years have witnessed an upsurge of interest in qualitative research approaches. The following factors have influenced this growing movement:

- the development of increasingly sophisticated, user-friendly computer packages designed to facilitate the management of

---

qualitative data and enhance the researcher's analytical thinking;
- recognition of the increasingly complex nature of classroom processes, as articulated in Breen's seminal article on the context of language learning (1986);
- a growing sense of dissatisfaction with the limited relevance to classroom practice of findings from narrowly focused classroom-based research;
- a desire to find ways of reducing the oft-lamented gap between theory and practice;
- the general postmodern climate of the times, with its rejection of traditional, positivistic, scientific research traditions in favour of softer, more flexible, interpretive approaches.

1.2 Conducting a grounded theory study

The decision to conduct a grounded theory study should not be taken lightly, since there are no half measures with grounded theory: one is either conducting a grounded theory study, or one is not. If a researcher decides to go down the grounded theory path, they need plenty of time and determination to learn and then follow the procedures necessary for the development of a grounded theory.

A book that outlines grounded theory development procedures in an accessible way is *Basics of Qualitative Research: Techniques and Procedures for Developing Grounded Theory* (Strauss and Corbin, 1998). With its user-friendly style, short sections, italicised key terms, bold print for emphasis and so on, this book appears to be the answer to every neophyte researcher's prayers: a manual that describes the steps that should be followed for the successful completion of a grounded theory study. Unfortunately life is not so simple. Although the book provides a readily accessible outline of grounded theory development procedures, thereby filling an invaluable niche, it does not do the researcher's work for them. Many researchers purchase the book and follow the procedures without developing full ownership of the process. When this happens they may be disappointed with the result: grounded theories do not always emerge. Another criticism levelled at this book is that it oversimplifies grounded theory development procedures. Nevertheless, it is an excellent starting point.

Conducting a successful grounded theory study involves understanding the principles that underpin the procedures. This process is a challenging one, since it involves rejecting certain assumptions about the nature of research and replacing them with others. It also involves forcing oneself to follow certain procedures – and ensuring that one does not cut corners when the going gets hard. Conducting a grounded theory study involves going down certain blind alleys and having to retrace one's steps when certain hypotheses prove incorrect. The process of developing a grounded theory is also highly engaging, particularly in the creative phase when it is necessary to reach a higher level of abstraction by creating superordinate categories, often through the invention of new words. The process sometimes becomes compulsive, with researchers taking their notebooks everywhere they go and sitting in corners scribbling furiously when potentially important thoughts suddenly flash through their minds. In the latter stages of the cycle, when the theory finally starts to emerge, the process is truly exciting.

In sum, grounded theory research is a highly rewarding endeavour for those who persevere with it. It need not take the form of a large-scale study, but can be used for studies of more modest dimensions. These can include studies that stop short of developing theory, having as their goal the development of conceptual frameworks. When embarking on a grounded theory study it is helpful to join a support group of like-minded researchers who are able to share experiences and insights, to keep one on the right path, and to offer critical input into one's work.

The following sections provide a brief outline of the procedures that led first to the identification of the phenomenon of class cohesiveness, and second to the selection of an appropriate framework for the book. These procedures are an integral part of the research process: only by following them can the researcher be certain that the framework that is eventually chosen fits the data as closely as possible.

Grounded theory interviews

Armed with a broadly framed research question (in my case, 'What is a good language class?'), the grounded theorist embarks on a series of focused, open-ended interviews. The purpose of these wide-ranging interviews is to open up the topic, by encouraging each informant to talk openly and honestly about their classroom experiences. While ensuring that the interview does not veer too far off track, the researcher must give each informant sufficient leeway to talk about whatever they appear most ready and able to articulate. It is often the case that one teacher has valuable insights into one particular aspect of being a language teacher, while another teacher has equally valuable insights into another aspect.

The insights provided by each teacher generate additional questions in the researcher's mind: questions that the next teacher can be invited to answer. This kind of questioning, which grounded theorists call 'theoretical sampling', enables the researcher to identify and explore the significance of additional phenomena that they may not have considered important prior to conducting the study. These phenomena may be central to an understanding of the totality of the experience. By asking subsequent teachers to elaborate on insights and observations provided by previous teachers, a composite picture of what all the teachers are collectively saying is gradually developed. The validity of the findings is also enhanced, since the researcher can check whether the insights provided by one teacher are unique, or shared by others.

Since the data provided through open-ended interviews form the basis for grounded theory development, it is essential that grounded theorists are rigorous in their questioning techniques. They must ensure that they ask open rather than leading questions, and constantly invite informants to expand on each point they make, by elaborating on specific circumstances, or by providing examples to illustrate what they mean. They must be prepared to accommodate repetition and redundancy and resist the temptation to cut informants off in mid-flow. They must also provide on-the-spot validity checks, by repeating back to each informant what they have said during the course of the interview, and ensuring that they have understood them correctly. Using a questioning tone of voice is a useful strategy for encouraging informants to elaborate further. Additional validity-enhancing question types can be used, including devil's advocate questions (presenting an opposite position or interpretation and inviting comment) and hypothetical 'what if?' questions.

It is essential to tape-record and transcribe all interviews in full. This is because the researcher cannot know until a much later stage in the research process the significance of many of the observations that teachers are making – let alone know where they fit in the overall jigsaw puzzle picture. Unless verbatim transcripts are made, many potentially significant pieces of information may be lost.

Most research traditions advocate a compartmentalised approach to data collection and analysis: collecting all the data and then, when the data collection is complete, commencing the analysis. Grounded theory development requires a different approach. The researcher must alternate between data collection and analysis in an ongoing way: the second interview is conducted only after the first one has been analysed, the third only after the second has been analysed, and so on.

Data analysis

Grounded theorists work through a series of coding procedures that open their minds to the many possible ways in which their data can be interpreted. It is essential that they do not develop a fixed view about what their data are indicating early on in the research process: to do so closes their minds to alternative interpretations that may eventually prove to be more valid. Grounded theorists first print out their transcripts and then follow a series of coding procedures known as 'open coding' (initial opening up of the data), 'axial coding' (putting the data together in new ways) and 'selective coding' (systematically relating categories to the emerging central phenomenon).

The first stage of the analysis involves making notations all over the transcripts. This process includes highlighting words that stand out from the surrounding text, jotting down words that are similar to or associated with those that appear in the text, drawing arrows indicating possible connections, and hypothesising about the possible causes, conditions and consequences of a range of reported classroom behaviours. While making notes on their transcripts, grounded theorists record their first tentative ideas about what the data may be indicating in memos, each one headed and dated, and written on a separate piece of paper – or coded appropriately on the computer for later sorting.

A key feature of grounded theory development is that it requires the researcher to think both deductively and inductively. Although analytical thinking is an integral part of the research process, speculative thinking is equally important – not as an end in itself, but as an interim step in the research process. There are three main ways in which grounded theorists can use their imagination as a research tool: through diagramming; through exploring the data through metaphors; and through creating new words for overarching categories under which lesser categories can be subsumed. These are considered in turn below.

Diagramming

When grounded theorists are in the final stages of their research they often look back at their first tentative attempts to represent schematically relationships between their data and are reminded of how naive their thinking then was. They forget how far they have progressed since those first tentative scrawls and scribbles. A requirement for each diagram is that it represents the researcher's current overall understanding of the data – and is a refinement of the previous one. An early diagram of the relationship between individuals in language classes looked like this:

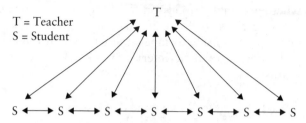

T = Teacher
S = Student

Figure 1.1   Early diagram

In contrast, a later diagram looked like this:

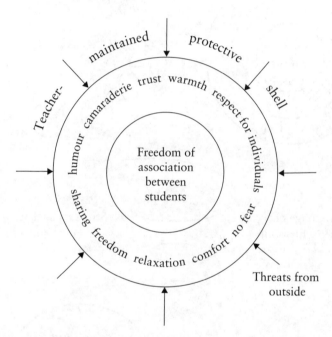

Figure 1.2   Later diagram

In the meantime I had explored the data with a variety of additional diagrams. Many of these were in the form of circles: circles interlinked as chains, small circles clustered around a central circle, overlapping circles, individual circles contained within one big circle, and circles nested inside one another like Russian dolls. The early diagrams had questions or problems attached to them. For example, with the links-of-a-chain diagram (which represented the hypothesis that a good language class might be defined as a series of good lessons), I broke the chain and speculated whether a single bad lesson would destroy a good class. Later I attached working titles to the diagrams and included descriptions of their component parts – using as labels the words that the teachers had used during the course of their interviews. Sketched below are some interim diagrams:

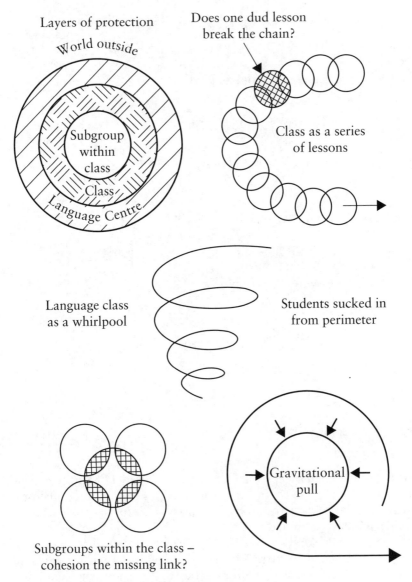

Figure 1.3 Interim diagrams

Exploring with metaphors

A key feature of grounded theory development is that the researcher switches readily between very different kinds of activities, each of which requires a particular kind of skill. One moment they are using their inter-personal skills by conducting an interview, the next they are thinking analytically as they sort memos into categories, and the next finds them thinking creatively with metaphors. This alternation between different activities and modes of thinking becomes second nature to grounded theorists. A new interview sparks new thoughts, which are recorded in separate memos and then sorted. The process of sorting the memos generates further memos, which in turn leads to the generation of further hypotheses. These can then be explored both with metaphors and in further interviews. And so the process continues in an ongoing, iterative way.

Exploring with metaphors is recognised as a powerful means of reaching a deeper level of understanding of specific phenomena. When analysing their data, grounded theorists think in terms of metaphors: concrete items from the real world that share certain features with the phenomenon under study. For example, a language class can be conceptualised as a ship of discovery, in the sense that everyone in the room is going on a journey into the unknown, with the teacher at the helm. Alternatively, it can be viewed as a swimming pool, with daring students plunging in at the deep end, while diffident students slowly let themselves into the water at the shallow end. In the fertile imagination of the grounded theory researcher, language classes can be compared to many objects ranging from playgroups to spinning tops: the possibilities are limited only by the imagination of the researcher. In each case, the process of comparing the incontrovertible features of the metaphorical item with the hypothesised features of the phenomenon under study enables the researcher to further refine their thinking.

> 'The metaphor is halfway from the empirical facts to the conceptual *significance* of those facts; it gets the analyst, as it were, up and over the particulars en route to the basic social processes that give meaning to those particulars.'   Miles and Huberman (1984: 221)

Developing hierarchical categories

As all qualitative researchers are aware, unstructured data have an annoying habit of not fitting neatly into the categories that have been created for them. There is always that extra pile called 'miscellaneous'

25

containing data that do not seem to fit anywhere – or that seem to fit equally well in several different categories. A key feature of grounded theory development is that categories must constantly be shifted around, adjusted, expanded, contracted or melded in order to accommodate new data. Just as in a jigsaw puzzle each individual piece has its place, so in a grounded theory study every single data item must be placed in an appropriate location in the emerging overall picture. In order for this to happen, hierarchical categories must be created. Such categories enable groups of 'pieces' to be shifted around together and positioned correctly in the picture. They may turn out to be part of the background or part of the foreground, to be located in the top left-hand corner or the bottom right – or perhaps they are part of the central image itself.

Hierarchies of categories work in the same way as the classification of living things, with lower-order sets being subsumed under higher-order ones: cats and dogs being classified as mammals and so on. In order to create hierarchical categories, grounded theorists must search for suitable abstract words – since higher-order categories need to be described in more abstract terms than lower-order ones. The category 'affective inhibitors', for example, contains the subcategories of 'worried students', 'reluctant students', 'temporarily distracted students' and 'culture-shocked students', while the category 'organisational inhibitors', contains the subcategories of 'levels too disparate', 'class too big/small', 'disparate objectives' and 'unsuitable classroom'. Both these categories can be grouped under the general heading of 'factors inhibiting the development of good language classes' – a branch on the hierarchical tree that contrasts with another branch of a similar level of importance entitled 'factors that enhance the development of good language classes'.

Because it is often difficult to find appropriate abstract terms, grounded theorists frequently resort to their dictionaries and the-sauruses. As they read the definitions of words, they come across a range of new words – words that can themselves be explored in terms of their overall 'fit'. This process continues until the most appropriate word for the particular category is selected. Sometimes grounded theorists find underused words particularly apposite, such as the unfamiliar word 'witting' (not surprisingly the opposite of 'unwitting'). The former can be used to describe the roles that students consciously choose for them-selves in the language classroom, while the latter can be used to describe roles that students find themselves playing without having chosen to do so. When they have difficulty in finding suitable words, grounded theorists often use words in unfamiliar ways. For example, they might describe individuals who draw their classes together as 'welders', 'uni-fiers' or 'coalescers'. Grounded theorists find that playing with words soon becomes an integral part of the creative data analysis process.

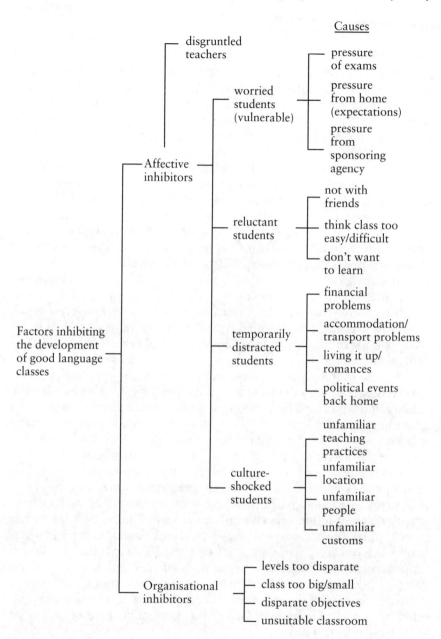

Figure 1.4   Hierarchical tree

Drawing the data together

The process of arranging and rearranging their data raises awareness in grounded theorists of emerging patterns and recurrent themes: they begin to realise that informants have been saying many similar kinds of things, albeit in many different ways. At this point they must start writing 'storyline memos': summaries of what they understand all their informants to have been collectively saying. Just as with their diagrams, grounded theorists find that their summaries grow in complexity over time: their initial summary will be relatively simple, while their final one will be considerably longer and more detailed. My first storyline memo was 300 words long, while the final one was almost 2000 words in length. In order to write storyline memos, grounded theorists must move from a divergent to a convergent thinking mode. Speculative thoughts and rapidly scribbled ideas are no longer required: they must write clearly and precisely, using measured tones and ensuring that no personal attitudes are revealed or value judgements made. Their task at this stage in the process is to create in words as accurate a picture as they can of the phenomenon they have been researching. They must then present this composite picture, accompanied by a diagram if appropriate, to those who supplied the data, and invite comments and critical feedback.

In grounded theory research, asking whether the executive summary makes sense to the people who provided the raw data (or to others who have undergone similar experiences) is a crucial means of enhancing the validity of the findings. If the findings resonate with the informants, who nod and say things like, 'Yes! That's how it is', or, 'Goodness! You've managed to put your finger on what I think', the researcher knows that they are on the right track. Grounded theorists invite critical input in order to fine-tune their summaries – so that nothing that they say in their final summary either grates with informants or seems not to ring quite true. In my case I modified both the executive summary and the final integrative diagram in one crucial respect: I removed the teacher from their position on the class circle and placed them outside the circle on an imaginary piece of elastic (see Figure 1.5 on page 29). This change reflected more accurately the teachers' perceptions of their roles: being able to switch readily back and forth between the more traditional role of authority figure and the more relaxed role of class group member. This adjustment proved to be a key factor in understanding teacher behaviour in language classrooms.

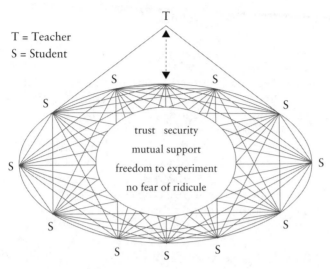

Figure 1.5   Integrative diagram

The class as group

The research for this book was begun with an open mind. Would language classes that were 'good' in the eyes of their teachers turn out to be collections of high-achieving students, collections of well-behaved students, or perhaps strings of perfectly executed lessons in which carefully planned teaching objectives were regularly achieved? By the end of the first study the answer was clear. In the minds of language teachers good classes were those that functioned effectively as groups. Although good classes might contain high-level, highly motivated students, or might be ones in which everything regularly ran like clockwork, the idea of perfection was not part of the equation. The kinds of classes that the teachers described as good included the most unlikely ones: classes containing unconventional students, classes that did not make particularly rapid progress, or classes that challenged the teacher's expertise in some way. In the eyes of the teachers these were, nevertheless, high-quality classes. The teachers described such classes with great enthusiasm, the behaviour of certain students and certain classroom events springing readily to mind.

The single feature shared by all classes that were highly valued by their teachers was that some kind of transformation had taken place. These classes had somehow metamorphosed from collections of disparate individual students into groups with happy, friendly and mutually supportive atmospheres – groups that appeared unified in their responsiveness to and liking for their teacher, and which, not surprisingly, were a pleasure to teach. In the minds of their teachers they operated in a highly cohesive manner.

Having identified class cohesiveness as being central to teachers' definitions of what constitutes a good language class, I could now formulate what grounded theorists call a 'substantive theory' (a localised theory that is grounded in a particular situational context). I could say that, in the minds of a sample of language teachers, good classes were those that function as cohesive groups. I now needed to turn my attention to the research literature. First, I needed to locate my findings within an established research tradition and, second, I needed to identify a framework that could be used to guide the collection and analysis of further data. In effect this framework proved to be sufficiently robust to function as the framework that underpinned the entire book.

1.3 Identifying a framework

Because the language teachers I had interviewed had made it so obvious that what was important to them was how well their classes functioned as groups, I was clearly going to have to examine the literature in the discipline of social psychology. Social psychology is the branch of psychology that focuses on how human beings function in relation to, rather than in isolation from, one another. An area within social psychology known as group dynamics is concerned specifically with how human beings both influence and are influenced by the groups of which they are a part. This appeared to be the most fruitful area in which to look for a suitable framework.

Since the pioneering work of Kurt Lewin in the 1940s much research has been conducted into how human beings behave in groups. Many findings are so well established that they are now largely uncontested. These include the notion that different leadership styles cause group members to behave in different ways, the fact that groups pass through different stages of development (though not necessarily in a set order), the fact that the behaviour of the group can influence the behaviour of individuals and so on. Many terms that were originally coined by researchers in the field of group dynamics have passed into general usage, such as the notion of group members playing different roles, the notion of group norms, the notion of peer pressure and the notion of groups having different levels of cohesiveness. The concept of different leadership styles – authoritarian, democratic, and so on – is also widely accepted. The applicability of group dynamics principles to language classrooms is now being increasingly recognised.

A well-established book by Schmuck and Schmuck, *Group processes in the classroom* (2001), outlines how group process theories can be applied both to school management and to individual classrooms, with highly positive outcomes.

Exploring the research literature

Although they must clearly have done extensive general reading in their subject area before starting their research, grounded theorists must avoid becoming immersed too early on in the specialised technical literature of their discipline. If they do this, there is the danger that their thinking may become so set in a certain direction that their minds will be closed to the possibility of using frameworks from other disciplines. In my case, once it had become evident that classroom interaction could usefully be interpreted from a group dynamics perspective, it was necessary to become familiar with the group dynamics literature.

It soon became evident that many frameworks could be used to interpret the data. Language classes could be examined in terms of the development of group norms, in terms of the evolution of an overall class culture, in terms of progress towards group goals, and so on. Although my general reading in the area of group dynamics has informed my interpretation of many of the classroom behaviours that are described in the book, it was still necessary to identify a single overarching framework. This was particularly important in view of the ambitious nature of the second study: to document the social–psychological evolution of eight different language classes through classroom observation and ongoing teacher interviews. Without such a framework it would have been difficult to decide which kinds of classroom behaviour to document.

The framework that I eventually selected was one that conceptualised leadership in a flexible way. Such a framework was needed because teachers had clearly indicated that enabling language classes to evolve into groups that they considered cohesive was a joint endeavour, involving initiatives on both their own part and that of their students: it was not their sole prerogative. Indeed, it seemed that the students themselves, behaving both individually and collectively, had equally important leadership roles to play. It also appeared that, when teachers and particular individuals in their classes interacted with one another in certain ways, they were engaged in collaborative leadership.

A functional approach to leadership

For many years leadership studies were based on the assumption that leaders led, while others followed: the responsibility for the progress of the group towards the achievement of its goals rested with the assigned group leader – who wielded considerable amounts of power. Unfortunately studies that attempted to isolate the qualities of effective leaders yielded disappointing results: there were as many effective individual leadership styles, it seemed, as there were effective leaders. It is now widely accepted that a dynamic conceptualisation of leadership provides a more helpful way of understanding how groups develop and function. This alternative way of viewing leadership, known as functional leadership, conceptualises leadership as a property of the group rather than of a single individual.

> Schmuck and Schmuck (2001: 228) believe that viewing leadership as a property of a group is a useful way of understanding how influence works within the classroom. They explain that this view frees us from believing that only teachers exert leadership in the classroom, enabling us to see that students also perform leadership functions. They point out that students wield great amounts of classroom leadership, with their behaviours sometimes facilitating classroom learning and at other times impeding it.

According to the functional approach to leadership, group members can play two major kinds of roles (Benne and Sheats, 1978: 53). The first of these are group task roles, which are related to the task that the group is to undertake (in the case of language classes, helping the class to progress towards its learning goals). The second are group building and maintenance roles: helping the group develop a feeling of unity and ensuring that it continues to feel united in an ongoing way. (In the case of language classes, group building and group maintenance roles are any teacher or student behaviours that enable the class to develop or to maintain its feeling of being a united learning community.)

This framework for interpreting the significance of the behaviour of individuals in group situations appeared ideally suited for my purposes. In particular it seemed likely to enable me to understand the significance of a wide range of spontaneous classroom behaviour that had seldom been the subject of classroom-based research. In addition, I felt justified in my choice of framework, since its relevance to educational contexts had already been recognised.

1.4 Conclusion

This chapter has described the steps that I followed to identify a framework for the present book. The first part of the chapter explained why a qualitative research approach was chosen, and why, from a number of qualitative research traditions, grounded theory was considered particularly appropriate. The second part of the chapter outlined the key features of the grounded theory approach. It showed that following grounded theory procedures in a step-by-step fashion led to the integration of large amounts of information into a composite picture of what a sample of teachers were collectively saying. The third part of the chapter explained how and why it was appropriate to select a framework from the discipline of social psychology. This framework could serve two purposes. First, it could guide the collection and analysis of data in the subsequent stages of the research and second, it could provide the organisational framework for the book.

Summary

Conducting a qualitative study with the objective of developing a localised theory that emerges from the data themselves involves following a number of procedures in a methodical way. These procedures form a series of incremental steps that must be followed in a set order and repeated in an ongoing, cyclical manner. In this way the researcher's understanding of the phenomenon under study is progressively both expanded and refined – until recurring patterns can be seen. The key processes involved in grounded theory development include the following:

- tape-recording focused, open-ended interviews and transcribing all the information verbatim;
- analysing each interview in detail, by using coding procedures which 'open up' the data (thereby sensitising the researcher to the many possible ways in which individual items of data can be related);
- conducting and analysing interviews sequentially, with hypotheses generated by the analysis of the information contained in each interview generating new questions that can be asked in subsequent interviews;
- starting to write about the data as early as possible in the research process, in the form of memos that can then be sorted into provisional categories;
- engaging in a range of processes that encourage the data to be conceptualised in different ways, including diagramming, exploring with metaphors and making word associations;

- creating categories to fit the data and then expanding, contracting and melding categories until the categories can be related to one another hierarchically, using appropriate abstract terms for higher-order categories;
- drawing the findings together in summary memos and checking their validity by inviting critical feedback from informants;
- incorporating all feedback into the revised summary so that the summary provides an accurate representation of what all informants are collectively saying;
- letting the data lead the researcher to identify a major framework (and additional subsidiary frameworks) that can enhance understanding of the data already collected, and frame subsequent research.

For further reading

A range of books is available on the grounded theory approach; many are relatively technical and not particularly easy to absorb. A book on qualitative research in nursing (Speziale and Carpenter, 2003) contains two chapters on grounded theory, the first of which provides a particularly clear introduction to grounded theory. One of the clearest books on grounded theory, edited by Chenitz and Swanson (1986), contains chapters by a range of well-regarded grounded theorists, while Strauss and Corbin (1998) describe grounded theory development in a manual-style format. A more recent book on grounded theory is by Dey (1999). A number of general books on qualitative research, including Denzin and Lincoln (1994) and Denzin and Lincoln (2003), contain specific chapters written by grounded theory specialists, some of which are relatively technical. Strauss has written specialised articles, while Glaser has written prolifically over the years on grounded theory, self-publishing his books, which tend to be detailed and somewhat emotive in style. There are also many articles reporting grounded theory studies in qualitative research journals such as *Qualitative Health Research*. These are often helpful in giving researchers an impression of the range of topics that lend themselves to grounded theory studies.

Looking ahead

The chapters that follow use the framework identified in the present chapter to describe the experience of classroom language teaching. The first of these, Chapter 2, describes the process of setting out as a language teacher: why people join the profession, and how they feel as they engage in learning their craft.

The relationship between the functional approach to leadership – the conceptualisation of leadership that provided the framework for the book – and the formulation of an explanatory theory of classroom practice will be discussed in Chapter 12.

2   Training to be a language teacher

The previous chapter described the nature of the research upon which this book is based, and outlined the steps that were taken to identify a suitable framework for the book. Chapters 2–10 present the experience of being a language teacher in a sequential manner. The sequence begins with this chapter, Chapter 2, which describes the experience of starting out as a language teacher. It concludes with Chapter 10, in which teachers reflect on the experience of being classroom language teachers.

This chapter is divided into four sections. Section 2.1 outlines some of the reasons why people choose to become language teachers. Section 2.2 describes the experience of training to be a language teacher on short, intensive courses. It highlights the pressurised nature of training courses and describes the challenges and pitfalls of teaching practice. Section 2.3 describes the shift towards becoming more student-focused, while Section 2.4 describes the feelings of newly trained teachers on entering the workforce.

2.1 The appeal of language teaching

It is now widely accepted that the scales have tipped in favour of English as the language of international communication – and that English is the preferred language of communication in the key areas of science, technology, trade and education. Because of the benefits that mastery of English brings with it, the learning of English is promoted in increasing numbers of countries throughout the world – with many education departments making the learning of English mandatory in primary and high schools. Growing numbers of people who are keen to upgrade their English language skills travel to English-speaking countries, either to attend short intensive language courses or to engage in tertiary studies in English-speaking institutions. Countries such as the UK and Australia accept significant numbers of migrants from non-English-speaking backgrounds who urgently need to learn English in order to function effectively in their adopted country.

The heavy demand for English language tuition has led to an exponential growth in job opportunities for English language teachers throughout the world. Native speakers of English find that, upon completion of an English language teaching course, they can readily find jobs either in their home countries or overseas. Although some language teachers complete postgraduate certificates or diplomas of a year's duration, increasing numbers of native English speakers begin their teaching careers by completing intensive preparatory courses in English language teaching such as the CELTA (Certificate in English Language Teaching to Adults).

> According to the University of Cambridge ESOL examinations website, CELTA is the best known and most widely taken initial 'TESOL/TEFL' qualification of its kind in the world. Over 10,000 people successfully complete a CELTA course each year. There are currently CELTA training centres in 135 countries around the world, with 118 in the UK and 20 in Australia. For a description of the background and details of the CELTA scheme see Roberts (1998).

The reasons why English speakers decide to obtain a language teaching qualification, with a view to teaching English on a short- or long-term basis, either immediately or at some point in the future, are extremely varied. However, the factors that influence their decision may be divided into two broad categories: 'pull' factors and 'push' factors.

'Pull' factors

Many young English speakers who have recently completed a university degree, and who are either unsure of what they want to do, or want a bit of fun and adventure before settling down, are attracted to the idea of English language teaching. A CELTA qualification, described by some young English speakers as a 'ticket to travel', enables English speakers to go to out-of-the-way places, pick up a job on a casual basis, and experience living and working in another culture for a period of time. The attraction of living and working in developing countries, where they feel their efforts will be highly valued, is particularly strong for some young people. In the words of one teacher:

> It's a great way to live overseas and get involved and get into the culture, and it gives you a good reason to be there, and you can do something useful and productive and really feel you're benefitting a local community.

The desire to teach English overseas is not limited to young adults. Older people who no longer have family commitments, and who perhaps feel that a change of direction will revitalise their lives, are increasingly attracted to the prospect of living and working overseas on a temporary basis. In the words of one mature-aged teacher, 'It allows you to keep the idea afloat that life is open-ended'. Again, a CELTA certificate opens doors: a quick surf on the Internet reveals the number of jobs available to an English speaker with an English teaching certificate and a willingness to travel. One retiree was delighted with his decision to spend six months teaching in sub-zero temperatures in Siberia – particularly since his artistic talents enabled him to win a local ice-sculpture competition.

People choose to go into English language teaching for a wide range of other reasons. Having a part-time English language teaching job is an attractive prospect for mothers of young children, for whom family commitments remain their number-one priority. Part-time English language teaching offers women in this category the opportunity both to remain in the workforce, and to have intellectual stimulation. One teacher remarked that she decided to become a language teacher because staying at home all day with a toddler was 'driving her nuts'. For women in this category the financial rewards of part-time language teaching are often of secondary importance. One explained that she was more than happy with her pay packet, saying, 'As long as it pays for the petrol, I'm more than satisfied'.

'Push' factors

Increasing numbers of people are being made redundant at an age when they consider they still have a great deal to contribute to society. Many such people take redundancy as an opportunity to reassess and redirect their lives. The prospect of readily available jobs makes English language teaching an attractive option. Others, including people in professions such as accountancy and law, can find their current jobs empty and unfulfilling. Acquiring a CELTA certificate gives them the option of leaving, or of taking time out, if they so wish. Other people do CELTA courses to open up new possibilities, when they become aware that career prospects in their current position are limited. Alternatively, people who are in established positions may feel bored by the routine nature of their jobs – and believe that teaching English will give them the mental stimulation they crave.

Trained teachers who have worked for a number of years in the primary or secondary sectors are increasingly tempted to move sideways into an area of teaching that they believe will give them more personal satisfaction than their present job. One teacher described such people as 'refugees from the failing public system'. It is a sad reflection on the state of the public education systems of certain English-speaking countries that many teachers feel that teaching in schools is a matter of survival – described by one teacher as 'going into a battlefield every day'. Describing her decision to leave high-school teaching, one teacher said:

> I thought to myself, 'I don't want to work in a school in London because it's going to be so much about discipline and so little about teaching'. You've got to be a bit heavy and behave in bossy ways – and I don't want to have to do that. It's not the way I want to be.

High-school teachers are aware that language learners, particularly adults, are on the whole highly motivated and unlikely to cause discipline problems. The prospect of teaching students 'who don't goof around all day' offers a refreshing alternative.

In sum, intensive English language teacher training courses contain the widest possible mix of trainees, ranging from recent graduates in their early twenties through to people of retirement age. They contain people with a wide variety of previous work experience, ranging from secretaries and conversation tutors to geologists, bankers and personnel managers. They often contain trainees with some kind of educational background, ranging from primary school teachers to head teachers or school administrators.

What is the experience of training to be a language teacher like for this varied collection of people, each with their individual set of life experiences and their own particular reasons for aspiring to be a language teacher?

Ferguson and Donno (2003: 31) point out that little is known about how beginning EFL teachers view their careers and talk about them, about what happens to teachers and what support they receive in their first post, or about how they view their certificate training in retrospect.

2.2 The training experience

Roberts (1998) provides a detailed description and analysis of the CELTA teaching qualification, which he describes as 'an initial, almost survival-oriented form of training'. He points to its value as a practical, classroom-based preparatory language teaching certificate that gives trainees the opportunity to teach real groups of learners and to receive immediate feedback on their personal pedagogic skills (1998: 211).

Sink or swim

One of the strengths of intensive English language training courses such as the CELTA is that trainees are given hands-on experience of teaching classes of language learners right from the start. There is no time to give trainees all the required input before having them teach classes. If they are doing a four-week course, trainees find themselves scheduled to teach their first lesson on the second or third day. Under such conditions it would be unusual for any trainee, regardless of inner reserves or high levels of self-confidence, not to feel twinges of nervousness and trepidation when required to stand up in front of a class to give a practice lesson. The situation is compounded by the fact that their performance is closely monitored. As one trainee commented:

> You've not only the learners all there in front of you – you've got your tutor and also all your peers looking on with pens poised, doing all this note-taking about your technique – so you just lay yourself open to criticism.

It is not possible to predict which trainees will cope best with what might be termed 'performance anxiety'. One teacher reported that she had been the least nervous of all the people on her course – attributing this to the fact she already knew what it felt like to be deeply hurt (having previously done a training course where her manner had been roundly criticised). A young woman who had recently completed a CELTA course estimated that her stress level during the course was a six on a scale from one to ten – regarding herself as more fortunate than her peers because, having recently obtained her degree, she was still in studying mode. She recalled watching a trainee sitting silently with tears rolling down his face when receiving feedback on a lesson that had gone drastically wrong – saying that she had felt like going over and putting her arms around him. She also recalled how wonderful it had been to see the expression on this man's face at the end of the course – by which time his teaching skills had much improved.

Sometimes older and outwardly self-assured people find the English language training experience particularly gruelling. In a sense this is natural: older people are used to commanding respect for being successful in whatever they do. The spectre of failing to give an effective lesson (however much the trainer assures them that making mistakes is a natural part of the learning process), and of facing public humiliation, looms particularly large in the eyes of some trainees. One such person, an experienced teacher, broke down in tears in the ladies' toilet prior to giving a practice lesson on more than one occasion – and said to the trainee who commiserated with her, 'I've been teaching for 25 years and

I've never felt like this before. I'm a grown woman and I don't understand why I'm so nervous.' Occasionally trainees fail to turn up to give their designated practice lessons, and have to be counselled by their trainer not to give up, but to continue to the end of the course. However, figures indicate that, in light of the rigorous selection process involving a detailed application and interview, provided they complete their course and complete the required assignments, trainees are unlikely to fail. According to Roberts (1998: 202) the pass rate for the CELTA course is approximately 97 per cent, with 2–3 per cent receiving an A-grade pass, 25 per cent receiving a B, and the vast majority of candidates (70 per cent) receiving a pass grade. Only 2–3 per cent of candidates fail the course.

Interestingly, the kinds of people who can most easily become stressed by the experience of participating in CELTA training courses are often teachers. There are a number of reasons for this. Teachers may feel that they know it all already – and may not agree with what might be termed 'teaching the CELTA way'. Even after making a determined effort to master the techniques that are required, they may find to their dismay that they do no better than trainees half their age who had never taught a lesson in their life prior to joining the course. Ex-teachers may also find it difficult to adopt the kind of persona that is appropriate for teaching adult language learners. They may find it difficult to discard authoritarian ways of behaviour or, if they have taught young children, to discard their primary school manner for issuing instructions, such as, 'Pencils down now, please – and all eyes towards me!' Finally, ex-teachers may resent having their lessons criticised or, in the words of one trainee, 'being roasted along with everyone else'.

Some trainees adopt a philosophical stance, taking the view that, provided they do what is required, they will pass the course and all will be well. In the view of one such person:

> It's a matter of realising how the CELTA people want you to teach. And then, provided you follow the pattern they want, you'll meet their criteria and they'll be happy.

Another, older, trainee had a similar attitude, saying:

> When you start anything, and it doesn't turn out right, you tend to think it's all your fault. But when you're older you decide it's not worth jumping off the balcony – you go and have another gin and tonic instead. Depression isn't worth the trouble.

For many people, however, the desire to learn how to do things properly and to avoid making mistakes in front of others is strong. Doing what they perceive as muddling through is not good enough.

So much to learn and so much to remember

The compressed nature of teacher training courses such as the CELTA, particularly when conducted in intensive mode over a four-week period, means that there is an enormous amount of information to absorb, and a wide variety of skills to acquire, in only a very short space of time. Trainees need to learn how to plan, organise and pace lessons; how to select, sequence and organise learning tasks; how to implement a range of specific language teaching techniques including eliciting, clarifying and concept checking; how to relate to students both individually and collectively, and so on. They also need to understand the principles underpinning vocabulary development and the teaching of reading, writing and phonology. Most challenging of all, it is necessary not only to start to understand how the English language is structured, but also to identify suitable ways of teaching it. All of this requires becoming familiar with a large amount of specific language teaching terminology.

Trainees need to ask themselves the following kinds of questions. What is the difference between TTT (teacher talking time) and STT (student talking time), and why is it important to think in terms of balance when planning lessons? What on earth is the information gap principle? What is TBL? What is the difference between PPP and ARC sequences, structures and functions, macro-skills and micro-skills, controlled and free practice, top-down and bottom-up approaches? Why is it essential to master MCQs (meaning check questions)? What is the difference between a proficiency and an achievement test? The list seems endless.

One of the biggest hurdles for trainee language teachers is coming to grips with English grammar. It is one thing to speak English fluently – and quite another to understand how the language functions as a system. Formal study of grammar has been unfashionable in English-speaking countries for many years. Unless they have studied modern languages, few native speakers are likely to have a sound overall knowledge of grammar or sentence structure – and may have only a hazy knowledge of parts of speech. Some trainees, realising from the pre-course test that their knowledge is limited, seek professional help to improve their knowledge of grammar before starting their course. One history graduate complained bitterly about having completed 15 years of full-time education without ever having been taught the difference between an adjective and an adverb. Another trainee explained how, feeling sorry for a fellow trainee who was struggling desperately to understand basic grammatical concepts, she spent time trying to explain what an infinitive was. In her view, 'Because he was in overload mode, something simple like that just didn't sink in'.

Teacher trainers impress upon trainees that they do not expect them to absorb all the information that they are given during the course – or to understand anything beyond the very basics of English grammar. They find themselves reiterating to trainees that it is important they revisit their notes on a regular basis once they are in the workforce – because this is the time when a great many concepts that were only half understood during the course will become clear. However, trainees are living in the here-and-now – and tomorrow's lesson must be prepared. If their lesson is to have a language focus, they need to understand how a particular structure works, and prepare a suitable context for teaching it – all before tomorrow. The situation is compounded by the fear that students will ask them questions about grammar points they may not be able to answer.

The importance of lesson planning is regularly stressed by teacher trainers, who may use the aphorism 'failing to plan is planning to fail' to impress upon trainees the importance of careful and detailed lesson planning, with a specific number of minutes allocated to each lesson segment. Learning how to develop and articulate lesson objectives, and then select and sequence tasks and activities that are likely to lead to the achievement of those objectives, is a fundamental part of learning how to teach. Lesson planning is not easy: it is time-consuming and requires a lot of thought. Then comes the business of organising and preparing teaching materials for the lesson. This can involve finding authentic materials or realia to stimulate interest, developing or finding appropriate worksheets and then photocopying the required number, checking that the tape recorder is working properly (and contains the right tape, wound on to the correct spot), and so on. All these preparations take time and need to be done well in advance to avoid last-minute panic.

The final hurdle is actually delivering the lesson. In the early stages of learning to teach, trainees find sticking to a lesson plan and actually teaching what is on the plan extremely challenging. Often timing goes out of the window, with individual segments of the lesson taking either considerably more or considerably less time than anticipated. Trainee teachers tend to view lessons as collections of discrete parts, rather than as integrated wholes. As yet unable to see which parts of the lesson are more vital than others, they are unsure whether or not to terminate an activity and move on to the next segment – particularly when the students seem interested and involved. Sometimes trainees let the warm-up activities run on too long, forgetting that their function is simply a lead-in to the main part of the lesson.

Common pitfalls

As a general rule, trainees tend to rush through their lessons relatively quickly, moving on to the next segment before students have been able to fully benefit from the previous one. Although they set up appropriate opportunities for learning, trainees find it difficult to exploit their potential.

Even if it is evident that a significant number of students may not have understood a vital part of the lesson, trainees tend to press on regardless. As one teacher recalled, 'When I was a trainee I went at one speed only: fast'.

Why is it that trainees appear so keen to rush through their practice lessons – apart from a natural desire to get something that they feel nervous about over and done with as quickly as possible? First, trainees are aware that most of their practice lessons are formally assessed – and know that 'achievement of lesson objectives' (which they interpret as covering everything they planned to teach) is one of the criteria against which they will be judged. (In fact trainers in certain centres are quite flexible, and are prepared to judge lessons in terms of the achievement of broad lesson goals.) Second, many trainees have a strong desire to give interesting lessons, and believe that if they spend too much time ensuring that students understand – rather than having students engage in the lively interactive tasks that they have planned – the students in the class may become bored. They do not yet appreciate that students who believe that they are learning and understanding worthwhile things are seldom bored. One teacher explained that in his early days of teaching he had failed to appreciate that 'fifteen minutes of getting there was better than going there straight away'.

A further reason why trainee teachers tend to rush through their lessons is that they cannot yet extemporise. Even when they sense that they need to expand, they are unable to do so. This is not only because they do not realise quickly enough that additional clarification or practice is needed, but also because they do not have at their fingertips alternative ways of clarifying concepts: additional examples, analogies, synonyms and so on. Finally, trainees may be wary about creating opportunities for consolidation or further practice for fear of interrupting the overall flow of the lesson.

There are good psychological reasons why trainee teachers find it difficult to improvise in their lessons. Tsui (2003:4) quotes Livingston and Borko (1989) who point out that, to improvise successfully, teachers need to have an extensive network of interconnected, easily accessible schemata from which they can select particular strategies, routines and information in interactive teaching. Livingston and Borko put forward two reasons why novice teachers have difficulties improvising when the lesson deviates from their plan. First, they do not have as many appropriate schemata for instructional strategies to draw upon and second, they lack sufficiently well-developed schemata for pedagogical content knowledge to enable the construction of explanations or examples on the spot. See Chapter 7 for a description of the ways in which experienced language teachers routinely improvise during the course of their lessons.

A key problem facing trainee teachers when they come to teach practice lessons is that there is just so much to remember – and so much that can potentially go wrong. The tape recorder can fail to work, a set of work-sheets can be misplaced, a pile of overhead transparencies can slither to the floor . . . Untoward events such as these can 'throw' trainee teachers, making them feel more nervous than they already were. Even though they have carefully planned their lessons, trainees can find themselves doing things differently from how they intended. They may spend a disproportionate amount of time explaining something to one particular group of students (thereby neglecting the rest of the class), or find themselves giving instructions in a confused way when they had resolved to give them clearly and succinctly. It is not uncommon for trainees to breathe a sigh of relief upon completion of their lesson – only to realise to their embarrassment that in the heat of the moment they forgot to teach a crucial segment of the lesson. As one trainee commented, 'When you're frightened it's easy for your mind to go completely blank'.

The experience of standing up in front of a class when things are going wrong, and not knowing whether or how to redress the situation, is one that trainees do not easily forget. In the words of one teacher:

> I was out of control – even though I'd prepared it. I was kind of stuck in this mire of self-awareness of how I'd gone wrong, and couldn't get out of it. I was floundering. It's like quicksand dragging you down. I was focusing on what was going wrong and how to fix it, and watching the other trainees watching me and thinking to myself, how much do they realise what a terrible mistake I've made?

A particular problem for trainees, especially when their lessons have a number of discrete segments, is knowing how to sequence the various segments so that they form an integrated whole – and how to organise smooth transitions from one segment to the next. Recalling his experiences as a trainee, one teacher commented:

> You weren't quite sure how you'd get through the pair work onto the dialogue build and then back to the skills activity. It would make you nervous – and the more nervous you were the less confident you were in the classroom and the more the lesson would go off track.

In effect most trainees do teach certain lessons when things fall into place, and when they have the satisfaction of seeing students fully engaged and on-task. When this happens, they experience that inner thrill familiar to all teachers when they sense that true learning is taking place.

In the words of one trainee:

> You feel so excited when the lesson is going well, and when you feel they're understanding. You get a real buzz when it all clicks and you sense that they've got it. It makes you feel so good.

When their lessons go well, trainees feel a whole lot better. Their self-confidence is restored – and they believe that they will make good language teachers after all.

Being inward-looking

A priority for trainee teachers is naturally to master as many language teaching skills and techniques as they can during the period of their training. There are so many new techniques and practices to master, and so many different things to remember, that a large amount of concentration is required. Not surprisingly, trainees tend to be inward-looking – focusing on themselves and their own performance, rather than on how well their students are learning. As one experienced teacher with ongoing contact with trainees commented, 'The novices who are coming out of those courses are so keen to put what they've learnt into practice that what the learner is getting out of it is secondary'. One trainee explained that she had literally tried to block the students from her mind:

> I'd prepare and prepare and prepare, and probably learn by rote how it was going to be. I didn't want to allow the students to interrupt, because it was like, 'This is what I have to do. How can I fit the students in around it?'

Despite concentrating hard on what they are doing, all trainees gain an overall feeling of how their lesson is going: well, okay or badly. The problem lies in identifying the reason why students are not reacting in the ways that they had hoped, but are sitting quietly with puzzled looks on their faces, or keeping their heads bowed and avoiding eye contact. When invited in post-lesson evaluation sessions to suggest reasons why students found the lesson confusing, trainees find it difficult to identify the main reason. For example, they may say that the class did not understand their grammatical explanation because they were speaking too fast – when in fact they had confused the students by giving an incorrect or incomplete explanation.

Some trainees may only be minimally attuned to the classroom 'vibes'. One teacher who regularly had trainees observe her classes remarked that often during the lesson she might say to them, 'I'm changing what I'm doing now because the students are not with-it and seem very tired' – only to discover that the trainees had not been aware that the students were in the least bit tired.

A key characteristic of trainee and novice teachers is that they tend to take negative feedback personally, construing it as evidence of their personal inadequacies. Reflecting back to her early days in the classroom, one teacher said:

> At the beginning of my teaching career I was very conscious if a lesson went well or badly. I took things personally and my self-esteem went up and down according to how well or badly the lesson went.

As subsequent chapters will show, a key characteristic of experienced teachers is that they welcome all kinds of feedback – whether positive or negative. For them, negative feedback is a crucial means of subtly adjusting their pedagogic behaviour to meet the immediate needs of their class. However, for the majority of novice teachers (both trainees and teachers at the start of their careers) the technicalities of teaching remain foremost in their minds. When explaining how she felt when she started teaching, one teacher used the analogy of driving a car, explaining that she was so busy listening to the engine and working out when to change gear that she could not take in everything else that was going on.

Comment

Johnson (1996) reports on the initial training experiences of a pre-service teacher during her 15-week TESOL practicum in a US high school. The experiences of this teacher were clearly different from the experiences of trainees participating in a four-week intensive course of English as a foreign language for adults, who found themselves teaching on the second day of the course. Nevertheless, the following observations can be made:

- For both types of trainee the practicum was what Johnson describes as 'shrouded in tensions'. However, while the high-school teacher attributed lack of knowledge of the students in the classes she was teaching as one of the causes of her tension, the CELTA trainees identified limited subject-matter knowledge as a major cause of their feelings of tension.
- Both types of trainees were inward-looking, tending to focus more on themselves than on their students.
- While the high-school teacher was given theoretical input prior to her practicum, but little in the way of practical preparation, the CELTA trainees were given much practice with ongoing support, but little theoretical input.

2.3 Awakenings

Becoming a language teacher is about far more than mastering a finite number of teaching techniques and skills: it is about understanding how to relate to students, and how to customise lessons to the needs and interests of students. As Chapter 3 will show, the ways in which teachers come to this realisation – and become committed to ongoing professional development and change – vary enormously. As described above, during their initial training trainees routinely prioritise the refinement of teaching skills and techniques, and direct their efforts towards delivering technically proficient lessons. It may not be until considerably later that they feel sufficiently comfortable to focus less on their own performance, and more on student learning.

However, many trainee teachers sense virtually from the outset of their courses that it is beneficial to be outward-looking, and not to teach in a blinkered way. For CELTA trainees, a preliminary step along this path is to get to know the students who have put their names down for free language lessons, and whom they will be teaching. One trainee explained how thrilled she had been to meet the students and to discover 'a whole flood of people from different cultures and different language backgrounds, with colourful clothes and customs'. While chatting informally to people from different countries is something that some trainees find difficult, others cannot wait to seize the opportunity. Recalling her training experiences one teacher said:

> I made an effort before every prac to be there half an hour early to talk to the students. And I made sure that my lessons were all complete the night before, so that I wasn't out there photocopying madly just before the lesson started. And I spent half an hour to forty-five minutes talking with the students. And I could relate to the younger adults because I've got kids of that age of my own. And a couple of the people on my course said, 'The thing that you've got is: you've made friends with them'. And I did – I made contact with them – and my interest in them was genuine.

Trainees such as this person tend to find teaching practice lessons less of an ordeal, because they feel they already know the students. As she explained, 'When I was in class and made eye contact with them, I knew who they were and what their names were – and I wasn't a stranger to them either'. Such trainees, finding that relating to adult language learners and empathising with them is something that comes naturally, have a head start when it comes to teaching. This is not to say that other trainees do not catch up.

Wanting to teach in individualistic ways

Even at an early stage in their professional careers, significant numbers of trainee teachers have niggling feelings that there is more to teaching than simply teaching lessons in a routine way. Even though they would like to teach more innovative lessons, many trainees do not yet have the confidence to do so. One trainee believed that her lessons could have been brought alive by the judicious use of music – but explained that she had not dared risk going with her gut feeling and designing a lesson that incorporated a musical element in case the whole thing was a disaster. Another spoke admiringly of a fellow trainee with a teaching background who had passed the course with flying colours, saying that she hoped one day to be able to teach like her.

Some trainers are sensitive to the potential of individual trainees, and encourage able candidates to design innovative lessons. Other trainers encourage all trainees to deliver lessons from the assigned chapter in the coursebook in a relatively mundane but technically proficient way. Trainees who feel ready to spread their wings can find the latter approach artificially constricting. One trainee, who had already completed a postgraduate teaching certificate prior to doing a CELTA course, complained that her trainer had criticised her for wanting to 'deviate from the coursebook', telling her that she suffered from 'text avoidance syndrome'. In the words of this young woman:

> You were not allowed to do things differently – and that was very difficult for me. I kept wanting to take the language from the textbook and teach it in my own way. I mean, I wanted to do the same thing – but in a different way that might be more appealing or more captivating for the students.

This trainee felt that she was being pulled in two directions. While feeling confident in her ability to customise her lessons to meet the needs of the students, she was also aware that she was a novice who did not have the right to criticise those whom she assumed knew better than she did. Talking about her trainers, she said:

> Their argument was, 'The people who wrote the textbook are the experts. Why are you recreating the wheel? They've done the hard work for you, they're the brilliant ones who have been in the industry for ever. Just use their knowledge.' Which is true – I mean, I'm a new teacher, so what do I know about it?

The stirrings in the mind of this trainee suggest that she was ready to enter the workforce and work in the kinds of independent, self-directed ways that are routinely required of newly trained language teachers.

2.4 Early days in the workforce

Upon completion of their courses, trainees are strongly advised by their trainers to go out and get a job as soon as possible, in order to develop confidence and consolidate their skills. Having completed an intensive course with a considerable degree of information overload, it is only too easy to forget what has been learnt. One trainee who did not heed the advice to find a job straight away made the following comment:

> I'm absolutely terrified of teaching now, because of the gap since I finished. I haven't been using what I learnt, so I don't have the confidence any more. The thought of being thrown in at the deep end and doing relief teaching – without having time to prepare lessons – scares me. My tutor has advised me to have three emergency lessons up my sleeve – one for beginners, one for intermediate and one for advanced. But I'm still petrified.

Significant numbers of trainees successfully complete their courses and then, if they do not find a job straight away or if it is inconvenient to start teaching immediately, never actually use their qualification. However, because of the large number of job opportunities available for native English speakers with a CELTA qualification, most trainees who are serious about finding a job eventually find one – even if it turns out to be in a language school with a dubious reputation.

Some trainees feel confident about joining the workforce and getting down to teaching as soon as – or even before – their courses have finished. One trainee rang round a number of local language schools before finishing her three-month part-time course, and was phoned two days later with the offer of a fill-in job. Not flustered by the fact that the only instructions left by the outgoing teacher were to 'teach current affairs', this teacher bought a newspaper, selected an article she thought might be of interest, devised some activities, and went off without more ado to teach her first 'real' lesson.

If there is work available, it is common for teachers who have obtained good grades to find themselves invited to stay on and teach in the same language school that has run the course. One teacher who had taught French in a high school for many years decided to retire early and do a CELTA course. Her language teaching background, coupled with the fact that she related well to people, meant that she found the CELTA course easy – and achieved a high grade. She was immediately offered a job, which she described as 'just heaven'.

Although they are on the way to becoming proficient language teachers by the time they complete their courses, most trainees take time to develop confidence and proficiency as language teachers. Not surpris-

50

ingly, a considerable number start teaching feeling that their teaching skills and subject-matter knowledge are inadequate for the task.

Feelings of inadequacy

When describing how they felt when they first started teaching, language teachers often recall feeling like 'fakes', 'frauds' or 'impostors'. They also talk about 'bluffing' or 'blundering on'. These terms suggest that in their early days of teaching they were far from happy with their levels of knowledge and expertise. As one teacher explained:

> I did the course and that got me into teaching and that was fine, but I felt like I was a complete fraud, like here I was teaching English and I just didn't know enough. I could manage a classroom and there was a lot I could teach – but I think particularly my weak grammar knowledge really undermined my confidence. I just really didn't feel up to what I was professing to be.

Time and again teachers describe their initial period of language teaching as being a steep learning curve – a time when they spend their evenings hastily familiarising themselves with the structure of their own language so that they can explain it to others the next day. As one teacher remarked, her familiarity with French and German was of little use when she began teaching English: she had to learn a whole host of new grammatical categories and concepts from scratch.

The reason newly trained teachers feel under pressure is that they realise that the students they are teaching expect them to understand how English functions as a system and expect them to be able to explain the rules of English grammar. The expectations of the students are not unreasonable: surely any native English speaker with a language teaching qualification has a full and detailed knowledge of how the English language works?

Teachers find themselves compelled to learn how to explain the structure of the English language using the terminology with which their students are familiar – which is usually that used in commercially produced textbooks. Until they have familiarised themselves with the rules such as those governing the use of the definite and indefinite article, or those that categorise the conditional into three broad types, novice teachers live in constant fear that their lack of knowledge will be exposed. One trainer recalled observing trainees becoming completely panic-struck when asked questions that they could not answer. Another described the experience dramatically as 'standing there naked in front of the class with your imperfect knowledge of the English tense system exposed for all to see'.

Training to be a language teacher

Newly trained teachers are aware that their knowledge in other aspects of English language teaching is also limited to the basic, introductory input they were given during their training courses. In the words of one teacher:

> When I first started in ESL I was very aware that I was entering a
> whole new profession and there was so much I needed to know. I
> mean you never stop learning, you never stop growing – but I felt
> that in order to be functioning competently there was a certain
> level of knowledge I needed to have. I needed to know about
> reading and writing and pronunciation and vocab and listening
> and speaking – all those sorts of things. And I remember thinking,
> Gosh! I've really got to swot up on all this before I go into the
> classroom.

Teaching in rigid ways

When invited to reflect upon how they taught when they first qualified, experienced teachers regularly point out that they taught in rigid ways. The following is a typical comment:

> When I first started, and I'd just done my EFL course, I followed
> very strictly what I'd done on the course. All my lessons if possible
> went exactly to plan, and I thought that I'd done really well if it
> went exactly to the plan – to the minute.

Many experienced teachers believe in retrospect that it was important to discipline themselves to follow lesson plans in their early days of teaching. They make comments such as, 'I think it was good for me then, because it helped me to realise that aims and objectives are important', or, 'especially when you've just started teaching, you do need to follow a plan so that you know where you're going – and can anticipate problems'. This reliance on lesson plans – a characteristic of novice teachers who are conscientious and aspire to teach well – is related to the perception that good teaching has to do with the flawless delivery of lessons. In the words of one teacher:

> I thought the perfect lesson had to consist of certain segments, and
> if I didn't go through these segments in order, and do the things
> that I'd been told I had to do – right from the beginning to the end
> of the class – it would be an inadequate lesson.

Certain teachers recall feeling angry and frustrated with themselves for teaching in such rigid ways. Reflecting back on her early days in the language classroom, one teacher commented:

> When I first started teaching I probably put all my focus on
> preparing the lesson, timing the lesson and so on – and always

being frustrated when it didn't always give you that satisfaction. You didn't always feel that it was a good lesson, and I used to think, 'What am I doing wrong?'

Questioning what they do is a vital step along the path towards becoming committed to ongoing development and change: the hallmark of the successful language teacher.

2.5 Conclusion

This chapter presented the first steps in the process of becoming a language teacher by describing the experiences of trainees and newly trained teachers. It began by identifying some of the main reasons that lead people from a variety of walks of life to take preparatory English language teaching courses, in terms of both 'pull' and 'push' factors. It then described key aspects of those courses, focusing particularly on trainees' experiences of teaching practice. It explained why this crucial element of teacher training courses is particularly challenging and often causes high levels of stress. The chapter described the kinds of difficulties that trainees typically experience as they teach their practice lessons, showing how their emotions are closely linked to the perceived success or failure of each lesson. It also identified the inward-looking focus of trainees who are struggling to master so much – and contrasted it to the more student-centred behaviour that gradually develops. The chapter concluded by focusing on the movement of newly trained teachers into the workforce, showing that, while they have the makings of proficient teachers, they are acutely aware of their limitations.

Summary

- Because of the growth in job opportunities, English language teaching is an attractive career option for native English speakers.
- Native English speakers at a range of different stages in their lives, and for a range of different reasons, participate in intensive English language teaching programs.
- Nearly all trainees find that participating in intensive language teaching programs is a demanding experience, even though virtually all of them pass in the end (see page 41).
- Trainees find it difficult to absorb fully the large amounts of information presented during intensive language teaching courses.
- Significant numbers of trainees lack a detailed knowledge of the structure of the English language, and find it difficult to identify contexts that demonstrate how particular structures are used.

- During practice lessons trainees find it difficult to put into practice all the different things they know they should be doing.
- Trainees can readily sense when their practice lessons are not going to plan but, rather than attempt to redeem the situation, tend to press ahead.
- During practice lessons the focus of trainees is on themselves and how effectively they are implementing their lesson plans – rather than on the students and how much they are learning.
- Trainees vary in the speed at which they absorb the key principles and techniques of communicative language teaching, and in the ease with which they relate to students.
- When they first enter the workforce, newly trained teachers find it necessary to disguise their lack of knowledge and expertise, and tend to teach in rigid ways.

Looking ahead

The following chapter focuses on the professional development opportunities available to language teachers, and on the processes that occur in the minds of language teachers as they mature and become committed to ongoing self-improvement.

3 Becoming a committed language teacher

The previous chapter described the collective experiences of prospective language teachers as they participate in intensive English language teaching courses. It focused particularly on the struggles that trainees have in developing, within a restricted time frame, sufficient knowledge and practical skills to teach a class of adult English language learners. The chapter ended at the point where newly trained teachers are ready to enter the workforce, armed with enough basic knowledge and skills to teach English – but aware of their limitations.

The present chapter continues the story of the professional development of language teachers. Section 3.1 describes the kinds of conditions under which language teachers typically start teaching, and identifies the priorities and concerns of language teachers at this early stage in their careers. Section 3.2 describes the kinds of professional development opportunities open to language teachers and how they take advantage of them. Section 3.3 moves on to describe the processes by which language teachers mature, showing that all teachers develop in unique ways, at different rates and in response to different catalysts. The final section of the chapter, Section 3.4, identifies the characteristics of language teachers who are reflective practitioners and committed to ongoing self-improvement.

3.1 Starting out

Typical first jobs

For newly trained language teachers, a first job in an English-speaking country often involves teaching on a temporary basis in a private language school. As described in more detail in Chapter 10, independent language schools run flexible numbers of classes, depending on student demand: when numbers are high, new classes are opened, and when numbers are low, classes are closed.

Many language teachers start their careers by finding a job in the summer months, when the demand for English language tuition is particularly high. The numbers of students from European countries ranging from Spain to the Ukraine who wish to spend part of their summer holidays having fun and learning a bit of English (or perhaps studying more seriously) have reached epidemic proportions. This means that language schools in English-speaking European countries from Ireland to Malta can suddenly find themselves in urgent need of additional teachers, whom they normally employ on a casual basis. Newly trained teachers fresh from CELTA courses are ready and willing to fill the positions – a situation that suits everyone all round. The language schools get their enrolment fees, the students get their tuition – and the novice teachers have the opportunity to practise their skills on classes of language learners who, being on holiday, are unlikely to be too demanding or critical. However, teachers have to be on their guard because, as one teacher remarked, 'There's always the odd poker-faced student who wants to do more than go shopping'.

Many other language teachers start their careers by being in the right place at the right time: contacting a language school at a time when additional teachers happen to be needed. Typically, newly trained teachers are given work, ranging from a few hours of teaching a week to a full-time load, with lower or intermediate-level classes. The director of studies will probably take them on a conducted tour of the building and classrooms, introduce them to other teachers who happen to be around, point out the resources and the photocopier, give them a copy of the coursebook – and leave them to it. Although they may receive help from other teachers, everyone tends to be busy – so to all intents and purposes novice teachers find themselves on their own. Reflecting back, teachers frequently talk about their early experiences as 'being thrown in at the deep end' or 'having to sink or swim' – images that suggest that, at this initial stage of their careers, survival is a key priority.

It is important for novice teachers to create a good impression in their first job: ensuring that their face 'fits' in the language school that has offered them temporary employment. If they get on well with the other teachers, and the director of studies is satisfied with their performance (either by observing them or by receiving informal feedback from staff or students), further work is likely to be forthcoming. Even if there is no further work immediately available, the name of the novice will be added to the list of people who can be contacted at short notice when more work becomes available, or if relief teaching is needed. If the impression they have created is less than satisfactory, they are unlikely to be given the promise of further work.

Although some novice teachers are fortunate to find jobs in language schools with good reputations and high levels of professionalism, others find jobs in lower-rung language schools where the pay and conditions may be far from ideal. Being new to the profession, newly trained teachers cannot afford to be choosy and in any case find it difficult to distinguish between the conditions and opportunities provided by different language schools. Even if they find themselves teaching in schools whose internal organisation they may describe as 'a shambles' or 'an impossible mess' – and their own experience as 'baptism by fire' – newly trained teachers with resilience and a positive attitude can still learn a surprising amount from negative experiences. In the words of one teacher:

> I knew I'd got a rotten job the day I started and I felt like walking out there and then. But I decided to stick it out because it's not like me to give anything up – and I learnt a lot in the end.

Traumatic initial teaching experiences, in which they find themselves teaching in stressful situations without the support that they need, can turn some novices off language teaching for good. Other more resilient souls put the experience behind them and start looking for better jobs.

Teaching overseas

Upon completion of their certificates, some newly qualified language teachers apply for and are given jobs in good-quality language schools in non English-speaking countries. Such schools recognise the potential of CELTA-trained teachers, and provide them with the professional development support that they need. Other teachers – particularly those in the older age bracket – may be offered contracts to teach overseas either on the strength of their previous teaching experience, or because of demonstrable life skills acquired through working in other areas. Many of these jobs work out extremely well – and if they do not the teacher can always jump on a plane and return home (which some do). It is also common for newly trained teachers, particularly those in the younger age bracket, to travel overseas and seek employment once they arrive in their country of choice. Again, there is a huge variation in the type of jobs available: some are highly satisfactory from the point of view of the newly trained teacher, others less so.

One problem that can arise is that newly qualified teachers may find themselves with restricted opportunities to implement the teaching approach that they have learnt and that they believe to be 'the best', or even 'the only effective way', for students to learn English. It can be very frustrating to find that students, within the comfort zones of their own cultures, are unwilling to engage readily in communicative activities. Sometimes teachers feel that their newly acquired teaching skills are wasted. As one recalled:

> The local teachers didn't want me to be there. They didn't see me
> as contributing to the system, but as a bit of light relief. The
> students' attitude was: 'Pete will entertain us and tell us all about
> Australia and draw pictures of koalas on the board and make
> kookaburra noises or something'.

In some ways it is not surprising that local language teachers sometimes
resent the presence in their schools of bouncy young native speakers of
English with introductory language teaching qualifications and breezy
personalities – and only allocate them conversation classes. How can
these young people know nearly as much about local conditions, and the
kind of teaching that is required to enable students to pass local exams,
as they do? The fact that fun-loving young people may speak English
more fluently than they do – while apparently knowing far less grammar
– can be particularly irritating.

Having fun

Happily, most newly trained teachers who start their teaching careers in
English-speaking countries are thrilled with their initial experiences in
the language classroom, particularly when they find themselves teaching classes of adult learners who do not require disciplining in traditional ways. Being in charge of a class of responsive and motivated
language learners is an exciting experience, especially for someone who
has moved out of a high-school environment, or has recently made a
career change in favour of a more people-oriented job. As one newly
trained language teacher remarked, 'it's a million times better than
sitting behind a desk'.

Armed with a range of techniques to encourage students to interact
with one another, novice teachers often find it relatively easy to create
classroom atmospheres that, in the words of one teacher, are 'abuzz with
excitement'. Most teachers find it exhilarating to watch language learners engaging animatedly in communicative activities set up by themselves. As one teacher remarked:

> When you first start off teaching you're a bit ignorant and it's all
> very exciting and stimulating and you just sort of go along and
> you don't know much about this area or that area, but you're just
> having such fun.

Many language teachers operate as enthusiastic amateurs for some
years, having developed a range of language teaching techniques for
energising their classes and convincing themselves that worthwhile language learning is taking place (see the 'party games syndrome' subsection in Chapter 8). Some readily admit that their attitude when they first

started teaching was less than serious, one teacher saying, 'I was just fluffing around', and another saying, 'After I'd finished the course I regarded the whole thing very flippantly and just enjoyed doing it and never took it any further'.

In view of the fickle nature of the profession and the relative lack of career paths (see Chapter 10), it is not surprising that many teachers are not particularly interested in working towards achieving a higher level of professionalism. After all, there are plenty of jobs to be had and, in the words of a contributor at a language teaching conference, 'Casually employed teachers tend to teach casually'. One teacher described her resolve to become a serious-minded teacher as 'turning sunbathing, drinking and partying into something much deeper'.

Being coursebook-dependent

Even though they have been taught how to organise individual communicative tasks, newly trained language teachers tend to breathe a sigh of relief when they learn that they are required to use a particular coursebook with the class they have been allocated. When asked how he taught in his early days in the profession, one teacher remarked, 'I would teach very much like we all started teaching – teaching from the book'. Following the structure of a coursebook is a natural thing for newly trained teachers to want to do. Well-structured coursebooks provide teachers with organisational frameworks, showing them how structures, functions, tasks, skills, topics and themes can be integrated. No matter that the coursebook may be linguistically or culturally inappropriate for some or even the majority of students in the class: it provides the novice teacher with a welcome blueprint – and a ready-made source of sequenced language learning tasks. As one teacher explained:

> I think when I first started I was much more reliant on published materials, because I didn't feel I understood what language teaching was all about. I relied far more on the teacher's notes to find out what the underlying aim of the activity was and what the language being represented was and how these things related.

The dilemma facing less experienced language teachers is the degree to which they should rely on the structure of a coursebook to give their particular course coherence. One teacher summed up the situation with the following comment: 'When I have a book I worry about getting through it – but when I don't have a book I worry about where I'm going'.

> In arguing for providing ongoing workplace support for less experienced teachers, Roberts (1998) points out that without this their isolation from other teachers could restrict them to a reliance on coursebooks to guide their teaching. As Roberts comments: 'While coursebooks are invaluable in supporting teachers, they may also push the teacher towards following recipes and routines (i.e. by following the book) and away from decision-making processes' (1998: 207).

Perhaps not surprisingly, newly trained language teachers tend to revere the superior knowledge and expertise of textbook writers. One teacher commented that he used to think that people who wrote textbooks were obviously far better teachers than he was, and that the materials and activities that they included in their books were naturally more relevant to his students' needs than anything that he himself could have devised. However, the more experienced language teachers become, the more prepared they are to criticise the texts and activities contained in their allocated coursebooks. As one teacher commented:

> At the point where I am now, I've found that I don't actually like a great deal of the stuff that's been written. It was a godsend when I started, but now I couldn't use it.

See Chapter 7 for a description of why language teachers regularly deviate from coursebooks, and the ways in which they do so.

Inner tensions

As described in the previous chapter, even trainee language teachers become aware that classroom language teaching is a dynamic process that involves far more than simply following the instructions outlined in the teacher's book that accompanies the allocated coursebook. In their early days in the classroom many language teachers sense, sometimes hazily and sometimes strongly, that they are not fully meeting their students' needs and expectations. One teacher described a turning point in her career in the following way:

> A few months into teaching I had to face things. I had to stop and say to myself, 'Hang on a minute here. This is not working. It's not what they want, it's not what they need. Just relax a bit, go more with them – let them tell you what they want to learn.'

This particular teacher was already moving down a path towards becoming an independent-minded language teacher who wished to be guided by her students' needs and teach in a more flexible way. She was moving away from a traditional model of teaching and learning, in the direction of a more collaborative one. When questioned further it became evident that this teacher held a process-oriented world view, seeing teaching as providing customised tasks through which students would learn, rather than as delivering a one-size-fits-all product.

Many language teachers find themselves facing similar situations, but do not yet have the confidence to modify their approach. Although they know that their lessons are not going as well as they had hoped, they lack the courage to experiment by doing things differently. One teacher explained that she would lie awake at night worrying that her lessons were boring – but was too scared to take the plunge and try something new. In her words, 'It's freaky for me to let go. I'm always wanting to be creative in teaching – but I don't trust myself to do so'. Although this particular teacher was dissatisfied with the book that she was using, she explained that she still required her students to complete the majority of the exercises contained in it. She justified her use of the book in terms of its power to validate her course, saying:

> If I rely on the book then the students will have confidence –
> because the book is written by experts, and they must be right. But
> I know the book's far from ideal . . . I suppose I can say that it sort
> of works for them, but it doesn't work for me.

Despite a number of years in the profession this particular teacher was not sufficiently confident to regard herself as the crucial variable that would affect the level of student satisfaction with her course. Like many language teachers in similar situations it seemed to be the case that the devil she knew was better than the devil she did not know. She preferred to play safe and follow the directions in the book, rather than, in the words of another teacher, 'teach in the way you think best, and win your students' confidence that way'.

3.2 Professional development

Unless they have a previous background in language teaching, it is rare for CELTA candidates to receive an A-grade pass for their courses. The majority of trainees receive a pass rating, with those who have achieved at an above average level being awarded a B-grade rating. Candidates in both the pass and B-categories receive comments on their certificates to the effect that, while they have successfully completed the course, they will benefit from ongoing support in their early days of teaching.

What form does the professional development of newly qualified language teachers usually take?

Ferguson and Donno (2003: 27) point out that the regulatory bodies of the CELTA are now more circumspect in the claims they make for the course. They say that CELTA is no longer seen as a preparation in itself for teaching, so much as an initial step along a longer road to professional development. This is evidently reflected in the recent CELTA syllabus, which requires candidates to develop an awareness of the need for continuing professional development.

Formal professional development: workshops

Some language teaching institutions, particularly ones that are located in cities in parts of the world where there is a concentration of language schools, bring in language teaching leaders from around the world to run professional development workshops. Such people regularly fly in and fly out, leaving behind a range of new theories and ideas for teachers to adapt to their local teaching contexts. Other institutions spend allocated professional development funds on presentations by experts in a range of related fields. A teacher who had worked for many years in the Adult Migrant English Program in Australia was full of praise for the fascinating talks and workshops that she had attended over the years, particularly about issues relating to migrant health. Local language teaching organisations often run professional development workshops, which may or may not be well attended – depending on how exhausted teachers feel by the end of the day or week.

Individual language schools sometimes provide formal professional development opportunities for their staff. When they do so it is typically in the form of lunchtime sessions in which experienced colleagues share their ideas with others. However, some language schools provide their teachers with no formal professional development at all. Professional development costs money because, apart from paying the speaker, the school must also pay teachers for time when they are not actually in the classroom and engaged in the business of teaching. In some language schools this is an ongoing bone of contention, with teachers demanding professional development sessions for which they are paid.

When they recall the professional development experiences that have had an impact on their teaching lives – stimulating them and making a long-term difference to the ways they teach – language teachers invariably remember speakers who have themselves been in the classroom. They sense that such people talk from the heart, recalling some as being 'inspirational'. One teacher talked in glowing terms about Thornbury's notion of 'plugging in' to students' lives – using information provided by students themselves as the raw data for lessons – and she resolved to put these ideas into practice as soon as she returned to her classroom (see the reference to the Dogme approach in the Box on p190). Other teachers value professional development workshops that affirm what they are already doing, thereby boosting their confidence that they are doing things right. As one teacher commented:

> When I go to meetings and people are talking about things they've tried in the classroom and are giving us demonstrations, I find it so reassuring, because I sit there and I think, 'I can relate to that. That's the kind of thing that I do in the classroom.'

For high schools and accredited language schools the provision of professional development for teaching staff is usually mandatory. Language teachers report that input sessions vary in quality, some being extremely valuable and others 'a complete waste of time'. Some language teachers admit to having become somewhat sceptical over the years, casting their eyes to heaven when recalling yet another workshop in which they were required to share their ideas and experiences in group sessions, with the facilitator bustling around but giving little in the way of solid input. Experienced teachers tend to be independent-minded and articulate and, if the things that they are told in input sessions do not accord with their experience of what happens in classrooms, are often more than ready to disagree with the speaker.

Learning from colleagues

When talking about their personal professional development, language teachers nearly always say that they learnt most from fellow teachers. One teacher who completed a nine-month postgraduate certificate in English language teaching (now no longer offered by the institution because of the popularity of the CELTA) recalled being asked at the end of the course who or what had contributed most to her professional development. Apparently she, along with everyone in her group, gave the same answer (quite independently of one another): they had been helped the most not by the staff, the lectures or the books they had read, but by fellow trainees more experienced than themselves who had been helpful and supportive.

One teacher who taught straight off the CELTA course (having been offered a job by the institution where she had trained) talked about how grateful she was to have been taken under the wing by one particular teacher, who functioned as her mentor. The mentor had lent her a file containing all the materials that she herself had used for the course, explained how she had used them, suggested alternatives, and shared ideas generally on how to be creative with materials. Evidently one of the techniques that the novice learnt from this teacher was that of putting words on cards and having students shuffle them around on the table for a variety of purposes: creating sentences, grouping words in sets according to meaning or grammatical category, and so on. The novice, who subsequently became a highly regarded teacher with particular skills in the teaching of vocabulary, said that in her view the card-shuffling technique was one of the best teaching tools she had come across 'because it gives the students the idea of the fluidity of the language'. The novice explained that she felt extremely fortunate to have had a mentor who had been so generous with her time and ideas, saying, 'Without her I'd have been completely at sea'.

Unfortunately it is rare for teachers to report being helped and supported in their early days of teaching to the extent that this teacher was. Although the value of the mentor system is widely recognised, and although mentoring systems are formally established in some language schools, it is common for the system to break down when things get busy, with meetings between the novice teacher and their mentor eventually petering out. In effect mentoring often seems to work best when it is done informally: when a generous-minded experienced teacher is prepared to devote time helping a novice teacher on a voluntary basis.

> Ferguson and Donno (2003: 31) report research by Helms (1999) which suggests that professional support to teachers in their first posts is variable and patchy. Ferguson and Donno make the point that, where the professional support of teachers is weak, the inherent limitations of the one-month courses can be exacerbated. As a result, while many teachers 'somehow muddle through and grow professionally', a few do not.

One of the most helpful things for newly trained teachers to do is to observe colleagues teaching and to glean ideas from them – not only about teaching techniques, but also about the kind of persona to project in the classroom. In reality, unless newly trained teachers are engaged in team teaching (a relatively rare occurrence), there is little opportunity for them to observe their peers. In most language schools everyone is teaching at the same time, and when people are not teaching they are busy preparing lessons. Unless a new teacher makes a special effort to visit the school at a time when they are not scheduled to teach, they are unlikely to have the opportunity to observe other people's lessons (something they found particularly helpful during their CELTA training).

Informal professional development: learning on the run

In reality the professional development of most language teachers occurs in a variety of informal ways. The most common one of these is chatting during lesson breaks, when teachers gather together for a cup of coffee or tea. Talking about the collaborative way in which teachers typically help one another out, one teacher said:

> At morning tea, if somebody brings up a problem, then the whole group gets very interested and we discuss and support each other, saying 'this works' and 'that works', and making suggestions: 'Why don't you try that?'

If teachers are sharing ideas in groups, those who are not central to the conversation tend to do what one teacher described as 'eavesdropping': listening in and picking up ideas that might be useful at a later date. In the words of one eavesdropper:

> You listened to people around you and thought to yourself, 'Gosh, is that really what they do?' I always reflected and I thought, 'This is the way I'd want to do it.' I didn't necessarily want to copy them exactly.

Another time that teachers commonly share ideas is after class, when they are preparing their lessons for the following day. Recalling a language school with a strong culture of sharing, one teacher explained how useful it was to have the photocopier located in the same room as the reference books, saying, 'You could talk to whoever was around and just bounce ideas off other people as you were waiting for the photocopier to be free'. Indeed, it could be said that places such as the staff kitchen, the coffee shop, the resource room or the space round the photocopier function as the professional hubs of language schools.

Lave and Wenger (1991: 29) use the term 'legitimate peripheral participation' to draw attention to the fact that learners inevitably participate in communities of practitioners and that the mastery of knowledge and skill requires newcomers to move toward full participation in the sociocultural practices of a community. They explain that legitimate peripheral participation provides a way to speak about the relations between newcomers and old-timers, and about activities, identities, artifacts and communities of knowledge and practice. It concerns the process by which newcomers become part of a community of practice.

Some language schools have much stronger cultures of sharing than others. One teacher, who had taught in high schools before transferring to an independent language school, recalled with pleasure working in a school that had a particularly strong culture of mutual support. In her words:

> It was lovely and I was just learning so much and I've never known such a collegiate atmosphere anywhere before. Someone would look at you and say, 'Oh, are you having problems with that?' And they'd all just come around and offer you suggestions and give you different things. And when people did lessons and creative things and made up cards and all the rest of it, it all went in files for everyone to use. And so everyone shared, shared, shared. There was a huge sharing atmosphere in that place, and it was a lovely way to learn about the communicative style of teaching and to develop as a teacher.

Unfortunately there are plenty of language schools at the other end of the spectrum, where teachers keep a close eye on their personal files of ideas and materials for fear of others appropriating their innovative ideas and favourite activities. There can be good reasons for teachers' unwillingness to share their materials, one of which is job insecurity. As one teacher commented, 'Nobody shares in this place because people with established positions are jealously guarding them'.

A further reason why teachers may be unwilling to share their ideas and materials with others is of a practical nature. Unless a language school has an effective system in place whereby resource books and supplementary materials are designated for use with classes at particular levels, teachers can find that the previous teacher of the class they are currently teaching has already used some of their favourite activities. There is nothing more maddening than to walk into a class with a lesson prepared, only to have the students say, 'We did that last week'. In reality most language schools lie somewhere between these two extremes, with language teachers helping their colleagues out on an impromptu basis whenever the need arises.

Some language teachers are highly creative, becoming adept at developing activities and worksheets. Often their good ideas become shared knowledge very quickly. For example, if they happen to leave the master worksheet on the photocopier, the next person may well pick it up and slip it into their file for future use. One teacher admitted feeling guilty at having 'squirrelled away' worksheets that she knew had been developed by a colleague. Some teachers are amused to find worksheets and activities that they developed many years previously being used by newly trained teachers, who have no idea of their origin.

In sum, because such a large proportion of the professional development of language teachers occurs through fraternising with colleagues, finding out what they do and exchanging ideas with others at the grass roots level, there is a vibrant folk culture of teaching. New ideas of things to do in the classroom are passed from teacher to teacher, from school to school, from country to country, and from continent to continent, as teachers travel the world taking their ideas with them. It is almost as if there are parallel cultures of teaching running alongside one another: a higher-level research-based culture that many busy teachers tend to ignore, and a lower-level practice-based culture in which newly trained teachers soon become immersed.

3.3 Maturing as a language teacher

> 'Some teachers, like fine wines, keep getting better with age.'
> Arends (2004: 29)

When listening to language teachers talking about their personal experiences in the profession, it is clear that the professional development pattern of each individual teacher is unique: some teachers develop quickly, others more slowly. Some report a change in behaviour that occurs as the result of a sudden realisation, while others report having gone through a gradual developmental process. Teachers also identify a range of catalysts that lead them to identify themselves as professionals and regard themselves differently.

It is relatively common for teachers to talk about personal transformations having taken place in a dramatic fashion, using expressions such as, 'It just happened overnight', or 'The lights were suddenly switched on'. Changes such as these can occur at any point in a teacher's career. One teacher talked about a personal transformation having occurred after she had been teaching for a few months, another after she had been teaching for several years, and a third after eight years.

The fact that it is common for language teachers to report either sudden or gradual changes in their perceptions of themselves and their levels of professionalism may be partly because many start teaching before feeling fully competent to do so. Although most teachers lack confidence when they first start teaching, those who have completed extended teacher preparation programs and who have thorough subject-matter knowledge do not report transformations as readily as do CELTA-trained teachers. One teacher who began teaching French and Spanish after studying these languages at university and then completing a year's teaching certificate reported no dramatic change in self-perception after starting to teach: she simply gradually became more proficient. In contrast, as pointed out in this and the previous chapter, CELTA-trained teachers regularly drew attention to the fact that they felt incompetent in their early days in the classroom and were often able to pinpoint key moments of change. In the words of one teacher:

> For eight years I just blundered on and then suddenly, bingo! It just came together a bit more. All that experience suddenly culminated in a qualitative leap, when I suddenly got the picture, got the overall idea a bit more.

This teacher was referring to the fact that she suddenly found herself able to select materials and tasks on a rational basis – rather than simply going to the resource room and, feeling overwhelmed by the large quantity of resources, selecting materials virtually at random.

Recognising the need to change

The ways in which teachers change are varied – and often involve feeling dissatisfied with how they are currently teaching and resolving to do things differently. In the words of one teacher:

> After about five or six weeks I was really feeling like I was trying too hard, and it wasn't happening. I think I was throwing too much work at them, and expecting too much. So I decided to find out what each individual student liked – their passions and interests – and started creating lessons and conversations about certain things that different people loved.

Another teacher described her personal transformation in terms of becoming a more instinctive teacher, saying:

> I would say I started to change very quickly into my first job – after about three months. I'd been so strung up and nervous after the course and so keen to keep to the principles and practices of the course that I was missing what my heart was telling me to do. It suddenly really hit me that I could do far better by forgetting what I'd been taught and going with my instinct. I decided to relax and not worry whether I was doing it right.

A high-school language teacher identified a key moment in her teaching career when she decided to change her classroom behaviour. She explained that she had felt dissatisfied with her teaching style and wondered why a particular colleague evidently was more successful than her despite not having such strong subject-area knowledge. She decided that the crucial difference lay in the fact that her colleague focused on developing a good relationship with her class – something that she herself had never done. She resolved to behave differently in class and experienced immediate success, recalling the transformation in these words:

> The day I decided to give focus to developing rapport with the students and giving that a priority – because that's what she seemed to be having success with – my whole teaching changed, and I've never looked back.

Other language teachers recall similar moments, one teacher resolving to 'establish intimacy with the class group' and another deciding to 'relax and be myself in the classroom'. As will be discussed in Chapter 4 and again in Chapter 12, establishing rapport is central to the success of language teachers who wish the students in their classes to engage readily in communicative tasks. Indeed, it may be that the ability to establish rapport between themselves and their students is a quality shared by all successful teachers. A language teacher from China believed this to be the case, saying that even in teacher-fronted lessons with large classes, where inter-student communication was not practicable, he believed establishing rapport with each class group to be essential.

The development of self-belief

It is common for language teachers' perceptions of themselves to undergo a process of gradual change. One teacher described this subtle shift in self-perception by saying that when he started teaching he did not regard himself as a language teacher but simply as 'someone who taught'. This particular teacher described his personal professional development journey in terms of three distinct phases: a phase of inexperience, a period of further study and a phase characterised by the feeling of 'having arrived':

> I started off as a graduate student. I was teaching, but I didn't really feel like a teacher. It was just a job I did. Then, later on, once I'd done that for long enough, I kind of identified with the role. But internally I felt I was a fraud, just getting away with it but making a reasonable income. For a long time it was like that. And I was feeling inadequate about my teaching, so I did formal study and that kind of helped me feel a little bit more confident about claiming to be a teacher – but even so I never felt like a real teacher inside. But then gradually, as I relaxed more about it, it dawned on me, 'Gosh! You're good at what you're doing.' *Then* I felt I could claim to be a teacher. And now of course I'm a passionate teacher, I love teaching . . . It's kind of gradual. You build up your confidence, your experience and your expertise, and then you feel you can claim to be a real teacher – not only in qualifications but also in outlook.

Another teacher regarded her professional development as a series of feelings that changed over time. She said that she began by feeling 'scared because of inexperience', progressed to a time when she felt 'more confident and perhaps too complacent' and finally reached the present period in which she felt 'in control and confident – but still knowing that there are better ways to teach'.

Clearly experience and length of time in the profession are factors that contribute to the overall levels of confidence of language teachers. The longer they have been teaching, the better they know their subject area, the more familiar they are with the kinds of classroom situations that are likely to arise, and the more strategies they have for dealing with those situations. As a result they are able to pay more attention to other things that are going on in the classroom. In the words of one teacher:

> Being experienced is about being so totally comfortable with your knowledge of the language that you don't need to study the worksheet or have the answer sheet. You can just do it on the spot while they're doing it – so you're not worried about your knowledge of the subject any more. And what you can do then is concentrate on other things. And that's when you start interacting with the class a lot more.

However, as described earlier in the chapter, length of time in the profession does not guarantee that language teachers will attain a higher level of confidence. Every teacher is unique, and not all teachers reach the point where they have strong feelings of self-worth and believe themselves to be true professionals.

Public recognition

People in any sphere feel good about themselves when their skills and talents are recognised, and when they sense that they are valued for what they do. Some language teachers recall specific moments in their careers when they received affirmation that they were committed teachers who were good at their jobs. Language teachers recognise that this affirmation, which comes in the form of positive feedback from administrators, directors of studies, colleagues or students, gives an important and often much-needed boost to their self-esteem.

Teachers sometimes report that being given additional responsibilities encourages them to regard themselves in a different light. One teacher said that she had considered herself to be 'a general dogsbody' until given the opportunity to become involved in setting up a master's program for the local language teachers in the country where she was currently working. Another teacher recalled being given sole responsibility for developing a government-accredited bridging program, which was then formally assessed. He described the growth of his professional pride in the following way:

> The program was proven over time to be a great success. There was lots of positive feedback going from the students to the director – so I felt very good about myself as a teacher. The skills that I developed through developing that course improved my confidence a lot. It was tremendous.

Language teachers also report that their view of themselves as effective teachers is affirmed when individual students thank them personally for their efforts and tell them to their face that they are good teachers. They feel particularly gratified when students make special requests to be placed in their classes. One teacher recalled feeling that all her hard work had been worthwhile when the director of studies told her that her reputation was 'legendary' – and that her writing class had a waiting list of students eager to join it.

It may be that regular affirmation of their teaching skills is something that all teachers need. For novice teachers who are as yet unsure of their teaching abilities, receiving positive feedback from students can mark an important turning point. A language teacher from China had vivid memories of a single incident that changed for ever his perception of himself – providing him with concrete evidence that his teaching skills were appreciated and enabling him, in his own words, 'never to look back'. The incident involved an electricity failure that required him to leave the classroom in search of help. On his return, instead of finding the class with their books packed away waiting to be dismissed, as he had expected, he found the students sitting with lighted candles waiting for him to continue the lesson.

Positive feedback from peers also encourages language teachers to rate themselves more highly. One teacher described how it was not until colleagues less experienced than himself started coming to him for help and advice on a regular basis that he came to regard himself as a senior staff member. His relatively low estimation of his personal knowledge and expertise prior to that time is reflected by his words, 'I surprised myself by how much I knew and how much I was able to help them'. It is perhaps a characteristic of teachers in general that they tend to err on the side of humility – underestimating rather than overestimating the skills and talents that they have acquired.

Engaging in further study

Catalysts for change also come in the form of opportunities for further study. One teacher found herself teaching in a language school in Japan at a time when a professional development package was offered. After completing the package, and becoming intrigued by the range of alternative teaching approaches and methods that were discussed, this teacher recalled saying to herself, 'This is exciting! I'm going to learn more about all this! This is just the tip of the iceberg.' She also reported that her self-esteem was raised when her assignments were returned with comments that revealed, in her view, a degree of closed-mindedness on the part of the tutors who had marked them.

Postgraduate or higher-degree programs often help to transform language teachers from what could be described as enthusiastic amateurs into people whose classroom practices are based on a sound theoretical knowledge of why particular teaching strategies are or are not effective. As one teacher commented:

> A sense of professionalism came when I had more of a sense of what I was doing and why I was doing it. I could relate the theory to the practice. I learnt which kinds of things that I do in the classroom engender learning – and which kinds of things undermine it.

Another teacher gave a practical example of how further study had informed her classroom practice. She explained that her knowledge of research into error correction gave her a theoretical basis for deciding when and how to correct her students' errors in order to maximise uptake of correct linguistic forms.

Further study not only enables language teachers to become more confident and self-assured, it may also lead them to become more independent-minded. Reflecting on the experience of teaching on a new program with an alternative syllabus framework, while at the same time completing a master's degree, one teacher recalled:

> I remember thinking, 'I know that! We do that!' It just confirmed and confirmed and confirmed everything that we'd been doing. But at the same time I was able to challenge some of the literature and say, 'That's a load of rubbish!' Because the person that's researched it isn't in the classroom from Monday to Friday. It's all very nice radical theory, but we are the teachers, and we know what we have to do when we get in there.

For this teacher, engaging in further study inspired her to consider her classroom as a laboratory and begin to experiment. She described the relationship between student feedback, her own confidence levels and her desire to innovate in the following way:

> It's when you start to experiment, and you get tremendous feedback or success from the students . . . that you think, 'Hey, I didn't pick that up from studying. I went out on a limb and I

experimented and I explored. The more risks you take, the more
confident you become. And the more confident you are, the
more adventurous you get. And so you push forward the
boundaries in methods and activities and what you do with the
students.

The way she talked about herself suggests that this particular teacher
found the prospect of teaching in innovative ways exciting and challenging. As the following section demonstrates, language teachers who
have undergone the kinds of transformations that have been described
in this section are driven by an ongoing desire for self-improvement and
change.

3.4 Ongoing development

One might have expected language teachers who have reached a high
level of competence to sit back, relax and take the easy path. Why do
things differently when classroom teaching comes easily, so that they
no longer have to think too hard about the structure of the language,
interaction patterns, or issues of classroom management? Why make
things more difficult than they need to be? Surely, having put in all that
hard work, experienced language teachers can take the easy option and
coast along, secure in the knowledge that they have worked out the
most effective ways to teach? To use a catchcry that is commonly heard
in language teaching circles, 'Why reinvent the wheel?'

The desire for self-improvement

The answer to the perennial question of why teachers who are confident
in their levels of professionalism routinely take the difficult as opposed
to the easy path lies in the fact that they are driven by a desire to seek
different and potentially better ways of doing things. For them it is not
enough to teach in the ways that they have always done: they want to
experiment, to try new things, to push forward the boundaries of what
they can do. One teacher with considerable experience in both language
teaching and adult training linked his willingness to experiment with his
desire for ongoing personal development, saying:

I'm always trying new ideas. Sometimes they work and sometimes
they don't. I think you're only as good as your last lesson. You
always develop and change. You should have a feeling that over,
say, the term or several weeks, your actual teaching style is
developing and changing. You're trying to become more relevant,
you're trying to engage students more fully. The way I feel about

> my teaching is that it's part of my personal development. And
> that's the key to my character.

Another teacher described the notion of commitment to change in terms
of striving for excellence. In her view, the difference between a good
teacher and a great teacher was that a good teacher could 'wing it' (do
things competently on the run), while a great teacher was one who constantly strove for excellence. Many other teachers express this commitment to change in terms of an ongoing desire to experiment, making
statements such as, 'I like to go forward and try this, have a go at that,
experiment with it and see how I get on'.

The desire for ongoing self-improvement expressed by the above
teachers reflects findings from research on the nature of expertise.
Bereiter and Scardamalia (1993), reported by Tsui (2003: 18), found
that experts set high standards for themselves and choose to put time
and effort into tasks, rather than completing them as quickly as possible. In comparison with non-experts, who tackle problems for
which they do not have to extend themselves, experts work 'at the
edge of their competence', tackling challenging problems and
thereby increase their expertise.

Bereiter and Scardamalia (1993: 34, reported by Tsui, 2003: 18)

The kinds of classes that language teachers are required to teach are to
some degree responsible for the evident willingness of teachers to experiment in an ongoing way. As will be discussed in Chapter 7, the heterogeneous mix of students in most adult language classes means that
teachers must constantly find new ways of meeting the needs of their students. No two courses can ever be delivered in exactly the same way
because the needs and interests of each student group are subtly different. In a sense, the nature of the job requires language teachers to be flexible and innovative throughout their careers.

A further reason why experienced language teachers continue to
experiment with ways of doing things differently, rather than delivering lessons in predetermined ways, is to avoid becoming stale. As one
teacher said, 'I'm still experimenting and trying out new techniques to
avoid getting bored. It's as much for my benefit as theirs.' This point
will be further discussed in the 'to thine own self be true' section of
Chapter 7.

This commitment to self-improvement is also demonstrated by the
common phenomenon of language teachers' teaching a certain class at a
certain level for a number of courses and then wishing to move on and
teach another class, either at another level or with a different focus.

Language teachers recognise the danger of becoming stale if they remain teaching the same kind of class and using the same kinds of materials for too long. Sometimes self-imposed change involves moving to a different institution. In the words of one teacher:

> Sometimes I've felt it's time for me to move on and do something different. Most of my contracts for jobs have been two to three years, and I find myself teaching different kinds of courses in each institution I've been to. I get pleasure out of trying a new kind of teaching and teaching different kinds of courses.

It is of course true that, like all teachers, some language teachers lose their enthusiasm and desire for innovation: it is simply too exhausting to keep on experimenting and trying new things. One teacher described this phenomenon as teachers 'plateauing out', while another described teachers in this category as becoming 'mummified'.

Being a reflective practitioner

A key feature of language teachers who are committed to ongoing development and change is that they are prepared to monitor the success or otherwise of their teaching practices on a regular basis. They recognise that, in the absence of anyone else to judge their performance (classroom observation of established teachers being extremely rare), they themselves must be the judge of their own performance. As one teacher said, 'I learnt a lot by looking at myself in the classroom and evaluating whether what I was doing was actually benefitting the students'. As another teacher explained:

> I feel the way I've developed over the years is to become a reflective practitioner. I think I'm very self-critical anyway, so I think it's a habit of looking at myself and saying, 'Am I doing that right?' And I learnt a lot by thinking about how students were reacting to what I was doing.

Teachers such as the person quoted above acknowledge that being a professional does not mean doing things perfectly all the time. Rather, it means accepting that there may always be a better way of doing things – and resolving to do things differently next time around. One teacher described her outlook in the following way:

> I always try to keep alert and identify the things that go well in lessons and the things that don't go so well. I see my professional development as an ongoing thing and I hope I'll never stop learning and growing as a teacher. The day I no longer want to keep on learning is the day I'll give up teaching.

Interestingly, even language teachers who are clearly proficient at their jobs are reluctant to place themselves in a 'highly experienced', or even an 'experienced' category, when it comes to how experienced they consider themselves to be. When asked why they rank themselves lower, teachers often make it clear that they regard themselves as 'arriving', rather than as 'having arrived', in terms of their professional development. Indeed, one teacher with five years of solid experience and a flair for innovation insisted on rating herself in the lowest category on a five-point level-of-experience scale, ticking the 'learning fast' box. This teacher's insistence that she still had a long way to go in terms of her professional development may have been partly due to false modesty. However, it also represents a view that is commonly held by experienced language teachers: that even though they regard themselves as professionals, they recognise that they cannot take anything for granted – and that there are always new things to learn and opportunities to do things better next time round.

Ongoing commitment to change

In sum, once language teachers have matured they regard themselves as genuine professionals who are capable of doing a professional job. They set high standards for themselves and work hard to maintain those standards. Even though they may behave in low-key ways they have the inner confidence of knowing that they have a better understanding of the students they are teaching than outside experts. This knowledge enables them to behave in independent ways, making executive decisions that may sometimes run contrary to current orthodoxy. Their extensive subject-area knowledge and broad experiential base enables them to teach with confidence. They readily acknowledge that they do not know the answers to the myriad problems that they face on a day-to-day basis, and know that they may sometimes make mistakes. However, they make an effort to redeem situations when things have gone wrong and to seek better ways of doing things in the future. They regard being a language teacher as an ongoing developmental process and wish to continue learning for the duration of their careers.

> **For further reading**
>
> Appel's *Diary of a language teacher* (1995) provides a fascinating account of the daily classroom experiences of a high-school language teacher. Each chapter contains selected diary entries collected under specific themes, followed by an analysis section in which the

author relates the diaries to relevant research and provides further thoughts and insights. In Appel's view the insights he provides highlight the complexities of school practice, and create a picture of development and change in a particular teacher.

3.5 Conclusion

This chapter began by describing the kinds of jobs that are normally available to language teachers who are fresh off CELTA or similar intensive language teaching courses, showing that some of these do not provide an ideal starting point. It identified the fact that, while many newly trained teachers find their jobs exciting and stimulating, they also have certain concerns. The chapter then described the professional development opportunities available to language teachers, emphasising the fact that for language teachers the most effective professional development takes place informally, through interaction with their peers. The chapter then identified the phenomenon of a shift in self-perception that typically marks the process of transformation of language teachers from inexperienced novices to self-directed individuals for whom ongoing professional development and change are part of who they are. It showed that this shift occurs in individual ways, in response to a range of catalysts, and can occur at any stage in a teacher's professional life. The chapter ended by describing the characteristics of teachers who have matured to a point where they are reflective practitioners who are self-critical and constantly seeking better ways of practising their craft.

Summary

- The kinds of jobs available to newly trained teachers are of varied quality, leading some novice teachers not to regard their jobs too seriously.
- In their early days of teaching, language teachers tend to rely on coursebooks to provide guidance on both what and how to teach.
- For newly trained teachers professional development opportunities tend to be limited.
- The most common way for novice teachers to develop and refine their skills is to learn from the teachers with whom they are working.
- The professional development pattern of each language teacher is unique.
- A significant number of language teachers identify critical moments in their teaching careers that caused them to regard themselves differently.

- A range of catalysts, including times when they receive positive feedback and periods of further study, can transform language teachers into self-confident and independent-minded practitioners.
- Whether it is a sudden shift in outlook or a more gradual developmental process, once this transformation has taken place language teachers become committed to ongoing development and change.
- Apart from an inner drive and a desire to do the best by their students, there are practical reasons why language teachers typically continue in their ongoing quest for self-improvement.
- Characteristics of language teachers who have developed and matured include: inner confidence; a willingness to be self-critical; independence of spirit; and a high level of autonomy and self-direction.

Comment

There is a large body of research on the development of expertise. Much of it focuses on contrasting the characteristics of novices with those of experts, or on identifying the characteristics of people at different stages in their professional development and categorising the stages of development in relatively fixed ways. Tsui (2003) provides a useful review of the field, examining in the second chapter of her book three prominent theories of expertise: Dreyfus and Dreyfus (1986), Chi *et al.* (1988) and Bereiter and Scardamalia (1993). As was revealed in the present chapter, the experiences of the language teachers who provided data for this book match most closely the Bereiter and Scardamalia model, although they also reflect features of the other two models. The Bereiter and Scardamalia model conceptualises expertise as an ongoing developmental process, rather than as a fixed point at which a person eventually arrives. In the third chapter of her book Tsui discusses the characteristics of expert and novice teachers that have been identified in the literature on teaching expertise. These findings are illuminating, since they help to explain why the newly trained teachers described in Chapter 2 of this book, and the more experienced teachers described in subsequent chapters, think and behave in the ways they do.

Looking ahead

The following chapter describes the classroom behaviour and practices of language teachers in the early days of each new course, as they seek to establish the classroom environments and behavioural patterns that they consider suitable for communicative language practice.

4 Establishing the learning environment

The previous chapter showed how becoming a competent and confident language teacher is an ongoing developmental process that involves being self-critical, learning from both positive and negative experiences, and constantly aspiring to higher levels of professionalism. It showed how, by following individual professional development patterns, language teachers gradually mature to a point where they feel confident about their ability to teach and manage their classes in self-directed ways.

The present chapter focuses on how language teachers go about creating the classroom environments they consider suitable for communicative language practice. Section 4.1 describes the kinds of activities that are typically set up in communicative classrooms, while Section 4.2 focuses on the fact that communicative classrooms in western settings are characterised by high levels of informality. Section 4.3 describes a number of important ways in which, in the vital first few lessons of each new language class, experienced language teachers establish rapport with their classes and create behavioural expectations for the students within them. The final section of this chapter, Section 4.4, outlines how experienced language teachers exercise authority in low-key ways. By so doing, they are able to maintain both the rapport that they have developed with their class and the overall atmosphere of informality and friendliness that they have cultivated.

4.1 What communicative classrooms are like

In language classrooms throughout the world there is a growing emphasis on oral communication. Clearly the ways that language teachers implement the communicative approach vary according to local contexts and conditions. This section describes the kinds of activities that are typically set up in communicative classrooms by teachers working in western educational contexts. However, it should be borne in mind that it may be neither possible nor appropriate for teachers in non-western educational contexts to implement the communicative approach in similar ways to those described here.

Activity-based lessons

Teacher training programs emphasise that learning a second or foreign language involves mastering a skill, rather than simply absorbing a body of knowledge: it involves developing the ability to communicate with others in an unfamiliar tongue. During the course of their training, language teachers learn a variety of techniques for encouraging students to interact with one another in the target language. These include communicative games and competitions, role-play activities, brainstorming activities (which require students to pool prior knowledge), information-gap tasks (which require students to share information amongst themselves in order to complete a task), problem-solving tasks, discussion tasks, and so on. Such tasks require students to speak with a partner, with a small group of fellow learners, with a variety of individuals (in mingling activities), in a chorus situation (such as a song or a group chant), or in front of everyone in the room (in a whole-class activity). Language teachers routinely require their students to swap seats, rearrange tables and chairs, gather together in small groups in different corners of the room, come up and write things on the whiteboard, and sometimes to rush around the room in competition with other groups. Language teachers may even take their students to different locations where language practice can more readily occur: in the hallway, in the courtyard, in the garden and so on – or send them out into the real world to practise their language with native speakers.

It is common to hear the scraping of chairs, a cacophony of excited voices and bursts of spontaneous whole-class laughter emanating from communicative classrooms. Teachers often remark that hearing sounds of animated behaviour coming from an adjacent classroom gives them the impression that the next-door teacher is more dynamic than they are. This can engender temporary feelings of envy or dejection – until they remind themselves that the learning activity that they are doing with their own class is equally valid, even though it may not generate so much noise or excitement.

Incorporating interactive games and tasks into language teaching programs is not the sole prerogative of primary and high-school teachers. Language teachers find that adult learners from overseas who have studied languages in very different ways respond equally well to the notion of engaging in interactive tasks. This is particularly so when learners have previously focused on the structure of the target language and on the development of reading and writing skills – with reduced opportunities for developing their speaking skills. Even when teaching reading or writing classes, language teachers regularly incorporate speaking activities into their lessons. Before asking their students to read a text, they may ask students to share with one another prior knowledge of the topic, brainstorm all the words they can think of relating to the topic, or predict the content of the reading from the title or other contextual clues. In writing skills classes language teachers may get students in groups to talk about what is happening in a series of pictures before describing the story, talk about their own experiences before recounting them, or discuss their views and opinions in small groups before committing their ideas to paper. In short, language teachers find it unnatural not to provide their students with opportunities to speak in their lessons, even in reading and writing classes. For them, speaking activities provide a useful and appropriate lead-in to reading and writing tasks.

In sum, language teachers place a high priority on oral interaction in their classrooms and are familiar with a wide range of games, activities and tasks that can engender classroom talk. What kinds of classroom environments do they consider appropriate for sustained language practice?

It is now widely accepted by educational psychologists that, whatever the subject taught, the psychological environment of the classroom, or 'classroom climate', is of vital importance. It is also accepted that teachers need to behave in certain ways for effective classroom climates to develop. According to Ormrod (2000: 601), teachers should do the following:

- communicate acceptance of, respect for and caring about our students as human beings;
- establish a businesslike, yet non-threatening, atmosphere;
- communicate appropriate messages about school subject matter;
- give students some sense of control with regard to classroom activities; and
- create a sense of community among the students.

4.2 Creating informal classroom atmospheres

Language teachers working in western educational settings commonly seek to establish informal atmospheres in their classrooms. They prioritise the establishment of informal atmospheres for a number of reasons. Firstly, common sense tells them that students will be more willing to practise speaking the target language in situations in which they feel relaxed and at ease. As one teacher said, 'I think, if the students don't feel secure and comfortable in the environment, they're going to put up all sorts of mental barriers and they're not going to learn as effectively'. For language teachers, classes with friendly, informal atmospheres provide just such environments. Secondly, classes with informal atmospheres provide teachers with plentiful feedback, allowing them to judge in an ongoing way the success of their teaching practices – and to adjust them as necessary. Thirdly, classes in which students behave informally and spontaneously can provide teachers with vital clues about interpersonal relationships and the wellbeing of individuals. Finally, classes with informal atmospheres enable students to behave in spontaneous ways. Such behaviours (provided they are ones that the teacher condones) can lead to the ongoing development and maintenance of a feeling of community within the class.

Language teachers go about establishing informal classroom atmospheres in a variety of ways. They encourage adult students to remain seated as they enter the room, to address them by their first names and to call out answers without raising their hands. They may call the class roll as they sit perched on the corner of the desk, perhaps making light-hearted remarks to the class as they do so. Alternatively, they may cast their eye around the room and say to the class at large, 'Who's missing?', possibly speculating jokingly with the class as to why a particular student might be absent or late. Language teachers sometimes create nicknames for students ('Superman' for the student called Clark, Señor Incognito for the student who wears sunglasses in class and so on), or they may encourage students to create their own nicknames. Some high-school language teachers encourage their students to adopt a nickname that they have chosen for themselves because, as one teacher pointed out, 'If you don't choose your own nickname the kids will create one for you anyway'.

Using humour to set the tone

Language teachers regularly say things in a joking manner to lighten the mood of their classes – and reinforce the notion that their classes are informal rather than formal learning environments. Many of them encourage their students to follow suit, showing appreciation by smiling, laughing or giving a quick response when they do so. Language teachers make it clear that they value humour and wish their lessons to be punctuated by regular small bursts of whole-class laughter. Over time language teachers develop individual, quirky ways of generating laughter that they use regularly in their lessons. Familiar with the kinds of words that could easily be confused through similar pronunciation or spelling, one teacher would regularly focus on key words with exaggerated intonation, saying, '*aid*, not AID*S*', 'topical, not tropical', or '*A*ustria, not Austr*a*lia!' Experienced teachers also have a sense of when a student has overstepped the mark and have at their disposal a range of low-key, semi-joking ways of expressing displeasure (see the final section of this chapter).

Many language teachers have extroverted personalities and a high degree of self-confidence, considering themselves to be 'people-oriented' individuals rather than dry academics. They have had plenty of practice at getting meaning across through exaggerated facial expressions, body movements, miming and so on, and are seldom self-conscious. As one teacher remarked, 'You've got to be prepared to jump up and down and stand on your head just to get your meaning across'. A middle-aged high-school teacher assured her students that she would never require them to do anything she would not do herself, joining in the games she set up for her students, including running around exchanging places in a game of 'language tag'. Language teachers regularly make quips or laugh along with their students when untoward classroom events occur, such as insects buzzing around the room or electricity failures. One teacher exclaimed, 'Ah, someone, trying to join the class!', when a window cleaner's ladder appeared outside the window.

Language teachers rely heavily on humour as a way of creating informal atmospheres in their classrooms. Humour is a powerful tool in the hands of experienced teachers and functions in language classrooms in a number of additional ways. Chapter 8 describes the key role that humour plays in vitalising the atmosphere of language classes, while Chapters 6 and 9 show how humour can be used to develop and maintain a feeling of community within language classes.

Korobkin (1988) provides a useful overview of some of the many roles that humour can play in the classroom. Quoting Ziv (1976) she says, 'An instructor who actively shares in the humor helps to cultivate freer interaction, idea generation and group cohesiveness while reducing social anxiety, conformity, and dogmatism'. Quoting Ziv again (1983: 74) she states, 'Once the authority figure has given approval and extended an invitation to laugh, the resulting contagious effect has a "... positive reinforcing effect on each member of the group, augmenting the enjoyment of all"'.

Alternating between roles

Although they are in positions of power in their classrooms by virtue of their assigned status as teachers, language teachers are keen to convey the impression that in another sense they are 'one of the crowd' and little different from anyone else. They want their students to consider them as real people with the same range of emotions as other people: the ability to have fun, the capacity to feel tired and grumpy on occasions and recognition that they too can make mistakes. One teacher explained that she hated creating the impression of 'being the teacher up on your pedestal and them being lowly students'. In order to demonstrate that the social distance between herself and her students was relatively small, she would make a point of saying to each new class, 'I'm no different from you: I just happen to know more English'.

A key characteristic of experienced language teachers, who are confident both in their levels of professionalism and in who they are as people, is their ability to switch roles in their classrooms. They are readily able to alternate between the more formal, traditional role of the teacher as the person who keeps control of the class and dispenses knowledge in time-honoured ways, and the less formal role of the class group member. One might have expected experienced language teachers, and particularly those who are no longer young, to maintain a degree of distance between themselves and their students. Why would they want to operate on the same level as their students? Surely to do so might mean losing control of their classes?

The key reason why experienced language teachers of any age find themselves operating on two distinct levels in their classrooms is that by so doing they enable a range of potentially positive social processes to occur. By behaving in formal, traditional ways – ensuring that their students are learning worthwhile things, and pulling their classes back before communicative activities get out of hand – language teachers enable their classes to feel united and confident in their ability to guide them with a firm and fair hand. By behaving in informal, less traditional ways language teachers facilitate the occurrence of a wide range of social processes that have the potential to unite their classes and help them to develop into unified classroom communities. As will be discussed in more detail in the final section of this chapter, and again in Chapter 12, language classes that function as cohesive groups can exert a powerful normative influence on the behaviour of individual class members. Teachers who behave informally therefore do not lose control of their classes – because the social processes that they have facilitated through their informal behaviour mean that the power of dissident individuals is reduced. It is difficult for a student to lead the class against the teacher if the teacher is not the enemy – but a friendly person to whom everyone in the room can readily relate.

In a sense it is the ability to maintain a balance in their relationships with their classes that provides a clue to the success of language teachers in communicative classrooms. If they are able to develop and maintain a high level of informality while at the same time retaining their authority and credibility as language experts, all kinds of potentially beneficial social processes can occur. High-school language teachers, who might have been expected to want to retain greater distance from their classes (because children tend to be more unruly than adults), also wish informal atmospheres to prevail in their classrooms. One young female language teacher working in a boys' high school recalled how she had initially started off by being very strict and projecting a 'tough woman' image. Later on she discovered that a far more effective way of managing classes of teenage boys was to chat to them informally as they dribbled into the classroom, get to know them as people, and 'always be prepared to have a bit of a joke'.

As early as 1980 Stevick drew attention to the fact that some of the best language teachers he had known readily switched roles in their classrooms, alternating between behaving conventionally as teachers and functioning as what he termed 'Fellow Human Beings' (1980: 28). Stevick used the image of masks to convey the idea of role-switching, talking about teachers coming out from behind their 'Teacher masks' and temporarily wearing their 'Ordinary Person masks'.

In the general field of education, Feiman-Nemser and Floden (1986: 508) draw attention to the same phenomenon: the duality of the role of the teacher. They state that an additional norm that governs teacher–student relationships contradicts the picture of the distant teacher, saying, 'The tension between these expectations for distance and closeness creates a fundamental ambiguity in the teacher's role.'

4.3 The vital first few lessons

Language teachers sense that the first few lessons of any new course are of vital importance. This is the time when they meet their students for the first time, when first impressions are created, and when norms of behaviour (of either a desirable or an undesirable kind) are established. During this period the kinds of questions that typically run through the minds of language teachers include the following: Are the students in the class going to be lively or withdrawn? Do the students look as if they are going to relate easily to one another and willingly engage in the kinds of interactive tasks that I plan to organise? Are there any bright sparks in the class who are likely to enhance the social development of the class group and/or help the class to learn? Are there going to be any tricky students whom I'm going to need to handle with care? Am I going to get on well with this class and enjoy teaching them?

Running through the minds of students is a parallel set of questions, which includes the following: Am I going to like and respect this teacher? Do they have a good level of knowledge of the language I want to learn? Are they going to make the lessons interesting? How strict will they be? What kinds of learning activities will I do in this class? Are there any of my friends in this class, or any students of my own nationality? Will I be able to sit next to them? Will the other students in the class be friendly towards me? Am I going to like this class and feel comfortable in it? I've paid a lot of money for this course: Am I going to get my money's worth?

The questions running through the minds of high-school language students are of a slightly different order and include the following: Is this teacher going to like us as a class? Are they going to be able to control us, or are they going to let us get away with messing around? Are they going to manage the class in friendly, firm ways, or in bossy, mean ways? Are they going to make language learning interesting by organising activities that allow us to express ourselves, occasionally let off a bit of steam and learn the language at the same time? Is the teacher going to be someone we can like and respect and do our best for, or shall we find ways of baiting them and have some fun that way instead?

Warm-ups/icebreakers

When describing the kinds of activities that they normally engage in with their classes on the first day of each new course, language teachers usually mention 'icebreakers': socially driven speaking tasks that require students to interact with a range of class members in a variety of ways. Most teachers have personal repertoires of icebreakers that they use on a regular basis, adding new ones that they try out and find to work well. These activities vary considerably in the extent to which they require students to 'have a go', or to reveal aspects of their personalities or private worlds. Relatively non-threatening activities include asking students to go round the class and shake hands with everybody, exchanging names and greetings, asking students to chat to a partner and find out selected pieces of information (ranging from how many brothers and sisters they have to their career aspirations), or having students engage in the popular 'find someone who . . .' activity, which requires students to mingle with others in the class in order to find out personal information (about habits, hobbies, likes and dislikes, and so on), which is then shared with the class as a whole.

Some icebreakers require a higher degree of personal revelation, such as those that require students to share with a partner a moment in their lives when they felt particularly embarrassed, proud or frightened. Other icebreakers are more adventurous still. One teacher regularly did a trust activity that required students to fall backwards into the arms of waiting students, while another teacher did a tension-building activity that required students to stare into the eyes of a partner until one of the pair 'cracked' – and talk erupted. Teachers use the kinds of icebreakers with which they personally feel comfortable, which they have used success-fully in the past, and which they believe are valid ways of encouraging information-sharing through oral interaction. In order to make ice-breakers work, language teachers often add an individual flourish. One teacher, for example, always demonstrated to his class the difference between a firm 'Aussie' handshake and a 'wet fish' one, before requiring his students to circulate and greet fellow class members.

The icebreaking principle holds good, even when teaching a class of complete beginners, no matter what their age. In such cases teachers often do a whole-class learning activity that involves a good deal of rep-etition, such as having everyone stand in a circle and toss a beanbag around, the person catching the beanbag having to introduce themselves. A teacher of Japanese explained that in her first lesson she always got students to introduce themselves and, if they were businessmen, to add at the end, 'Here is my business card'. The ice was broken when people made incorrect deductions about what the teacher was saying, became befuddled, forgot how to say things, mispronounced words and so on – with the result that everyone burst out laughing. In the view of the teacher, 'You need lots of relaxation, play-the-goose kinds of activities, just to loosen everybody up'.

Comment

There is always the possibility that warm-up activities, designed to make students feel relaxed and comfortable with their peers, will have a different effect to the one that was intended. Atkinson (1989) suggests that language-learning activities that involve deep, affective investment by learners in the learning experience make excessive demands on students, while Widdowson makes the following comment (1990: 13):

'The individual may not *want* to reveal his private life in a public role. Thus, encouraging learners to explore and share their own personality can actually be seen as an unwarranted intrusion on privacy, and as the imposition of alien attitudes, in some cultures and in some indi-viduals. In which case it may lead to a *dis*engagement from learning.'

Apart from giving students the opportunity to get to know one another in unusual and sometimes unexpected ways, activities such as these serve a number of additional purposes. First, they provide teachers with pre-liminary information about the linguistic proficiency, the personalities, the interests and the learning goals of the students in their classes. Second, they provide teachers with some indication of how malleable their classes are going to be, in terms of the willingness of the class members to engage in communicative tasks. Third, because everyone in the room is engaged in social interaction, activities such as these encourage the class to begin to consider itself as a group rather than as a collection of individual learners. As one teacher put it:

> You need to work on the corporate dynamic first, before you begin to work on the language. And then, once you've got the class functioning as a happy unit with all that interaction happening, then you'd begin to identify some of the individual learning needs. . . . I'd take the class as a whole first and say, 'How are these individuals going to work together?'

Establishing rapport with the class

The relationship that language teachers have with their classes is extremely complex and multifaceted. It begins the moment the teacher and class meet for the first time and continues for the duration of the course. In order to set in motion the kinds of social processes that will enable their classes to develop into unified groups that include themselves, language teachers see it as important to establish personal relationships not only with individuals, but also with their classes as wholes. High-school language teachers talk about the importance of 'getting on the same wavelength as the students', of 'developing a connection with the class' or of 'winning the class over'. As one teacher said, 'If they're not with you, they're against you'. As outlined in the final chapter of this book, establishing and maintaining rapport with classes of language learners is a key goal for experienced language teachers – and one that drives much of their classroom behaviour.

In the first few lessons of each new class language teachers of adults often reveal selected aspects of themselves and their personal lives. For example, they may divulge information about marital status, number of children, personal interests, likes and dislikes, language teaching experience, knowledge of other languages, countries visited, and so on. Teachers may volunteer such information spontaneously, or they may invite students to ask them questions about themselves – having asked their class first of all to work in groups to devise suitable questions. Activities such as these encourage students to interact with one another for a genuine purpose – to find out about the teacher – and help set the tone of the class: that everyone is going to be open, friendly and interested in one another as individuals.

Language teachers provide their classes with selected information about themselves for a number of reasons. First, it is a way of establishing professional credibility: showing that they are not only friendly people but also people with qualifications, relevant life experiences and knowledge of other languages and cultures. They may let slip, for example, that they have a working knowledge of several languages – or that they are currently learning another language in evening classes (and can therefore empathise with their students' situations). Second, they sense that it may be important for their class to know at what stage they are in their lives. An attractive young female teacher may want to ensure that her students know that she is engaged to be married, whereas a mature-aged female teacher may believe it appropriate to let her class know that she has grown-up children and wishes to be considered as a mother figure. Third, when teachers share knowledge about themselves, students are encouraged to follow suit.

Experienced language teachers often reveal one additional aspect of themselves: their beliefs about language learning. They do this because they sense that students find it helpful to understand why they teach in the ways that they do. One teacher described how she established a relationship with her class in the first lesson of a five-week intensive course by typing out a sheet entitled 'All about me', which contained 17 assorted statements about herself. These provided information not only about the teacher's living arrangements ('I live with my teenage son and two dogs') and personal indulgences ('I love chocolate ice cream'), but also about her weaknesses ('When I get excited I talk very quickly, so you have to ask me to slow down'). Equally importantly, this teacher indicated her beliefs about learning ('I believe that learning is most effective when everyone in the class is pro-active'; 'I love reading books and think that it is one of the best ways to learn'). She also forewarned her class that she would not be following the syllabus in a slavish fashion ('I think it's useful to have a syllabus, but it should be flexible and allow students to choose some content').

Demonstrating approachability

Closely related to their desire to establish rapport with their classes is the desire of language teachers to impress upon their students that they are friendly facilitators who will do their best at all times to help them in their efforts to develop proficiency in the target language. They wish their students to understand that they will behave in a sympathetic rather than dismissive way whenever anyone has difficulty in comprehending what they are trying to teach. Talking about encouraging students to ask questions, one teacher made the following comment:

> I work very hard at trying to make myself a person who can
> be interrupted, or who makes you feel you won't be regarded
> as a prat for asking a question. I think I try to create an
> atmosphere in the classroom where it's okay to ask questions,
> it's okay to catch the teacher's eye – not stick your hand right
> up, but wave a finger to indicate 'What?' or 'Can you say that
> again, please?'

Some language teachers are prepared to go to considerable lengths in the
early days of their classes to convey the message that they wish their students to feel comfortable enough to approach them when they do not
understand. This may even involve teachers admitting past errors of
judgement to their classes. One teacher described how she had once
taught a high-level English class containing engineers from a variety of
European countries. Fearful of making her lessons too easy she had
ploughed on, saying to the class at the end of each lesson, 'Did you
understand today's lesson?' – to which the students had invariably
responded, 'Yes'. Evidently in a class outing to the pub at the end of the
course the students eventually told her the truth: they had understood
very little of what she had taught – whereupon she felt so mortified that
she had burst into tears.

This particular teacher explained that she told this anecdote on the
first day of all her subsequent classes – as a way of getting the point
across to each new group of students that she wanted them to feel free
to tell her whenever they did not understand. She would tell the anecdote in a theatrical manner, getting the students to laugh by having
them nod when she said, 'Do you understand?' and then shaking her
head slowly from side to side as she imitated their words, 'Yes, I understand'. Recounting what she would then say to the class, this teacher
said:

> So I say to them, 'Don't be afraid to say if you don't understand,
> because if you don't I can guarantee there are ten others who are
> not courageous enough to put their hand up who didn't understand
> either.' And by telling them that story, I've set the ground rules.

In sum, experienced language teachers who wish to encourage the students in their classes to communicate freely and in uninhibited ways with
one another are sometimes prepared to go to considerable lengths to
make it clear where they position themselves in their classrooms. They
wish to convey the impression that they view themselves in a support role
– rather than in a position of power and domination.

The fact that they view themselves as facilitators in their classrooms, and the fact that they regard themselves as caring teachers (see Noddings, 2001: 99, for an analysis of this concept), suggest that language teachers of adults are humanistic in their class management approaches. Williams and Burden (1997: 30–38) provide a useful overview of the psychological bases of humanistic approaches in education, explaining the considerable influence that humanistic approaches have had on English language teaching methodology, particularly through the championing work of Stevick (1976).

Creating 'safe' learning environments

Mastery of any skill, whether it is learning to ride a bike or play the violin, involves much trial and error and a great deal of practice. Language teachers are aware that trying to communicate in an unfamiliar language – getting your mouth round awkward sounds and trying to use unfamiliar language patterns – is by no means easy. They are also aware that making errors in public is threatening to one's self-esteem. In the words of one teacher:

> It seems to me that language learning is fundamentally an exercise
> in risk-taking, because every time you open your mouth you run
> the risk of making a fool of yourself by saying something
> completely stupid. To me I feel very happy when I've got a class
> where they're not worried about that risk-taking and they're just
> relaxed and they'll say things and they don't care whether it's right
> or wrong.

In order to encourage the students in their classes to practise communicating with one another freely in the target language (and make the errors that will inevitably occur), language teachers model desired behaviour. Whenever they make small slips themselves (something that inevitably happens during the course of classroom teaching: misspelling words on the board, inadvertently providing incorrect answers and so on), language teachers acknowledge what they have done, gaily make light of it and move swiftly on. They routinely invite the students in their classes to spot their own errors and reward them for doing so. One high-school teacher said to her class, 'Double jelly babies for anyone who can spot a mistake!' while a teacher who often used worksheets containing the odd typing error would take the opportunity to say to her class, 'Quick! Who can spot the typo in the second sentence?' Whenever a student pointed out that he had made an error on the whiteboard one particular teacher would swivel round, grin and exclaim to the class at large, 'I am not the Buddha!'

Clearly language teachers cannot afford to make errors too often: to do so would be to undermine their credibility as language experts. Nevertheless, by encouraging the students in their classes to identify their own errors, and by showing that they are not embarrassed when caught out, language teachers are giving students permission to make their own mistakes. By making light of their own mistakes language teachers are also, of course, saving face.

Another way that language teachers attempt to cushion students from potential damage to their self-esteem as they struggle to master the target language in front of their peers is to ensure that their classrooms function as far as possible as sheltered environments within which all students feel comfortable and protected. Language teachers of both adults and children often go out of their way in the early days of each new class to stress that they expect the students in their classes to be friendly and supportive of one another. They make it abundantly clear that they will not condone ridicule, teasing, sniggering or derisory laughter. One teacher explained to each new first-year high-school language class that her classes were not like any others in the school, that everyone would make mistakes (including herself) and that everyone must be supportive of everyone else's efforts. She would then explain to the class that there was 'good laughter', which she welcomed, and 'bad laughter', which she defined as 'knife-in-the-back stuff', and which she would not condone. This teacher would encourage her pupils to applaud the efforts of others. Another teacher would call a student to the front of the room to engage in a role-play activity in the early days of a new class and would then ask them how they felt. When the student said 'embarrassed' she would proceed to tell the class a story of a successful businessman who was mortified to discover that he'd given a speech with wet marks on his shirt. She would then talk to the class about vulnerability, and explain that her class would be a safe place in which no one need feel nervous or threatened.

In sum, experienced language teachers are aware of the ego-threatening nature of practising interacting in an unfamiliar language in classroom situations. They make considerable efforts to convey the impression that their particular classes, with their relaxed and friendly atmospheres, function as sheltered environments within which students can feel that threats to their self-esteem will be minimised.

The beliefs that language teachers hold about the negative effect that anxiety can have on learning are amply supported by research findings. In a useful book on affect in language learning Arnold (1999: 8) observes, 'Anxiety is quite possibly the affective factor that most pervasively obstructs the learning process. It is associated with negative feelings such as uneasiness, frustration, self-doubt, apprehension and tension.' In the above book Oxford provides an overview of research into different types of anxiety associated with language learning.

Establishing professional credibility and a sense of purpose

A key issue for adult language learners who may be investing a lot of time, effort and money in attending a language class is the level of professionalism that their language teacher displays. Students can pick up much from the way their teacher walks into the room at the start of that very first lesson. Does the teacher survey the class as a whole in a smiling, welcoming way, looking relaxed and confident as they put down their books in an ordered way? Or does the teacher rush in a few minutes late and dump their books down in an untidy pile, looking smiling and friendly but, if anything, *too* relaxed? Does the teacher have a groomed appearance, or do they look as if they had a late night and got out of bed in a rush? How does the teacher introduce himself or herself? Do they say, 'Hi, I'm Joe', and lounge on the desk with one leg crossed over the other? Or do they write their full name on the board and say, 'Hello everybody, my name is Joe and I'm going to be teaching you for the next six weeks. Welcome to the class. I'm sure we're going to work well together and achieve a lot.'?

As described in the 'party games syndrome' subsection of Chapter 8, experienced language teachers are aware that informal classroom atmospheres are a necessary but not a sufficient condition for successful language practice. Most experienced language teachers make a point of giving their class something 'meaty' in the very first lesson. Highlighting the importance of beginning each new course with a learning activity that students saw as purposeful, interesting and relevant to their needs, one teacher explained:

> If I don't grab them with something on Day One, I never grab them. They go away disgruntled . . . I must grab their interest. They must think, 'This class, oh yes! There's something in this class for me!' . . . so if they know the focus of the class is 'this', they're more patient.

93

Establishing the learning environment

In the very first lesson of a new course language teachers are to some extent feeling in the dark, because they do not yet know what the specific needs and interests of the students in their class actually are. One teacher routinely did a whole-class information-gathering activity in the first lesson of each course so that she could gain a composite profile of her class as quickly as possible. This involved dividing the class into four groups and having each group collect data and present it to the class on an overhead transparency. The first group had to gather information on the language learning strengths and weaknesses of the class, the second information on the students' past experiences of learning English, the third on the students' future aspirations and the fourth on the students' living circumstances and opportunities to speak English outside class. In the plenary session that followed, after the groups had presented the data they had gathered, the teacher would assure the students that she would satisfy as far as possible the specific needs and wants of everyone in the class. In this way she established confidence in her ability to 'deliver the goods', together with a sense of purposefulness and relevance for the course that was to follow.

A further way that experienced language teachers establish and maintain their professional credibility is by creating a sense of purpose and direction at the start of each lesson. Even though they may deviate during the course of lessons (see Chapter 7), certain teachers make a point either of writing their lesson goals in a corner of the whiteboard, or of stating what the focus of the lesson is to be, as soon as they walk in the room. As one teacher, who had completed a graduate diploma of teaching, commented:

> The students have got to know what it is they're supposed to be
> learning. You've got to let them know your goals. For me that's
> total common sense: they've got to know where they're going.
> That's one of the key things you learn when you do your Grad Dip.

However, many language teachers make their lesson goals known implicitly rather than explicitly.

Negotiating the syllabus

Most language courses are pre-designed in the sense that there is an allocated coursebook, an articulated syllabus containing designated structures, functions, skills, topics, themes and so on, a set of specified learning outcomes that students are to achieve and a particular examination to prepare for. Only relatively rarely are teachers expected to negotiate with their students the nature and content of the syllabus itself.

Experience tells language teachers that it is usually safe to assume that the students in their classes will readily accept the courses that they plan to teach. Language teachers know that they will have to supplement their courses with additional materials and activities once they get to know their class and identify particular needs and interests (a process that is described in detail in Chapter 7). They also know that they may have to change the coursebook, for example if the level of the book is inappropriate for the class, or if certain students have already studied the book elsewhere. Generally speaking, however, language teachers do not find it necessary to negotiate the nature of the syllabus itself with their classes.[1]

There are, nevertheless, exceptions. Language teachers sometimes find themselves facing classes of reluctant or rebellious students who make it plain through their overall demeanour and general behaviour that they are not interested in the language course that their teacher is required to teach. Indeed, they may not want to attend the class at all. The class might contain a critical mass of teenagers who have been sent overseas to study English when they would far rather have stayed at home. Alternatively it might contain a group of disenchanted migrants unaccustomed to formal study, whose previous teacher has given the impression that their learning skills are poor. When such situations arise experienced language teachers take drastic action and put the ball back into the students' court. What would *they* like to do? A high-school teacher of Spanish, forewarned that a particular group of students was highly disaffected, went into class and was up-front with the students, saying, 'We've got to be together for a whole year, so let's find a way of working together'. After failing to identify any spark of interest through word-association games, the teacher noticed that one student was looking at a stamp with a soccer player on. Was the class interested in soccer? 'Yes.' Would they be prepared to study soccer for a whole year? 'Yes.' The teacher then devised a whole course around an imaginary soccer tournament set in Spain, bringing in the names of countries, nationalities, colours (through sports uniforms), directions (how to get to the stadium), numbers (because you need money), food (because you'll get hungry), and so on. In the words of the teacher, 'The kids were really enthusiastic – and totally conned'.

Another occasion when language teachers find themselves negotiating with their classes is when they are teaching in contexts that differ significantly from the ones with which they are familiar (to which their

---

[1] Some language schools provide 'elective' afternoon classes, in which students can choose from a range of options, which might include classes with an academic focus, such as 'writing skills' or 'grammar extension', or classes with a less-defined focus, such as 'drama', 'the media', 'reading for pleasure' or 'vocabulary extension'. With classes such as these, which are not as pressured as other classes, teachers are more likely to negotiate with their students the specific content of the course.

accustomed teaching practices are attuned). When teaching overseas, teachers may find themselves negotiating their very teaching approach. One teacher described her experience of teaching in Vietnam as thinking about what the students wanted and adjusting her teaching to the students' expectations, or of 'meeting them halfway'. She described the process of negotiation in the following way:

> I could feel the students and me pulling at either ends of a rope, because of our different expectations of the teacher's role. But bit by bit our relationship grew and we could relate – we were understanding each other more: I could understand their needs, and they could understand mine. In the end we both gave way: they could see the benefit of pair work, and I could see the benefit of chorus work . . . Yes, I did some chorus work with them, with them following what I said and chanting in unison. That was my compromise. I didn't do quite so much of what I normally do in class in the way of interactive stuff.

This teacher described the gulf that she believed existed between what her students expected of her and how she actually taught, saying, 'I was someone from the moon to them: they had no experience of my approach'. This teacher also made a point of saying that she explained to the students the assumptions underpinning the communicative approach, upon which her accustomed classroom practices were based:

> I told them they weren't going to get pearls of wisdom out of my mouth: they would have to learn for themselves. I explained how we teach in Australia, saying, 'In Australia we teach like this and the students really do improve'. I said to them, 'I won't be here for long, so you'll have to get going on your own. You'll find you subconsciously pick up correct structures from the radio, from the TV, from the Internet.'

Harmer (2003: 292) points out that there is a sense in which all classroom language teaching is a matter of negotiation. In Harmer's words, 'Successful methodology arises when teachers and students reach an accommodation between their differing expectations and hunches about what is best for them'.

Breen and Littlejohn (2000) provide a collection of practical accounts of negotiated work with language learners in a range of geographically and culturally diverse contexts around the world. Their book includes accounts of negotiated work with children in primary and secondary schools, with adult learners in universities and language schools, and in teacher education programs.

4.4 Exercising authority

A key reason given by ex-primary school and high-school teachers of other subjects for moving into the area of teaching English as a second or foreign language to adults is that they no longer want to be compelled to behave in authoritarian ways. They want to devote their time and energy to teaching grateful and responsive students, rather than to policing unruly students – a practice dubbed 'crowd control' by some teachers. Those engaged in teaching language to adult students can reasonably expect their class to behave in socially appropriate ways. They can expect students to remain seated at their desks unless requested to do otherwise, to listen attentively to instructions, to treat fellow students with respect, and so on. High-school language teachers can make no such assumptions. Young people are naturally high-spirited and full of fun, and cannot be guaranteed to behave in socially acceptable ways. It is great fun to stick a foot out as someone walks past your desk, to hide someone's bag and assure the teacher that you have no idea where it is, or to hurl a beanbag at another student in a question-and-answer activity with more force than is strictly necessary. Other young people have severe behavioural problems that can render them beyond the control of even the most experienced teacher. If a language teacher who is inexperienced and lacking in confidence tries to set up communicative activities with a class that they are not able to manage, the class can rapidly degenerate into chaos.

Establishing norms of behaviour

Successful high-school language teachers know that they must avoid class management problems by setting standards early. Such teachers focus on training their students to behave appropriately, making it clear that there are certain rules that must be obeyed. These include simple things like lining up outside the door before entering the room, waiting to sit down until instructed to do so, or stopping talking when the teacher claps hands or gives some other designated signal. Language teachers also make threats and make sure they are carried out. These include moving students to other seats if they continue to behave inappropriately after having been warned, isolating them or sending them outside the door for a few minutes to cool down. Language teachers may speak in direct, brusque terms, making statements such as: 'I'll tell you once, otherwise you're wasting my time – so I'll waste yours: stay inside during recess and clean the chewing gum off the bottom of the desks!' They may even threaten to lose their temper, such as the teacher of Italian who informed each new class (with a twinkle in her eye) that Italy had not three but four volcanoes: Vesuvius, Etna, Stromboli – and an additional one that erupted occasionally, but extremely forcefully. Above all, language teachers know that they must behave consistently and fairly and, most important, avoid direct confrontation. The latter is crucial because, in the words of one teacher, if they confront a student in full view of the class, 'the battle lines are drawn'. Once this happens, the relationship of mutual trust that they have sought to develop with their class for the purpose of enhancing language learning may be permanently damaged.

Despite their gruff exteriors and on-the-spot disciplinary behaviour, experienced high-school language teachers try to manage individual students in sensitive ways. They may take them aside and attempt to ascertain the underlying cause of the unacceptable behaviour. As one teacher explained:

> For both younger and older kids you discipline them politely, quietly, and you don't embarrass them. You never make an example of them. Your interaction with them must be subtle, so that no one else knows what's really going on. If you want to keep them on side, you don't visually take them aside. And you get *them* to articulate their problem.

Another strategy used widely by experienced high-school language teachers is that of rewarding children for appropriate behaviour, rather than punishing them for inappropriate behaviour. Apart from regularly 'praising kids in strategic ways', a technique that one particular teacher considered she had got down to a fine art, most high-school language teachers have developed their own personal reward systems. One teacher had a basketball basket at the back of her classroom and when a boy had done something praiseworthy, would allow him to have a shot at the basket. If successful, he would be given a jelly bean. Another language teacher who worked in a school that contained large numbers of disadvantaged children would award coupons for good behaviour of any kind. All the coupons then went into a lucky-dip box that was ceremonially dipped into at the end of each term. The beauty of the system was that it was egalitarian, with any student who had been awarded even one coupon having a chance to win a prize.

Low-key ways of registering disapproval

'Educational psychologists recognise that handling minor behaviour problems that interfere with classroom learning as unobtrusively as possible is an effective classroom strategy. They use the term *cueing* to describe the practice of letting students know, through a signal of one kind or another, that they are aware of the misbehaviour and would like it to stop.' Ormrod (2000: 615)

The class management practices of teachers who teach language to adults are somewhat different. When teaching adults it is seldom necessary to articulate classroom codes of behaviour, or to develop complex reward or punishment systems. Students can be expected to arrive on time, to switch off mobile phones before entering the room, to show respect to other students, and so on. Language teachers of adults tend to register disapproval of undesired behaviour at the point at which it occurs, rather than beforehand. They often do so quickly and with a degree of lightness and humour, before returning quickly to the focus of the lesson. For example, they might register mock horror when a student's phone goes off, or exclaim 'Good *afternoon*!' when a student arrives late yet again for a morning lesson. One teacher made it clear that there were two classroom behaviours that he would not condone. One was carrying on speaking to a partner when he was addressing the class at large, and the other was speaking in the class in any language other than English. If anyone contravened either of these rules he would mime shooting them with an imaginary rifle. The reason that teachers of adult language learners use low-key, humorous strategies for registering disapproval of undesired behaviour is that by doing so they hope to avoid compromising the friendly, informal relationship that they wish to maintain with both the individual student and the class as a whole.

> 'Humor constitutes a symbol of disapproval – a subtle way of sanctioning the deviant and at the same time providing him with an opportunity to accept the humorous definition of the situation, acknowledge the incongruity of his behavior, correct his behavior, and rejoin the group without "losing face".' Martineau (1972: 117)

Experienced language teachers of both adults and children sense that classrooms with informal atmospheres are ultimately easier to manage than classrooms with formal ones. This is because classes in which spontaneous student behaviour is accepted and valued are more likely to evolve into cohesive groups than classes in which spontaneous student behaviour is repressed or openly disapproved of. Once classes begin to operate cohesively, classes as wholes can exert a normative influence on the behaviour of individuals. As a result undesirable behaviour is likely to become less frequent. In contrast, if language teachers behave in authoritarian ways, meting out punishments without demonstrating their human side, they are reinforcing the divide between themselves as teachers and their students as learners. As a result their class groups may well become unified – but it will be against a common enemy: themselves.

In sum, when it comes to establishing acceptable norms of behaviour in their classes language teachers must tread a careful path. If they are overly rigid in their responses to student behaviour they run the risk of being unable to develop a productive, informal classroom environment. On the other hand, if they are overly relaxed or familiar with the students in their classes, they run the risk of not being respected as professionals.

4.5 Conclusion

The present chapter has focused on the fact that language teachers working in western educational contexts believe that classes with informal atmospheres are the most suitable environments for communicative practice. It has identified and described the kinds of strategies that experienced language teachers routinely use in the early days of their classes to establish informal atmospheres and to encourage students to behave in relaxed and spontaneous ways.

The chapter has drawn attention to the kinds of relationships that experienced language teachers wish to build with their classes. It has shown that, while setting behavioural parameters and keeping control over their classes, language teachers also strive to be accepted by their students as integral members of their class groups. By alternating readily between 'distant' and 'close' roles, experienced language teachers set in motion the kinds of social processes that facilitate the development of a sense of community within their classes.

Once the learning environment has been established in the first few days of each new class, students can predict with some degree of accuracy the kinds of learning activities that their teacher will set up. They also know the kinds of interpersonal and learning behaviours that their teacher will value and encourage in an ongoing way.

According to Candy (1991: 337), the need for a supportive climate for learning has been recognised as a central feature of good adult education practice for decades. Candy refers to Knowles (1984), who points out that almost all learning theorists – behaviourists, cognitivists, humanists and personality theorists – endorse the need for an 'atmosphere of adultness' in which 'conditions of mutuality and informality' combine to provide a supportive human and interpersonal climate. Candy identifies the elements of such a climate as low threat, unconditional positive regard, honest and open feedback, respect for the ideas and opinions of others, approval of self-improvement as a goal and collaboration rather than competition.

The kinds of classroom environments that language teachers seek to set up in the early days of their courses resemble the classroom environments identified by Candy as being appropriate for adult learning.

Summary

- Language teachers in western contexts require the students in their classes to engage in a wide range of interactive games, activities and tasks.
- For a number of reasons language teachers consider that classes with informal atmospheres are the most appropriate environments for communicative language practice.
- Language teachers rely heavily on humour to set the tone in their classes.
- During the first few lessons of each new course language teachers use a variety of techniques to encourage the students in their classes to relax and get to know each other. Students may find some of these techniques disconcerting.
- Aware that students may be diffident about performing in front of their peers in the target language, language teachers assure their students that making mistakes is part of the learning process.
- High levels of self-confidence enable language teachers to model desired behaviour, including revealing aspects of themselves and laughing at their own mistakes.
- Language teachers tread a careful line between being relaxed and friendly with their classes, and maintaining their credibility as competent professionals.
- Language teachers are able to switch readily between more 'close' and more 'distant' roles. By so doing they encourage their classes to develop into social groups of which they themselves are an integral part.
- Experienced language teachers are sometimes able to get tricky classes 'on-side' by negotiating the content of the syllabus.
- Experienced language teachers of both children and adults prefer to regulate the classroom behaviour of their students in non-authoritarian ways, believing that by so doing they will be able to retain an ongoing positive relationship with their students.
- In language classes with informal atmospheres the behaviour of the class group can exert a positive normative influence on the behaviour of individuals.

Looking ahead

The following chapter describes the diverse backgrounds, concerns and expectations of adult students joining language classes in an English-speaking country such as Australia. By so doing it emphasises that each language class is a unique collection of individuals, some of whom may need to be handled with particular care and sensitivity.

5 The diversity of the language classroom

The previous chapter focused on how language teachers in western contexts go about establishing the kinds of classroom environments that they consider most suitable for language practice. It drew attention to the fact that language teachers value informal classroom atmospheres, encouraging their students to behave naturally and spontaneously as they engage in whole-class activities and small-group interactive tasks. The chapter identified the kinds of communicative tasks that language teachers regularly set up in their classrooms, and showed how language teachers typically behave in order to set the students in their classes at ease.

The focus of the present chapter is on the raw material of language classes: the students themselves. Section 5.1 describes the wide range of backgrounds, learning experiences and expectations that adult learners typically bring with them to their classes – and which make each language class a unique entity that can never be exactly replicated. Section 5.2 describes the kinds of factors that can impinge on the ability of individuals to maximise their learning opportunities, while Section 5.3 describes some of the ways in which students can aggravate one another within the confines of the language classroom.

The data for this chapter have been gathered in Australia, a country with a tradition of providing English language tuition to a range of students including migrants, refugees, fee-paying students on short intensive courses and students from non-English-speaking backgrounds who aspire to enter Australian tertiary institutions. The majority of students studying on intensive English language courses in Australia come from Asian countries, with the minority coming from a range of other countries around the world. Even though the situations that are reported in this chapter refer to students studying in Australia, it is likely that similar situations occur in classrooms in other English-speaking countries.

5.1 Students: the raw material of any language class

The unopened package

When they walk into their classrooms on the first day of each new course, language teachers of adults usually find between 12 and 24 students awaiting their arrival. As they walk into the room the students typically fall silent, waiting for the teacher to begin. If the class roll does not include the country of origin of each student, teachers are normally able to deduce the class composition from the characteristics of the names on the roll. A language class may contain students from a wide spread of countries (perhaps from as many as ten countries in the one class), with no country represented by more than three or four students. Alternatively it may be composed of a block of students from one country, with only a smattering of students from elsewhere. There again, it can consist of students from two major cultural groups, such as Bosnia and China, or Japan and Switzerland. It is often the case that single students, the sole representatives of their countries of origin, find themselves in classes that are dominated by particular cultural groups: a solitary Korean in a class of Swiss German and Swiss French students, or a single Romanian in a class of Chinese students.

The variations in class composition are infinite in number and clearly have the potential to affect the dynamics of the class group. Language teachers are accustomed to teaching classes that contain a unique and often unbalanced combination of adult learners from disparate linguistic, ethnic, cultural, educational, political, social and religious backgrounds. Language classes may also contain students of widely differing ages and with very different life experiences. For example, a middle-aged Japanese gentleman with a superb knowledge of the structure of English but poor pronunciation found himself in the same class as an 18-year-old Belgian boy who was fluent in English and keen to display his considerable knowledge of English swear words.

Many other ingredients must be added to the mix that makes up the unique flavour of each individual class. Apart from the linguistic strengths, weaknesses, needs and wants of each student, other variables include students' educational backgrounds and learning expectations, their past circumstances and present living conditions, and their innate personality types. A final crucial variable in the complex classroom equation is the degree to which individual students are prepared to fit into the class group, and to meld their own learning goals with the overall learning goals of the class as a whole. The personality of the teacher, of course, must also not be forgotten.

5.2 Factors influencing student behaviour and performance

Students' learning expectations

All adult language learners bring to their classes memories of earlier learning experiences from their home countries. Based on these experiences they have certain preconceived ideas about what classroom language learning will be like. Students from China, for example, who have studied English in classes of 50–60 students, are accustomed to listening quietly and attentively while their teacher dispenses knowledge. They are used to becoming active participants in the learning process *outside* rather than *inside* the language classroom – when discussing points with their peers in the comparative privacy of their university dormitories, or when practising speaking English in informal 'conversation corners' in public places. Chinese children are taught from a young age that learning is not meant to be easy, but requires persistence, hard work and considerable intellectual effort (including sustained bouts of memorisation). Despite generational changes in attitudes towards education, parents wishing their children to achieve highly still teach their children that 'learning means piercing your thigh with an awl'. This well-known Chinese proverb promotes the view that pain is an integral part of the learning process.

Comment

There is currently an ongoing debate regarding the degree to which students are able and willing to adapt to the culturally specific norms of interaction that typically prevail in 'western' communicative classrooms. This issue was initially raised by Thorp (1991), who argued that, where there is a mismatch between students' expectations and those of their teachers, teachers should be explicit about the interactional demands of their classes. Littlewood (2000) states that the overall message that emerges from his research is that Asian students do not wish to be spoon-fed with facts from an all-knowing 'fount of knowledge'. In his words, 'They want to explore knowledge themselves and find their own answers. Most of all, they want to do this together with their fellow students in an atmosphere which is friendly and supportive'. Meyer (2003) discusses the actions and reactions to group work of students from China. Her findings support Littlewood's position: that Asian students actually wish to behave (and do behave if given the chance) in ways which differ from the classroom behavioural norms they have been taught to follow.

Young adults from European countries are likely to be familiar with the kinds of classroom practices routinely used by language teachers in Australia, including the emphasis on learning by doing and the notion that learning should involve engagement of the whole person rather than simply the intellect. However, older students from European countries, particularly those from former Soviet bloc countries such as Poland, Czechoslovakia, or those from the former Yugoslavia such as Bosnia and Croatia, are likely to have been educated in relatively traditional ways. Such students, particularly if they left school in their teens and now find themselves back in the classroom after a gap of 20 years or more, are likely to be in a similar position to their Asian counterparts.

> 'There is much less difference between the average group responses of students in Asia and Europe than there is between the individual responses of students within the same country.'
>
> Littlewood (2000: 34)

For language students from traditional educational backgrounds it comes as something of a surprise to find that their teachers in Australia expect them to relax in class and actually enjoy the process of learning (see Chapter 8 for further discussion on this point). Many classroom practices commonly used in western language classrooms are quite alien to such students. These include being asked to express personal opinions (on topics or issues that may be quite new to them), being encouraged to disagree with the teacher, being expected to help other students, being invited to suggest topics for study, and so on. The list of educational surprises goes on and on.

> 'Many adult learners, especially those with good metalinguistic knowledge, express a preference for structure-based approaches.'
>
> Lightbown and Spada (1999: 119)

Many students adapt easily to informal western teaching practices, happy to be in classrooms where active participation is encouraged and where there is little danger of falling asleep through weariness or lack of engagement. A considerable number of students, however, remain uneasy about the situation. They value the friendly, lively, informal atmospheres of their classrooms, but often wish that their teacher would push them just that little bit harder – or make lessons just a little bit more teacher-centred so that they have the opportunity to hear 'correct' English more often.

Cortazzi (1990) points out that students have common educational and cultural assumptions about what teachers should do, saying, 'Unexplained violations of the expected norm by teachers enthusiastically embracing communicative approaches may lead to the diminution of their status and perceived competence in learners' eyes. The teacher is not behaving in ways that learners have come to expect good teachers to behave' (1990: 59).

Most adult students, being polite and restrained and not wishing to upset or offend their teachers, keep their thoughts to themselves. Occasionally, however, a vociferous individual may choose to make their views more widely known. When this happens the gap between the student's learning expectations and what the teacher actually provides becomes apparent to everyone in the room. In one class a student from the former Yugoslavia made it clear at regular intervals throughout a ten-week course that he believed his learning expectations were not being met. His responses included 'Don't ask us! *You* are the teacher!' when the teacher gave the class a choice as to which activity to do next, and 'I was *born* alone, I shall *die* alone – and I *learn* alone!' when invited to do a collaborative task with a partner.

Students who feel that they are being short-changed by the language teaching institutions in which they are studying (and from which they cannot move, if they have prepaid their fees) sometimes take matters into their own hands. One group of highly motivated Korean students booked out of their language school for a week, ostensibly to take a holiday, but in fact so that they could spend their time in the school library going through old TOEFL exam papers and testing their knowledge of idioms and phrasal verbs.

The Test of English as a Foreign Language (TOEFL) is a test to measure the level of English proficiency of non-native speakers that is required primarily by English-language colleges and universities in the USA. The multiple-choice format of three of the four sections of the test means that students can self-test their knowledge of English.

Another Korean student walked around with a two-month-old yellowing copy of the *West Australian* under his arm. He had set himself the goal of translating one new article into Korean each day, filling the margins of the paper with meticulous notes as he did so. Behaviours such as these suggest that students sometimes remain unconvinced that the communicative approach is capable of satisfying their perceived language-learning needs.

Comment

The students described in the above paragraph appear to have a transmission view of education. According to Cortazzi (1990: 58), citing Barnes (1976):

'Such a view sees the teacher's knowledge as being transmitted to learners and it can be contrasted with the more innovative view that learners creatively build up knowledge and concepts through activity, participation and the experience of verbal expression. These two views reveal a major contrast between education as cultural transmission or as innovation and social change. The first is closely associated with cultures stressing continuity, stability and group identity. The second is linked in the West with an emphasis on individual development and personal experience, which is a different cultural emphasis.' Cortazzi also points out that both aspects are present in most cultures but receive very different emphasis, with the result that varied expectations come about, affecting presuppositions about learning and teaching.

Students' current circumstances

Most adult students embarking on a course of intensive English language tuition in Australia find themselves under a certain amount of pressure. This is often the result of hoping to make a large amount of linguistic progress within a limited timeframe. The parents of young adults who come to Australia to study on short courses often have unrealistic expectations of what their children can achieve – and limited funds to subsidise additional courses. Migrants whose level of English has been assessed as being below functional level receive 510 hours of language tuition (for which they must pay), while refugees get this same service free. Either way, after completing their designated 510 hours, all new Australians are launched along pathways leading towards employment or further study. For migrants and refugees wishing to engage in further study, higher-level language classes may be available.

Unless they have achieved a sufficiently high level on the IELTS test, students aspiring to enter Australian universities (at either undergraduate or postgraduate level) must complete intensive English language bridging courses. Such courses operate as gatekeepers, denying students who do not reach the required level the opportunity to pursue their chosen careers or to upgrade their professional qualifications. Students who have only achieved the minimal band score on the IELTS test prior to starting their intensive pre-university courses feel particularly pressured. Unable to derive full benefit from the courses in which they are enrolled, often because of limited speaking or listening skills, such students can easily fall further and further behind. Circumstances such as these suggest that it is rare for language classes to be composed entirely of pressure-free students.

The International English Language Testing System (known as the IELTS test) is a test of English language proficiency jointly managed by the University of Cambridge ESOL Examinations, the British Council, IDP Education Australia and IELTS Australia. It is taken by increasing numbers of students on a worldwide basis – particularly those who wish to do tertiary studies through the medium of English in a tertiary institution in an English-speaking country. For further information see http://www.cambridgeesol/schools/index.htm

---

Language teachers often find that particular individuals within their class groups seem upset, distracted or generally not as committed to learning as they might have expected. Although the reasons underlying this apparent lack of receptivity are limitless, many behaviours such as regular absences, persistent late arrivals, constant requests to leave the room, general lethargy or an inability to complete homework can often be related to the immediate circumstances of individual students. For young adults in the 18–24 age group, problems often relate to the fact that they are living away from home for the first time in a new country where everything is strange: the accommodation, the transport system, the food, the suburban way of life and so on. Students who are suffering from loneliness or homesickness, who have fallen desperately in love, who have had their mobile phone stolen, or who have squandered their allowance at the local casino (a mecca for overseas students because of its bright lights and familiar crowds), are unlikely to be model students. During lessons, thoughts entirely unrelated to language learning may be running through their minds.

Personal circumstances may also impinge on the ability of older students, particularly migrants, to take full advantage of the intensive English language classes available to them. Sometimes refugees from war-torn countries who have been in Australia for a matter of weeks find it too stressful to attend language classes at all, particularly if they have been tortured or suffered other traumatic events such as seeing family members killed or injured.

In Australia a number of handbooks have been produced that give teachers specific guidance on how to cater in class for the special learning needs of migrant students suffering from their experiences of torture and trauma. These include Henesey-Smith (1997) and Martinez (1997).

Several students from the former Yugoslavia withdrew from a beginners' class within the first two weeks for mental health reasons, while some of those who remained had difficulty concentrating. As one teacher explained:

> Many of these people have lost everything when they come here, and they've got to pick up their lives again – and they feel homesick, and they feel guilty and worried about the family members they left behind. And they're having to cope with lots of settlement issues as well, and perhaps marital problems, and children adjusting at school, and language, and different food – and a different attitude too. Particularly for Moslem guys who haven't seen women with bare arms before, and here we all are in Australia with short skirts and bare midriffs. But they're still applying the same mores and customs and feelings about what's right that they had in their own country. It takes them a long time to reconcile the two cultures.

Even the most well-adjusted migrants may experience difficulties when forced to juggle attendance at language classes with attending to the needs of their families. One woman with four young children had to leave two at pre-school and two at primary school before catching two different buses to get her to the city, where classes began at 9 am. Added to this she had to take one of the children, who had received gunshot wounds during the civil war in her home country, for regular hospital appointments. Evening commitments, ranging from casual cleaning jobs to feeding babies, can leave migrants feeling exhausted and unable to do themselves justice in class. For some the social support offered by an amenable class and a sympathetic teacher is more important than the language they are meant to be learning. On the other side of the coin, some migrants use language lessons as an opportunity to fraternise with their compatriots. One teacher who had had difficulty managing a particular migrant group complained that 'all they wanted to do in class was to party in their own language'.

Certain articles in *Prospect: An Australian Journal of TESOL*, report on issues such as student vulnerability (Wajnryb, 1988) and the problems faced by overseas students (Nixon, 1993).

Books of a more technical nature include Furnham and Bochner (1986), which deals with psychological reactions to unfamiliar environments, and Watts and Horne (1994), which deals with the issue of coping with trauma.

Certain factors make it particularly difficult for migrant men to maximise their learning opportunities in the language classroom. Many have held down jobs in their home countries for some years – and have enjoyed the status that being successful providers and established members of their communities brings with it. Some men (and also some women) find it particularly demeaning to find themselves once more in a classroom, particularly when they are regularly outshone by younger students who are both quicker at picking up new language and better at retaining new information than they are. Some younger men are desperate to enter the workforce, seeing the best years of their working lives being whittled away by yet more time spent studying when they could be earning a living. Another factor that can influence the behaviour of some older men in language classes is the experience of being taught by a young, attractive, female English teacher. Some feel uneasy at the role reversal, since it challenges their understanding of the relative positions of older men and younger women in the power hierarchy.

Student personalities

Clearly the personalities and attitudes of individual students are additional factors that can contribute to the social wellbeing (or otherwise) of language classes. Some students are naturally more outgoing than others, and are prepared to behave in a friendly, inclusive manner towards many students in the room. Others are more guarded, preferring to remain within the comfort zone of their immediate circle of friends. Some students are by nature generous-minded, while others are naturally competitive and inclined to feel resentful when others do better than they do. Some students have high levels of self-confidence, while others are by nature shy and reticent.

Brown (2000: 147) identifies self-esteem and the closely related concept of inhibition as being factors within a person that contribute in some way to the success of language learning. He talks of those with weaker self-esteem maintaining 'walls of inhibition' to protect what is self-perceived to be a weak or fragile ego, or a lack of self-confidence in a situation or task. Brown explains that the human ego encompasses what Guiora *et al.* (1972) and Ehrman (1996) have called 'language ego' a term that refers to the very personal, egoistic nature of second language acquisition. In Brown's words: 'Meaningful language acquisition involves some degree of identity conflict as language learners take on a new identity with their newly acquired competence. An adaptive language ego enables learners to lower the inhibitions that may impede success.'

Some students have highly positive attitudes towards their adopted country – particularly when they have made a carefully considered decision to migrate to Australia. One Russian student made it known that he was thrilled with his decision to emigrate – recounting to his class that he had walked past the Australian embassy in Moscow on his way to work for three years before realising where his destiny lay. In contrast, other students have not yet come to terms with the fact that they must rebuild their lives from scratch. Some students who come to Australia are still in the stage of lamenting the lives they have left behind. As one student commented, 'Before the war we had a good life, our own car, a beautiful apartment, many friends. Everything seemed so good. Now we have nothing.' Although most migrants who come to Australia under the refugee program are extremely grateful for everything that their adopted country has to offer, by no means all migrants think that the way of life in Australia is superior to the one they left behind. One group of Bosnian students took the opportunity of a communicative activity that required them to role-play moving house to criticise the poor quality of Australian housing. They talked in lyrical terms about the well-constructed apartment blocks with their high ceilings and polished floors of their home cities, comparing them favourably with the cheaply constructed single-storey suburban houses in which they now found themselves living.

The term 'culture shock' is used to describe 'the disorientation and unhappiness caused by an inability to adapt to a culture which is different from one's own' (The Macquarie Dictionary). Arnold (1999: 22) refers to research that suggests that culture shock may inhibit language acquisition.

Oxford (1999: 64) quotes Adler (1987: 25), who states that culture shock can involve some or all of the following symptoms: emotional regression, physical illness, panic, anger, hopelessness, self-pity, lack of confidence, indecision, sadness, alienation, a sense of deception, a perception of 'reduced personality', and glorification of one's own native culture. According to Adler, if handled effectively, culture shock can become a cross-cultural learning opportunity involving increased cultural awareness, increased self-awareness and reintegration of personality.

For an alternative description of culture shock in relation to second-culture acquisition see Brown (2000: 183).

Clearly the personalities and states of mind of students within language classes, and the ways in which they interact with one another, have a bearing on the quality of the class groups that language teachers are required to teach.

5.3 Tensions within the language classroom

Communicative language classrooms are intimate places in which everyone learns a great deal about everyone else. When an adult student enrols in an intensive language course they can expect to be with the same group of students for a considerable length of time – particularly if they join an examination preparation class such as one that prepares them for the Cambridge First Certificate in English. Language students can find themselves studying with the same set of classmates for up to 23 hours a week. Typically they will study for three hours on five mornings a week with their 'core' teacher, and for a further two hours on four afternoons a week with one or more supplementary teachers. Students may or may not combine with students from other classes in their afternoon lessons. Over a 12-week period language students can find themselves with the same group of learners for as many as 276 hours. This is a long time to be with students who may not have the same priorities, interests or goals as their own – particularly when interpersonal communication is the order of the day.

> 'There exist many layers of intricate cultural transmission and transformation constantly taking place in multicultural classrooms. . . . Individuals have many identities, and which ones come into the foreground depends on specific aspects of the context and on personal background variables.'
>
> Ehrman and Dörnyei (1998: 170) summarising
> research by Duff and Uchida (1997)

Interpersonal and intercultural tensions

There are many language classes in which interpersonal and intercultural tensions are never an issue. The students within such classes get along with one another straight away, giving the impression of being an outgoing, happy and harmonious learning group right from the start.

However, just as in families individuals can rub others up the wrong way, so students in language classes can, sometimes deliberately and sometimes unwittingly, irritate their classmates. Some students have personalities that their classmates find overpowering. A student in a lower-intermediate class became excited during a role-play activity in which he was a 'doctor' giving advice to students who came to him with their 'symptoms'. After listening to a set of symptoms he proclaimed to one student, 'You will die!' and burst into uncontrollable laughter. The patient was not amused. Other students are reluctant to fraternise with even their own compatriots. A Swiss girl said of one of her fellow countrymen:

He's a typical Swiss boy. He thinks he's the most important person
in the class and he wants his questions answered. I decided I didn't
want to work with him – and I don't.

Clashes between value systems, even between students from the same
cultural background, can sometimes come to the fore in language classes.
For example, Korean students in their mid-twenties who have completed
national service consider themselves in a different league from younger
Koreans, and expect deference from their 'juniors'. They are particularly
disapproving of 'younger generation' Koreans who have adopted more
flexible codes of behaviour and liberated sexual mores. One student even
expressed disapproval of his teacher, saying 'no good, no good' to the
class when she described her own domestic arrangements to exemplify
the term 'de facto relationship'.

Sometimes teachers may be unaware of subtle undercurrents swirling
around their class – particularly when social processes are occurring
between students from the same cultural background. One teacher was
at a loss to understand why the communicative activities that she set up
in one particular class never seemed to go well. Some time later she discovered that there was an ongoing battle between the Japanese girls in
her class, one of whom had refused to fraternise with the others, preferring to develop a friendship with a French girl. It transpired that the
other girls, with their strong group-centred culture, felt that the girl in
question had behaved disloyally and had betrayed their trust. The
teacher had misread the situation, believing that the independent-
minded, extroverted Japanese girl was an asset to the class.

Taking an ecological perspective Arthur *et al.* (2003: 8) explain how
socio-cultural factors inform not only the practices within families
and wider social groups, but also classroom dynamics. They state
that teachers and students can be seen as cultural beings who are
embedded from birth in the traits, mores, values and attitudes of
their own cultures and that, as a result, in any classroom there will
be a diverse range of attitudes and values about relationships and
behaviour. They point out that students, or even groups of students,
may have quite different views on other students based on gender,
class or ethnic and racial markers.

Sometimes language classes contain students with similar levels of linguistic proficiency, but with different levels of maturity and areas of
interest. It is difficult for teachers to identify suitable topics when some
students are of the 'sunshine, sand and sea' brigade, interested in relatively frivolous topics such as sport, sex and fashion, while others wish

to discuss more weighty topics such as nuclear testing or press censorship. As one student explained:

> We are university students. We like to talk about serious topics like politics and economics . . . We can't speak English very well, but we think about serious problems. We don't want to talk about daily life.

Another factor that can affect the social harmony of language classes is the development of subtle pecking orders within classes. For example, Europeans may consider themselves superior to non-Europeans, Asian students may look down on students from Africa, or students with 'city values' may behave dismissively towards less sophisticated students from rural areas. Students demonstrate their perceived superiority over others in language classrooms in a range of obvious and less obvious ways. An easily discernible way that students can create a feeling of exclusivity is by choosing their classroom 'territory' and indicating, through the placing of chairs, the patting of seats or the strategic placement of bags, who is welcome to sit next to them – and who is not. Reasons that students give for not wanting to associate with certain groups of students can also be indicative of innate feelings of superiority. One student informed his teacher that there was no point expecting him to work with 'those' students, since the way they pronounced English meant that he could not understand a word they said. Communicative tasks can also provide subtle indications of racist sentiments. One student told his teacher that it was a waste of time to go round the room asking everyone whether they preferred bread, pasta, potatoes or rice, since he already knew what the answer of half the class would be.

When given an appropriate opportunity, and when they sense that the person in whom they are confiding will understand their viewpoint, language students sometimes openly reveal racist attitudes. On one occasion, when funding was made available for students to evaluate their classes orally through interpreters (as opposed to the normal practice of ticking boxes on evaluation sheets), an unexpected outcome resulted. In one class, which contained seven or eight Polish students and a similar number of students from Kampuchea, the Polish students informed their interpreter that they did not consider it appropriate to be learning English in the same class as people from Kampuchea: they expected to be segregated. The teacher recalled the irony of the situation: that one of the students from Kampuchea was linguistically far more able, and had a far better world knowledge, than any other student in the class.

Apart from occasional pronouncements such as, 'I am a European with high culture; I don't want to mix with students with less culture,' students rarely make openly racist statements to their teachers or to researchers. However, racism undoubtedly lies below the surface in many language classes, and may manifest itself in subtle ways that teachers do not notice.

Often, of course, as soon as they mingle with students from different ethnic groups during lessons, students find that any preconceived ideas they may have had about particular races or cultures quickly dissipate: they recognise that the similarities they share with students from other cultures far outweigh the differences. Even students who find themselves studying in classes with students from countries with whom they have recently been at war are normally prepared to put ingrained prejudices behind them once they enter the language classroom. Sometimes studying in the same room may involve reaching an entente cordiale, such as the Bosnian and the Serbian who, through mutual agreement, never spoke to one another in class. They did, however, unexpectedly find themselves having fun together in the final week of term – during an inter-class soccer game.

The above examples are indicative of the highly complex, ever-changing pattern of human relationships that can occur in any language class.

5.4 Conclusion

This chapter has identified some of the variables that give each language class its own particular flavour and unique social character. In so doing it has demonstrated the complexity of the task facing classroom language teachers, who must find ways of working with the raw material of their classes – the students themselves – whoever they may be and however receptive they are. To be successful in this unique environment language teachers need to be not only highly skilled at their craft, but also adept managers of people.

Summary

- Classes of adult language learners in an English-speaking country are typically multicultural, containing students from a range of ethnic, linguistic and cultural backgrounds.
- Language classes are seldom balanced, in the sense that they are unlikely to contain balanced numbers of students from different countries of origin.
- No language student joins a language class as a blank slate: each one brings to class a unique personality combined with an individual set of circumstances, priorities and concerns.

- Students frequently enter language classes with sets of learning expectations that differ from the expectations that their teachers have of them.
- Personal circumstances may make students less receptive or responsive in their classes than their teachers would like.
- Tensions can develop between groups of students from both similar and different cultural backgrounds.
- Certain groups of students in language classes may consider themselves different from or better than other groups of students.
- Although in most language classes a satisfactory accommodation is reached, some students harbour racist attitudes that may or may not be detected by their teachers.

Comment

The whole area of students' impressions of their classes, and the degree to which they are satisfied with the tuition that they receive in communicative classrooms, merits further investigation. Anecdotal evidence suggests that some students may not be as satisfied with the communicative approach as their teachers assume them to be. In a section entitled 'Countering learner resistance' Willis (1996: 140) pinpoints the most common complaints articulated by students as follows:

- 'We don't do enough grammar';
- 'We'd like to be corrected more when we speak';
- 'We've been doing this course for some time and don't feel we're making progress';
- 'We find the recordings of natural speech hard to understand'; and
- 'We don't like doing pairwork with people who speak our own language'.

It now appears that certain students' impressions may be justified. Lightbown and Spada (1999: 150) report research which suggests that learners in programs where there is no guided focus on form continue to have difficulty with accuracy. In their words, 'Because this approach emphasizes meaning and attempts to simulate "natural" communication in conversational interaction, the students' focus is naturally on *what* they say, not *how* to say it. This can result in a situation where learners provide each other with input which is often incorrect and incomplete.'

Looking ahead

The following chapter describes how language teachers respond to the challenges outlined in this chapter. It shows how they deal with individual students in ways that enable language classes to function as collaboratively and harmoniously as possible.

6 Managing individuals

The previous chapter showed how each language class is composed of a unique meld of students, in terms of their countries of origin, linguistic backgrounds, personalities and so on. It showed how each student's state of mind, which is often related to personal circumstances and immediate concerns, can affect their classroom behaviour. It also showed how groups of students can differentiate themselves from other students, thereby posing potential problems for their teachers.

The present chapter focuses on how language teachers manage individuals and groups of students in their classrooms. Section 6.1 shows how experienced teachers, recognising the leadership roles that students with strong personalities can play in their classes, attempt to harness for the good of the class the energies of potentially disruptive students. It also demonstrates how the behaviour of individuals or cliques is related to the overall wellbeing of language classes. Section 6.2 outlines the different ways in which experienced language teachers are alert to classroom 'vibes': behavioural clues that are indicative of students' states of mind. It suggests that language teachers are particularly alert to potential threats to the self-esteem of vulnerable individuals. Section 6.3 describes some of the pro-active and reactive ways in which experienced teachers seek to maintain or restore a sense of social equilibrium within their classes when they sense that the emotions of individuals or groups of students are running high.

6.1 Coping with individuals

> 'Success depends less on materials, techniques and linguistic analyses, and more on what goes on inside and between people in the classroom.'
> Stevick (1980: 4)

When they walk into any new class language teachers confront a sea of unfamiliar faces. It is not long, however, before certain students begin to emerge from the crowd: able students, lively students, attention-seeking students or perhaps individuals with challenging looks on their faces.

119

However, at this early stage in the life of each new language class most students have not yet entered the viewfinder of the teacher. They are the compliant, silent majority – happy to wait, watch, listen, absorb the ambiance, and go with the general flow.

Identifying allies

Language teachers know that in the early days of each new class it is possible to identify students who, through their confident manner and outgoing personalities, have the potential to operate as class group leaders. As one teacher remarked, 'You always get your natural leaders coming out – and you can tell virtually from the first day who they are going to be, just from your experience in the classroom'. Language teachers value such students highly because, in the words of another teacher, 'It takes the pressure off you. Things are happening naturally. *You* don't have to be the one making things happen all the time.'

The leadership roles that students assume in their classes can take a variety of forms. The most crucial one is that of being openly friendly to everyone in the class, as demonstrated by the following description:

> This dear little Vietnamese girl was just a caring little thing and she loved the teacher and she loved the other students, she loved everybody, and she used to go round arm in arm with some of the Bosnian women. She was able to relate to everybody, so she brought the Asians together with the Europeans.

Some students are quick to assume the role of teacher's helper, hastening to carry books, hold open doors, set up the room, operate the slide projector, and so on. One student consolidated his role as teacher's aid by performing these tasks with a quick click of the heels, a small bow, and a broad smile to the class at large. Other students are generally enthusiastic and willing to put themselves forward for high-profile learning tasks such as performing role-plays with the teacher, thereby setting an example for others to follow.

Students in leadership roles often have higher language levels than those of other class members – and the confidence that knowledge of their superior proficiency brings with it. One class contained two students whose English skills were well above the rest of the class, but who for logistical reasons could not be promoted to a more advanced class. One of these students sat in a corner of the room studying quietly and keeping her own counsel, while the other played a role that the teacher considered 'pivotal' to both the social wellbeing and the linguistic progress of the class as a whole. She sat in the centre of the room (next to the only non-European student in the class), from which position she could interact readily with individuals all around the room. She also voluntarily assumed a teaching role, catching the teacher's eye from time to time and moving around to help weaker students with their work as required.

Another leadership role that is relatively common in language classes is that of operating as the teacher's foil. Certain students develop bantering relationships with their teachers, thereby providing an opportunity for the rest of the class to play the role of amused onlookers. Self-assured teachers value such relationships, construing 'forward' student behaviour positively, rather than as a threat to their authority. One teacher described a class that did not contain any feisty students as being 'bland, with no spice'. This led him to recall with pleasure another class which had contained a particular student, a Polish nun, with whom he had developed an ongoing relationship based on word-plays and the literal meaning of certain parables in the Bible. Once students notice that the teacher responds to such initiatives positively, others sometimes try to follow suit.

Natural student leaders often continue their roles outside the classroom. For example, they may behave in inclusive ways towards the shyer and more retiring students during coffee breaks, or take the initiative to organise a party or group activity for the class outside class time. Students with leadership qualities may distribute lists of the phone numbers and email addresses to all class members so that everyone can keep in touch. They also tend to be the ones who organise the traditional purchasing of cards or gifts for the teacher at the end of the course.

Harnessing the headstrong

Of course forceful individuals have the potential to exert a negative as well as a positive influence on the class group. The early days of language classes are crucial times. This is when students who may prove difficult to manage make their presence known, and when teachers must make on-the-spot decisions about how to respond to their challenging behaviour. Adult students are often quite subtle in the ways in which they assert their individuality: they may isolate themselves from the class group by electing to sit on their own, or they may make excessive demands on the teacher's attention by asking a flood of questions. Young adults who are, in the words of one teacher, 'still in high-school mode', may behave in more openly defiant ways. Typical behaviour can include muttering asides within earshot of others, pouting when not selected to do something they want to do, or scraping their chairs and groaning when required to change seats.

Teachers sense that it is important to treat potentially tricky students with care – and perhaps to pay them a little more attention than is strictly their due in the early stage of a course. They know that there is often a small window of opportunity during the first few lessons of each new course when they may be able to get a tricky student on side – which can often result in a dramatic behavioural change. Recalling a particularly problematic student from Singapore a teacher remarked:

> He was such a dominant leader type. He started off really wanting to assert that he was the one in charge, and challenging all the time and often not doing the task that he was set, mumbling a lot under his breath, and trying to get a lot of attention.

The teacher recalled that after a period of time the student unexpectedly stopped challenging her, and eventually became very supportive of the weaker students, particularly when they were giving individual oral presentations to the class. In the words of the teacher, 'He still had this strong role, but in a much more positive way'. Although the teacher was at a loss to explain the radical transformation in the student's behaviour, it seems likely that she had indicated to the class that she valued the strong personality and high level of academic ability of this particular student. Public acknowledgement of his strengths may have been enough to encourage the student to focus his energies in a positive direction for the remainder of the course.

One teacher even went so far as to keep a diary about her struggle to manage one particular student over a ten-week period, entitled 'My ongoing battle with Stavros'. The reason that management of this particular student was so difficult was that the student challenged not only the teacher's level of expertise, but also the information provided in the teaching materials. He insisted, for example, that prototype computers were first developed in the cotton mills of England in the 18th century – rather than in the mid-20th century. The student eventually toned down his behaviour, to the point where the teacher viewed him as an asset to the class. Interestingly, as she gained control over the situation, the teacher's confidence in herself (which had been diminished because of the student's challenging behaviour) gradually returned. Towards the end of the course she wrote:

> He can still be controversial and challenging, but I think the other students find he makes the lessons interesting – and they feel comfortable because they can see that he doesn't get the better of me. He can't destroy my confidence any more.

In her diary the teacher recorded the strategies she'd used for managing this particular student:

Acknowledging that he's better than the rest; paying him extra attention; using him as a resource (consulting him about the Greek derivations of English words, for example); not losing my cool; showing him that I am the boss and that I will not let him dominate the class; gently teasing him for being unreasonable; showing the rest of the class where I stand, ie. that I think he is over the top and that I appreciate their position; trying to remain on the fence and not taking sides; playing the role of peacekeeper and diffusing confrontational situations between him and other students.

Teachers are sometimes aware of having missed a vital window of opportunity to get a forceful student on side. A high-school language teacher recalled having prepared a song to teach the students in her class how to say the date in Italian. When she mentioned the song a bright student who was new to the class called out, 'I can teach the class that song! I know it!' Instead of taking the student up on his offer the teacher brushed the student aside, saying, 'Maybe another time' – and instantly regretted her decision, recalling that at that point she could feel the student 'drifting away', his enthusiasm for learning Italian dampened.

> The insights provided by the teachers in the above section suggest that they have acquired an understanding of the kinds of roles that students can play in the social evolution of their class groups. For a description of the many roles that students can play in language classes, see Dörnyei and Murphey (2003: Chapter 7). See Senior (2004) for a description of both 'witting' and 'unwitting' student roles in language classrooms, and of how teacher reactions to spontaneous student behaviour can affect the dynamics of the class group in either positive or negative ways.

Ongoing problems

Just as they can handle problematic students in ways that lead to positive outcomes, so teachers can manage students in ways that can lead to ongoing negative behaviour. It is easy for language teachers to behave in ways that they later regret – particularly when their patience is wearing thin. Causing a student to lose face in front of their peers is a sure-fire way of creating ongoing problems. In one class a vibrant young migrant woman with excellent communication skills made it known that she thought the class was too easy for her, and was slack with her work. In the second week of the course the teacher chastised her in front of the class – fully aware that it was 'a bitchy thing to do' and that it might have ongoing consequences. It did indeed, with the student behaving in a resentful manner for the remainder of the course. Had the teacher handled her differently, and perhaps taken up some of the suggestions for discussion topics that she had put forward in the first week, the outcome might have been different.

Often what might be construed as demanding behaviour is nothing more than students demonstrating concern about whether or not their learning needs will be met. Language students who ask their teachers tricky questions early on in their courses are often testing their knowledge rather than challenging their authority. One student asked his teacher a detailed question about a specific grammar point in the second lesson of a course. When the teacher interrupted the flow of the lesson to answer the question in some detail (which included saying that the information provided by a previous teacher had been incorrect), the student nodded and sat back, visibly relieved. Some students whose questions are not answered to their satisfaction continue to be highly demanding throughout their courses.

Teachers try many additional strategies for pulling tricky students into line, including private chats to identify problems and offer advice, appeals to their better natures, humouring, cajoling, praising, singling out for special jobs, and so on. They are also aware of other students in the room sometimes attempting to induce classmates whose behaviour they disapprove of to conform. Often, however, once students are in recalcitrant mode they remain that way for the duration of the course. There are countless reasons behind their seemingly negative behaviour – many of which their teachers never discover (which is fair enough, since a teacher's job is to teach, not to be an amateur sleuth, psychologist or social worker). However, a prime cause for difficult student behaviour is often resentment at having been 'wrongly placed'. One student who had attended an intermediate class in one school transferred to another school where she was tested and placed in a lower-intermediate class – where she was one of the weakest students. Her teacher reported that she cast her a 'venomous look' as she passed her in the corridor on her way to request promotion to a higher class. When the promotion was denied the student behaved in a withdrawn manner for the remainder of the course, gazing out of the window, examining her hair for split ends or playing with her electronic dictionary.

Sometimes language teachers attribute ongoing problems with their classes to the fact that they failed to take the necessary steps to meld their classes into cohesive groups early on in their courses. One highly experienced teacher continued to be angry with herself for mismanaging a particular class long after it had disbanded. In her view she had misread the level of social maturity of the class group, believing that she did not need to do rapport-building activities at the beginning of the course because the students were of a high linguistic level – when in fact she did. In her view she lost the opportunity to 'glue the class together' at the beginning of the course – an opportunity that never returned. Social relations within this class evidently went from bad to worse, with new students joining the class and sensing that 'it was a class divided, not a class united'. This teacher lost confidence in herself to such an extent that she would abandon tasks halfway through and 'leave things hanging'– a classroom practice normally only seen in novice teachers. The teacher was highly embarrassed by the whole episode, since she was a qualified trainer and realised that in this particular instance she had failed to practise what she preached.

Sometimes, of course, language teachers find themselves in situations where the task of inducing their classes to behave in amenable ways seems impossibly difficult. These situations most commonly occur in high schools, notably in schools where language learning is not highly valued and where overall discipline is poor (see Chapter 10). When they find their classes virtually unmanageable teachers may resort to behaving in repressive ways for their own survival.

Irredeemable situations

Language teachers have learnt from experience that the behaviour of even a single student with a negative attitude can upset the social equilibrium of the class group – particularly when that student has a strong personality and is prepared to make their feelings known. A student who calls out 'This is boring!' or 'Why are we doing this?' can sow the seeds of mistrust in a class, while a dominant student who is determined to make their presence felt can totally destroy the class atmosphere. One teacher described the situation by saying, 'When you have one dissatisfied student it's like having a rotten apple in the midst of the class – it sours the whole group'. Teachers notice a marked difference in the classroom environment when problem students are absent. In the words of one teacher:

> Those two weren't there and the atmosphere was completely different. It was a delight. The other students were laughing and getting on together and interested in each other – in a way that they wouldn't have been if those two had been around.

Language teachers are aware of their own powerlessness in the face of a closed circle of students who are determined to pursue their own private agendas within the classroom. Talking about a particular clique, one teacher said, 'Those three unsettled the class, no matter what I did. They had no regard for the other students and were arrogant as people.' Students such as these can often be seen talking or whispering to one another in their mother tongue, or laughing together at some joke that nobody outside their linguistic group can understand. Such students are often more concerned with the impression that they are giving to their peers than they are with learning the target language or interacting with other class members. Sometimes they are reluctant to pronounce the target language in a more native-like way, for fear of sounding affected to their friends. The behaviour of students in closed circles such as these can have a highly detrimental effect on the social dynamics of class groups – particularly when the circle is a large one that encompasses a significant proportion of the class. Students outside the circle naturally feel excluded. Sometimes the teacher feels excluded too.

Other students cause offence without intending to do so. One student regularly responded to his teacher's requests with a terse 'Of course!', uttered briskly and without sufficient modulation to soften its effect. He appeared surprised when informed that his words sounded offensive to an English ear, then recalling that he had recently caused offence in the coffee shop because he had not said 'please' when ordering his coffee ('please' being used more frequently in English than in other tongues). It is likely that this student's gruff manner, combined with his over-use or under-use of phatic language, meant that he conveyed the impression of being more aggressive than he actually was. The same may be true of other students whose subtle misuse of the target language suggests a belligerent attitude.

Despite intractable problems with certain individuals or cliques, as their courses progress experienced language teachers are usually able to draw increasing numbers of students into the ever-expanding classroom 'fold'. Once high-profile students are drawn in, others will usually follow, with the shyest and most diffident students being drawn in last. Language teachers hope that everyone in the room will eventually feel comfortable in the knowledge that they are integral members of the 'inner circle' of their particular language class.

6.2 Tuning in to class behaviour

'Standing alone in their classrooms, teachers have little to guide them except what they know, what they observe and understand, what they sense and feel . . . They must be sensitive to what is going on while they work, somewhat as artists, in moving towards learning–teaching objectives . . . Teachers must learn to trust their own senses, their own observations. They must recognise the realities of group life as well as the complexities of individual personality.'

Luft (1984: 182)

Potential for interpersonal damage

One way in which language classes differ from classes in which other subjects are taught is that interpersonal communication is a goal in itself – rather than being a means by which students internalise concepts and understandings through discussion with fellow class members. Because they are required to be highly interactive in their classrooms, language learners are in possession of a powerful tool: the ability to say things to other people, or to react to what others say to them, in ways that might cause hurt or distress. Within the parameters of communicative activities, however carefully they are set up, students who feel so inclined can find creative ways of making other class members feel upset, indignant or exasperated (as in the 'You will die!' example in the previous chapter). Students can also anger or demean others without meaning to – as indeed can language teachers themselves. How do language teachers react in situations when they sense that a student's emotions are running high? Do they ignore the situation and pass swiftly on, or do they try to do something about it? The next sections indicate that, although they sometimes choose to ignore student behaviour, or may fail to notice key behavioural clues, for the most part experienced language teachers not only notice the behaviour, but also take some kind of remedial action.

Sensitivity to classroom 'vibes'

Experienced teachers are able to do two very different things simultaneously. They are able to register how students, both individually and collectively, are feeling at any given moment, and they are able to proceed smoothly with the business of teaching. There are two things that experienced language teachers routinely do when they sense that certain students may be experiencing feelings that are likely to impede their language learning. First, they intuitively make a split-second adjustment to what they are doing: deciding not to put two particular students together, congratulating in passing a low-profile student (within earshot of the class), or interrupting what they are doing to make a statement to the class at large. Second, they make a mental note of the occurrence, resolving to take certain steps when a future opportunity presents itself. One teacher described this process in the following way:

> The people I think are quieter and that I've got a query about in my mind, I might watch their reaction next time round – because I've made a mental note to do so. These are the sorts of things that are running through your mind all the time as you're teaching.

In one warm-up activity a teacher caught a fleeting glimpse of one student being hesitant to shake the hand of a student with a different skin colour from his own. This split-second observation raised her awareness of the fact that certain students in the class might be unwilling to work with this particular student, who had a high level of English but was naturally shy. For the remainder of the course the teacher monitored carefully where students chose to sit and whom they were friendly with. When an opportunity arose later in the course to allow the darker-skinned student to tell the class how he had cleverly countered the racist comments of a fellow passenger on a bus, she grasped it eagerly.

Because the process of adapting what they are doing in response to ongoing student feedback is such a subtle, organic process, teachers may not notice what caused them to react in the way that they did until after they have reacted. Sometimes, of course, the process is conscious. One teacher of an examination preparation class was aware that the patience of a highly focused student could quickly wear thin whenever she relaxed and had a bit of fun with the class. Reflecting back to a previous lesson she said, 'I could just feel his anxiety, his unhappiness, with where the lesson was going – so I quickly brought the lesson back on track'.

Language teachers describe their general alertness to behavioural clues in terms of keeping their eyes peeled, of having eyes in the back of their head, or of noticing things out of the corner of their eye. Most experienced teachers have had a good deal of practice at deducing how students are feeling from external clues including general behaviour, body language and facial expressions. When a student suddenly rushes from the room in tears there is little doubt that they are upset, although the cause may not be immediately apparent. Body language, too, is relatively straightforward to interpret. Students who look at their watches, yawn or furtively make their worksheets into paper darts are likely to be bored, while students who lean back in their chairs with chins lowered and arms folded are likely to be feeling angry, affronted or frustrated. The precise nature of these feelings, or what caused them, again may not be clear.

However, teachers are used to acting on hunches. The better they know the personalities and normal behavioural patterns of the students in their classes, the more likely they are to make accurate guesses about how particular individuals are feeling. The alarm bells ring when they notice a student behaving in an uncharacteristic manner, such as a student with a normally sunny disposition looking downcast and hanging their head. When this happens they sense that remedial action may need to be taken at some point in the future. Language teachers also notice when groups of students are behaving uncharacteristically. At a time of political tension between China and Taiwan, one teacher noticed a knot of Chinese students huddled together and talking in an animated fashion. As a result of this chance observation she made a mental note 'to watch it a little bit and wait till the crisis is over' (before doing a planned discussion activity).

Language teachers also glean information about students' feelings from what they write in their class diaries, or from casual chats before or after class. It is often possible for teachers to manipulate the situation so that it is not obvious to others that they wish to have a private talk with a particular student. Classroom tasks can also reveal students' feelings. One teacher was shaken by the level of intercultural misunderstanding between the students in her class which became evident when, as part of a research project, she devised an activity that required students to share their impressions of other cultural groups within the class. As a result of what she discovered she built this tolerance-building task into her regular teaching program.

It is far more difficult to read students' facial expressions accurately, particularly in the context of multicultural classrooms. One of the advantages of setting up interactive tasks is that students' faces tend to become lively and animated as they interact with their peers, providing teachers with the kind of feedback that they want and value. Language teachers, particularly those from western countries, expect to see a range of expressions on students' faces – and feel uneasy when these are not readily forthcoming. Talking about a particular student, one teacher said:

> His almond eyes just stared at me and I thought to myself, 'What are you thinking, mate?' . . . It throws us when we can't judge their facial expressions. I think I'm getting better at registering different looks on faces. Students from some countries don't use their faces like us – but you can usually tell from the eyes.

Language teachers tend to assume that facial expressions and head movements that are common to all human beings have universal meaning, and can be surprised and dismayed when they find that their assumptions are wrong. One teacher discovered to her cost that a student who always sat at the front of the class nodding sagely in fact absorbed very little of what she was saying, while another came to realise that smiling could be indicative of nervousness rather than friendliness. Occasionally a language teacher can misinterpret student behaviour and then react to it in such a way that their professional image is damaged. One teacher had the following recollection:

> When I first started teaching I blew up this Vietnamese guy for coming in late all the time and he started laughing, and the more he laughed the more cross I got and the more I blew up. I completely destroyed that class because the Vietnamese guy laughs when he is embarrassed and I wasn't able to read that. . . The class

was mostly Asians – and the Asians consider that it's inappropriate for a teacher to behave in that way. So after that they considered me a somewhat unbalanced person.

Physical proximity is also an area where teachers can sometimes behave inappropriately. One teacher recalled putting her hand on the shoulder of a male student and exclaiming, 'Oh, but you're lovely when you're angry' – only to have her hand shaken off and the student turn away from her.

Experience leads language teachers to conclude that different cultural groups behave differently in language classrooms. It is commonly accepted that students from western countries, including those from the former Soviet bloc such as Poland or the former Yugoslavia, tend to behave more assertively than their eastern counterparts from countries such as China, Indonesia or Japan. In the view of one teacher, part of the success of being a good language teacher involved being able to read what he called 'the culture fuse' of each cultural group. Another teacher demonstrated the cross-cultural complexity of language classrooms by explaining how difficult it was to reach a consensus decision if you were teaching a class composed of Japanese and Swiss students. This was because, while the Japanese students would wait to give their views till they sensed what the group wanted, the Swiss students would quickly assert what they wanted. Unless the teacher actively intervened on behalf of the more group-centred Japanese students, the Swiss students would always get their way.

Awareness of student vulnerability

When language teachers start out on their careers, the fun and excitement of teaching in communicative classrooms tends to sweep them along. As their experience grows, they become increasingly sensitive and, as a result, more careful in their handling of individuals. One teacher expressed this phenomenon in the following way:

Sometimes the more experienced you are the more you can feel things. . . As I've got to know more about what I should be doing and how complex it all is, the awareness, the sensitivity increases. I'm very aware of things I didn't use to worry about so much.

Language teachers become increasingly aware of how vulnerable students can feel in language classrooms, particularly competitively minded adult learners who have been high achievers all their lives and who have previously found learning relatively easy. (Such students are unaccustomed to failure: they are used to getting things right first time round.) One teacher who had a student who behaved in a particularly aloof manner in class believed that his behaviour was due to overweening pride, coupled with a deep fear that his peers might not regard him as highly as he regarded himself. Language teachers sense that making the smallest slip, whether it is mispronouncing a word, misunderstanding an instruction or stumbling as they read a sentence, can cause a student to feel mortified. One student became so upset on perceiving that someone in the class was sniggering at her errors that she requested to withdraw from the course. Her teacher said:

> Part of her problem is that she's too busy trying to put on an impression, and then the students keep pricking her bubble, or she keeps pricking her own bubble by getting it wrong – and so she's setting herself up to fail.

Dörnyei (2001: 88) refers to Covington's (1992) 'self-worth theory', which explains the basic human need to maintain a sense of personal value and worth, especially in the face of competition, failure and negative feedback (which are typical in classrooms). Dörnyei points out that this basic need generates a number of unique patterns of face-saving behaviours in school settings. Although he suggests that issues of self-esteem and self-confidence are particularly significant for learners who have not yet reached adulthood, it appears that these issues are equally, if not more, significant for adult language learners who find themselves once again in school-type situations.

6.3 Handling students with care

Because of their awareness of the vulnerable position in which students can find themselves in language classrooms, a key goal for language teachers is to minimise the potential damage to students' self-esteem that may be caused by the routine practices and activities of communicative classrooms. As they go about their daily teaching, these teachers subtly adjust the ways in which they manage not only individuals, but also their class groups. These subtle adjustments – a private comment here or a public statement there – are best understood in terms of the teacher's desire to protect the sensibilities of individuals. This motivational force appears to be a strong one for experienced language teachers, whose minds are constantly on high alert as they scan their classes for evidence of damage to the self-esteem of individuals. They can often intuit, based on their assessment of the current situation and on their knowledge of what has happened in similar situations in the past, either that damage is about to happen, or that it has already happened. In the former case they take preventive action to avert or reduce potential damage, while in the latter case they take remedial action to minimise the effect of such damage. For both these categories experienced language teachers have at their disposal a range of strategies that they have used successfully in the past – those that did not prove effective having been discarded along the way.

Behaving pro-actively: minimising damage to self-esteem

Language teachers describe a range of ways in which they subtly adjust their pedagogic practices in order to minimise threats to the self-esteem of vulnerable individuals. Teachers are conscious that students are likely to be feeling particularly nervous in the early days of their courses. As one teacher explained, 'For the first couple of weeks you really have to protect the students who are at a lower level than the others because they're more self-conscious and they feel intimidated'. Experience has taught language teachers that there are myriad ways of adjusting their pedagogic practices so that individuals can feel more comfortable and less threatened. These often involve adjustment of questioning techniques: only asking questions to diffident students once everyone else has had a go first, for example. Language teachers routinely find themselves having to balance the psychological wellbeing of individuals against their learning needs: students may be feeling vulnerable, but at the same time they need to be encouraged to become more fully integrated into the corporate life of the class group. Students who maintain low profiles in their classes for the duration of their courses report feeling 'invisible' or 'forgotten', particularly when their teacher never asks them a question, never singles them out for a high profile task – and perhaps never even addresses them by name.

Language teachers find ways of enabling vulnerable students to participate in the collective learning experience of the class group, while at the same time limiting potential damage to their self-esteem. One teacher explained that over the years she had become increasingly sensitive to students' feelings, and increasingly wary of putting individuals 'on the spot'. As a result she now gave her classes more chorus work (thus giving students opportunities to practise their pronunciation in unison with others), and encouraged students to call out answers to grammar exercises collectively rather than individually. Another teacher had developed the practice of always asking the students in her class to provide answers to exercises by going round the class in a predictable order. She explained that she did this to protect individuals, who would have time not only to prepare their answers, but also to check with their neighbour that their answer was correct before giving it. Practices such as these allow students to participate, while at the same time maintaining a low profile.

When students do make errors in front of the class, experienced teachers have at their fingertips a number of ways of responding that minimise damage to students' self-esteem. One teacher would routinely thank individuals for making errors, explaining to the class that the student in question had provided a valuable opportunity for everyone in the room to revise something important. Another would not correct the error, but would turn the event into a learning opportunity for the class as a whole, saying, 'Now, let's see: who can suggest what might be wrong with this sentence?' A third teacher, who routinely had students produce a piece of writing for the whole class to read, would sometimes enable the student under the spotlight to save face by saying, 'Now you put that error in there deliberately for people to find, didn't you?' The student would naturally agree. When learners have particular difficulty with certain sounds, some language teachers deflect attention from the student to themselves, by showing how difficult it is for *them* to articulate certain sounds in the *student's* mother tongue. Responses to student errors such as these suggest that many experienced language teachers regularly try to shield vulnerable language learners from threats to their self-esteem.

> The sensitivity they typically display as they try to minimise damage to the self-esteem of students who may be feeling nervous or vulnerable provides further evidence that language teachers are humanistic in orientation. Williams and Burden summarise the messages that humanism has for language teachers, one of which is to minimise criticism (1997: 38).

Controlling the atmosphere of the class group

An important way in which language teachers ensure that individual students feel protected is by keeping close control over the social atmosphere within the classroom. Language teachers, intuitively aware of the power of the group to influence the behaviour of individuals, work hard to ensure that the prevailing atmosphere is one of tolerance and mutual respect. Apart from modelling the kinds of behaviour that they expect and demonstrating approval when students are friendly and helpful towards each other, experienced language teachers make it clear that they will not condone certain kinds of behaviour. By so doing they instil a feeling of security in the minds of students, who know that steps will be taken to eradicate petty behaviour that can lead to social division within their classes.

One of the most crucial steps that language teachers take is to ensure that students do not develop the habit of talking to their compatriots in their mother tongues in the classroom. There are strong pedagogic reasons for discouraging mother-tongue talk in multilingual classrooms: valuable time spent communicating in the target language is lost (although occasionally it is beneficial to allow students to translate words or explain concepts to their peers in their mother tongue). However, there are even stronger social reasons for not allowing mother-tongue talk in language classrooms: students outside the linguistic group feel uneasy, since there is always the chance that they may be the subject of the conversation. Another problem with mother-tongue talk is that it tends to become increasingly prevalent: a quiet remark here or a quick comment there can quickly escalate into a situation in which mother-tongue talk becomes the norm. One teacher saw his class polarise into two distinct groups: a 'western' group composed of students who shared the same mother tongue, and an 'eastern' group composed of students from a variety of Asian countries. The eastern students became increasingly irate as the course progressed, particularly when the western students began to mutter asides to their compatriots during the course of small-group activities, and to shout comments across the room that caused their compatriots to laugh. The teacher observed in retrospect that, although he had stated at the beginning of the course that students should not converse in their mother tongues, he had not been sufficiently rigorous in ensuring that they did not do so as the course proceeded.

The ways in which language teachers ensure that classroom codes of behaviour are complied with vary considerably according to individual personalities and preferred class management styles. One teacher 'growled' at students, another would open her eyes wide with an expression of mock horror on her face, while a third would wag a finger in an exaggerated way whenever he noticed a minor transgression. One teacher would let forth a torrent of Italian (to remind students what it feels like not to understand a word of what someone else is saying), while another would exclaim, 'That sounds interesting – please translate!' when a student began talking in their mother tongue. A common feature of these quick responses is that they serve as instant reminders to the class at large that the teacher is monitoring not only student learning but also student interaction patterns. Such responses also convey the message that certain behaviours will be regularly noticed – and regularly discouraged.

Conscious of the fact that being chastised in public causes the offending student to lose face (and perhaps to behave defiantly in the future), experienced language teachers tend to pull students into line quickly before returning to the business of the lesson. They often do so with the proverbial twinkle in the eye – sensing that all eyes are watching and that their interaction with the errant individual is being monitored by everyone in the room. As one teacher said, 'If you're speaking quietly to a student and perhaps reprimanding them, there's nothing more attention-getting for everyone else'. This teacher recalled how after chastising a particular student she switched the conversation quickly to the student's holiday plans, deliberately talking in a slightly louder voice so that the rest of the class could overhear what was being said (and with what tone of voice). She explained that she did this so that the class would get the message that there were no hard feelings between the student and herself, concluding '. . . so she laughed and I laughed – and the matter was closed'.

> The awareness that experienced language teachers have that their management of individuals has an effect on the overall dynamics of the class group suggests that they have a high degree of 'withitness'. In a classic study of discipline and group management in classrooms Kounin (1970) coined the term 'the ripple effect', to refer to the way that a teacher's method of handling the misbehavior of a student influences the other students, who are audiences to the event but not themselves the target. Kounin defines the term 'withitness' as 'a teacher's communicating to the children by her actual behavior (rather than by simple verbal announcing: "I know what's going on") that she knows what the children are doing, or has the proverbial "eyes in the back of the head"' (1970: 80).

Behaving reactively: damage limitation

A key feature of the communicative approach is that students are provided with opportunities to interact freely with one another in the classroom – usually after having first practised new language in a more restricted, controlled way. At this point they are on the third 'P' of the 'PPP' (presentation–practice–production) continuum, or in the 'A' (authentic) phase of Scrivener's (1994) 'ARC' model of classroom interaction. At many points in language lessons, but particularly at this final 'free' stage, students are expected to use the target language for genuine communication. A large number of resource books containing the widest possible range of interactive tasks are currently available. These books line the shelves of resource rooms in language schools, providing easy and welcome ways of supplementing the activities provided in the assigned coursebook. In a hurry to find something that will engage the interest of sleepy students on a hot afternoon, language teachers readily pluck two or three activities that they think will go down well with their class, quickly make the requisite number of photocopies and rush off to teach. Although lessons based on such materials usually proceed smoothly, there is always the chance that students will complete interactive tasks in unanticipated ways. (They can be very creative in this regard.) Experienced teachers are normally quick to take palliative action when they sense that students have behaved inappropriately and offended their peers. They have at their disposal a range of strategies for reducing the impact of such behaviour and, hopefully, for restoring the social equilibrium of their class groups.

Strategies commonly used by teachers who have switched to damage limitation mode include shifting the focus of the activity ('angle-shifting'), broadening the focus of the activity ('broadening'), changing the tenor of the activity ('lightening') or outlining general lessons to be learnt ('moralising'). Teachers may also decide to cut an activity short, or to abandon it altogether, if the going gets too tough. In general, however, they prefer to try to redeem situations – perhaps sensing that, if they are too quick to abandon learning activities, they will appear unprofessional.

The strategies described by the teachers in this book are in many respects similar to those recommended by Jiang (2001) for handling 'culture bumps'. The term 'culture bump' was originally used by Archer (1986: 170), who defines it in the following way: 'A culture bump occurs when an individual from one culture finds himself or herself in a different, strange, or uncomfortable situation when interacting with persons of a different culture. This phenomenon results from a difference in the way people from one culture behave in a particular situation from people in another culture.'

Often experienced teachers combine several of these strategies in one single response. For one afternoon class a teacher selected an interactive activity entitled 'A human zoo' in which students were required to imagine that humans were inside cages, with animals peering in at them, rather than the other way around. Then, in groups of three, students were to select a 'species' for their particular cage (politicians, teachers and football fans were given as examples) and write a description of its characteristics. The class was composed almost entirely of Swiss-French and Swiss-German students – between whom little love was lost. While other groups described artists, comedians, sumo wrestlers and so on, three Swiss-French students jointly composed and presented to the class the following text: 'If you want to see animals that are strict, cold, serious, humourless, narrow-minded, conservative sausage-eaters – go to the Swiss-German cage'. The teacher was quick to diffuse the situation. She rapidly looked towards a Swiss-German student who happened to have a French name and none of the clichéd characteristics suggested by the gang of three, and exclaimed to the class, 'Oh dear! Where does that put André then?' She then invited the class to brainstorm a clichéd view of Australians – which the whole class did collectively, with great enthusiasm and mirth. She then talked in general terms about how misguided and offensive the whole notion of cultural stereotyping was.

Occasionally language teachers embark on a course of action with the very best of intentions – but with unforeseen and sometimes unfortunate consequences. One teacher of a high-level class composed largely of Japanese and Korean students decided that it would be appropriate on 6th August (the anniversary of the dropping of the atom bomb on Hiroshima in 1945) to focus her lesson on the events of that fateful day. She planned to end the lesson with one minute's silence in which the class would collectively remember all the Japanese civilians who had died at Hiroshima. The lesson did not go according to plan. The Korean students saw it as an opportunity to present the Korean view of this cataclysmic event, thereby correcting what they saw as public misconceptions. They emphasised that the tragedy was as much Korean as it was Japanese, since large numbers of Koreans (who were being used as forced labour in Japan) had also died. They even had at their fingertips the precise figures of how many Koreans had died at Hiroshima. The teacher realised that emotions in the class were running high, particularly when several students packed up their bags and noisily left the room before the minute's' silence took place. Both during the lesson and on the following day she sought to repair the situation. She talked in general about how all wars in all countries were tragic events mourned by everyone, and how all countries had national days to honour their dead. She invited all the students in the class to share with others information about similar special days in their countries, commenting that the Hiroshima anniversary was symbolic of all commemorative days throughout the world. In other words, she did her best to broaden the topic.

Just as they rush to smooth things over when they realise that the sensibilities of groups of students in their classes have been offended, so language teachers are quick to take palliative action when they sense that individuals are feeling hurt or demeaned. A common way of boosting the self-image of a distressed or disheartened student is to find something to praise them for – and to offer that praise either in front of the class, or else within earshot of other class members. Sometimes teachers allocate high-status roles to students who are feeling dispirited. One teacher had in her class a student who threatened to leave the course because she believed that she was being mocked by a student who was younger and quicker to answer questions than herself. The following day the teacher decided to invite the student to chair a whole-class 'debate' – having noticed from her body language that she was particularly keen to do so. This event evidently restored the student's faith in herself to the extent that she completed the course.

Sometimes teachers neglect to take palliative action when students appear angry or upset. Often interpersonal confrontations blow over naturally, with students feeling a good deal better the next day. In one class a communicative task that required students to rank crimes according to their degree of heinousness, and then agree on appropriate punishments, led to a serious clash of student values (some supporting capital punishment and others not). By the end of the day certain individuals were sitting back to back with their arms folded, refusing to speak to each other. The teacher, who had briefly left the room when the event occurred and returned at the very end of the lesson, did not take any particular action. However, by the next day cordial inter-student relations had been restored. It seemed that the students themselves had decided that it was in the best interests of everyone to put the incident behind them and get on with the business of learning.

In sum, there are an infinite number of ways in which, during the course of everyday lessons, students in language classrooms can feel upset, affronted or aggrieved. However sensitive language teachers are, they cannot be expected to notice even a small fraction of such feelings – let alone determine the root cause. Even if they were able to do so, language teachers would not be in a position to protect all students from all potential threats to their self-esteem. As one teacher remarked, 'You can't cottonwool everybody's ego all the time'.

6.4 Conclusion

Experienced language teachers are aware of both the positive and the negative roles that individual students, particularly those with strong personalities, can play in the lives of their classes. They welcome students with leadership qualities and work hard to encourage potentially problematic students to direct their energies in positive directions. When they are unable to influence the behaviour of individuals or cliques, the social wellbeing of their classes is compromised. Aware of student sensibilities, language teachers are on constant alert for evidence that the self-esteem of individuals is being damaged. They take pro-active steps to ensure that interpersonal relations within their classes are as harmonious as possible. When they sense that student feelings are running high they are quick to try to minimise any damage that may have occurred, using a range of different strategies.

Summary

- Language teachers, aware that students play different kinds of leadership roles in their classes, are quick to identify students who can influence their classes in either positive or negative ways.
- Experienced teachers who provide 'difficult' students with opportunities to redirect their energies in positive directions can sometimes see a dramatic change in student behaviour.
- Certain individuals and cliques within language classes remain outside the sphere of influence of even the most experienced teacher.
- Language teachers are alert to student body language, particularly when they believe it to be indicative of feelings of nervousness or distress.
- Language teachers do not always interpret behavioural clues accurately, and may often be unaware or unsure of the root cause of students' feelings.
- Aware that students in language classes often feel vulnerable to threats to their self-esteem, language teachers take particular care to treat individuals sensitively.
- Language teachers encourage the maintenance of classroom codes of behaviour that minimise potential damage to the self-esteem of individuals.
- Language teachers are quick to move into damage limitation mode as soon as they perceive that individuals are being demeaned by the deliberate or unwitting behaviour of others (including themselves).
- Language teachers have personal repertoires of tactics for dealing with interpersonal and intercultural problems in their classrooms.

Looking ahead

The following chapter focuses on the pedagogically oriented behaviour of language teachers, showing how they behave in flexible, opportunistic ways in order to enhance their students' learning.

7 Teaching flexibly

The previous chapter described the ways in which language teachers manage individual students in their classes. It showed that many of the strategies of experienced language teachers can be understood in terms of a desire to channel the energies of individuals in positive directions, while minimising the negative effect that the behaviour of individuals can have on the social wellbeing of their class groups. It also drew attention to the fact that the spontaneous classroom actions of experienced language teachers are based on noticing behavioural clues and rapidly responding to them in ways that they consider appropriate.

The present chapter focuses on pedagogic aspects of classroom language teaching, explaining how and why language teachers teach in such flexible ways. It is divided into four sections. Section 7.1 dispels two myths: that teachers teach in pre-planned ways, and that teachers teach from textbooks in the prescribed manner. Section 7.2, which occupies the major part of the chapter, presents a key premise of the book: that it is their capacity to draw on all their previous classroom experience that enables language teachers to make so many executive decisions in their classrooms with such speed and assurance. This section explains how sensitivity to students' learning needs enables experienced language teachers both to deviate in major ways from their lesson plans, and to digress in minor ways during the course of classroom activities. It also draws attention to the relationship between long-term goals and teaching flexibly. Section 7.3 identifies the ongoing need of language teachers to teach creatively in their classrooms, while Section 7.4 identifies the relationship between teaching flexibly and the maintenance of a sense of community within language classrooms.

7.1 The reality behind the myth

In 1970 large-scale research was conducted in the USA on the effects on student learning of three different foreign language teaching methods. The major conclusion came as a surprise to everyone (and a disappointment to those who had assumed that the audio-lingual approach would prove to be more effective): there was no significant difference in the levels of achievement of the students in the different groups. In other words, all three methods were equally effective. However, certain incidental findings were intriguing. One was that numbers of teachers admitted that they had not adhered strictly to the approach they were meant to be using, but had taught in the ways they thought best. This finding highlights the fact that teachers find it extremely difficult to limit themselves to teaching in prescribed ways: pedagogic eclecticism is, it seems, a key feature of effective teaching.

For a discussion of the findings of the Pennsylvania Project see Clark (1969).

Clearly, there are many reasons why no two teachers ever teach in the same way. Many of these are deep-seated ones quite unrelated to the immediate context of the language school, the program or the particular class being taught. The classroom behaviour of every teacher is subtly influenced by a unique combination of factors: their personality, their interests and life experiences, their previous learning experiences, their attitudes, values, assumptions and so on. A description of how these factors combine in myriad ways, enabling each language teacher to develop a unique world-view that in turn both informs and influences their classroom practice, will be presented in Chapter 11.

Comment

The infinitely flexible ways in which language teachers behave in their classrooms can be examined from a number of theoretical perspectives. References are given later in this chapter to schema theory and social constructivism, both of which go some way to explaining how and why classroom language teachers find themselves compelled to behave in such a range of unanticipated ways in their classrooms.

The present section focuses on two specific aspects of classroom teaching where the classroom practices of experienced language teachers confound expectations. These are (1) not making or following lesson plans in time-honoured ways, and (2) not following textbooks in a slavish fashion.

Doing away with the lesson plan

The practical component of teacher training programs requires trainees to decide what they want to teach in a number of practice lessons, plan and deliver each lesson, and then reflect on how each one went. It is emphasised right from the start that detailed planning is essential. Apart from creating a sense of security and minimising the risk of things going wrong, lesson planning enables trainees to appreciate the importance of sequencing activities, and of relating them all to the overall aim of the lesson – so that the lesson forms a coherent whole. By having the importance of lesson planning emphasised so strongly, trainee language teachers complete their courses believing that meticulous planning is the key to successful language teaching. On successful completion of her course one trainee decided not to go into language teaching after all – explaining that she felt daunted by the prospect of having to spend so many hours laboriously planning each and every lesson.

Once they enter the real world of everyday language teaching novice teachers find the situation very different. They notice that few teachers around them spend time writing detailed lesson plans – and certainly not ones containing formal aims and objectives. They notice that it is far more common for teachers to be making lists of items in the order in which they intend to teach them, or jotting down rough notes or reminders to themselves about what they intend to cover. They notice that many teachers happily go to class with piles of photocopied materials (but no apparent plan), while others go to class with nothing more than a short text, or perhaps even a single picture, to last for a two-hour lesson. What is going on here? Are teachers not fully planning their lessons because they are lazy or because of lack of time? Or is detailed planning not so essential after all?

It is the same story with longer-term teaching plans. Although they may complete weekly outlines of linguistic items, skills or topics to be focused upon, language teachers often complete such outlines retrospectively (as a record of what they have covered, as opposed to what they intended to cover). And if asked whether they plan whole courses in any kind of detail in advance, experienced language teachers regularly throw up their hands in horror and exclaim, 'Impossible!' or 'No way!' They may have an overall plan or framework for their course – but are often reluctant to specify the individual components of the course in advance.

It is not surprising that some language teachers (particularly those who do not intend to remain in the profession for long) are happy to grab materials off the shelf and rush off to teach without either a lesson plan or any particular teaching goals in mind. What is surprising, however, are the number of committed language teachers who explain that they go to class with their lesson plans in their heads – often in the form of general ideas about what they *might* do, rather than specific ideas about what they *will* do. The lesson plans of experienced language teachers are likely to reflect the following description:

142

My lesson plans are definitely in my head or on scraps of paper – or often I'll plan half the lesson and then, when I'm in the lesson, I'll see how what I wanted to do is developing. That's not to say that I don't go in with a clear set of activities, but I don't necessarily think through, 'X minutes on this', 'Y minutes on that' and rigidly stick to it. So if I do go in with a plan, it's likely to be a fairly rough idea of what I want to do, rather than a strict plan that I follow. And I'm very happy to deviate and amend it as I go through.

In his book *Beyond training* (1998) Richards has a useful chapter on lesson plans, in which he reports on a study of how experienced and less experienced ESL teachers used lesson plans. The study revealed that the experienced teachers reported less frequent use of lesson plans than the inexperienced teachers, made greater use of mental plans than written plans, and, because their plans were much briefer, included less information in them.

Language teachers put forward a number of reasons for their reluctance to engage in detailed lesson planning. The first one is practical: why bother to write out a detailed lesson plan if it's highly unlikely you'll follow it? One teacher recalled a transition moment early in her career when she looked at her beautifully written lesson plan and said to herself, 'It's a lost cause trying to stick to a set structure – so I'm not going to bother to write detailed plans any more'. Another teacher explained that, whenever she was inspected, she would always design and then follow a carefully planned and timed lesson plan – because she knew that this was what was expected of her. However, as soon as the inspectors' backs were turned she would go back to doing what she always did: teach lessons according to her gut feeling of what was right for her class, adjusting the length and focus of activities as she thought fit.

Language teachers believe that another limitation of lesson planning is that lesson plans compel them to focus on their lesson delivery rather than on the responses of their students. In the words of one teacher, 'When you keep referring to your lesson plan it dulls your sensitivity – the teaching antennae you've opened up are wilted or blunted'. A further criticism of lesson plans is that they take the excitement out of teaching, making it a more mundane exercise. One experienced teacher believed that he taught far more effectively when he didn't know in advance precisely the direction that his lessons would take. In his view, 'If you're in a state of reasonable anxiety, with an adrenalin rush – and having to think on your feet as you go – you'll produce more exciting and engaging lessons'. Comments such as these suggest that, although they recognise that lesson planning is an integral part of the process of learning to teach, many experienced language teachers find rigid adherence to lesson plans artificially restricting and, ultimately, self-defeating. They find that they prefer to go with the flow and, in the words of one teacher, 'respond to what's happening with the students – rather than plodding on with the plan'.

> Cognitive psychologists have identified that one of the roles of experience in expertise is acquiring the ability to foresee and exploit future opportunities to satisfy one's goals. Seifert *et al.* (1997: 105) describe the ability to take advantage of circumstances to solve problems as 'opportunistic planning', saying that the planner should exploit the current opportunity and change his or her expectations to properly anticipate and exploit the future opportunity.

Picking the eyes out of textbooks

In many language schools specific coursebooks are allocated for use with specific classes at specific levels. Most recently published coursebooks are colourful and attractive. They have clear organisational structures and contain carefully balanced and graded grammar, vocabulary, skills work and tasks. Topics and themes are selected with attention to what is likely to be of interest to the presumed users of the book. The accompanying teacher's book, written on the assumption that teachers will go through the book in a sequential manner, gives clear instructions as to how it should be used. Language teachers, it seems, are in a fortunate position. If they are teaching a course for which a particular book has been assigned, they apparently have at their disposal a complete package designed to be used as it stands.

Language teachers recognise the value of coursebooks. They recall how much they relied on them in their early days of teaching, one teacher describing coursebooks as 'an incredibly useful prop for inexperienced teachers'. Language teachers appreciate that coursebooks give a sense of direction, coherence and continuity to language programs. They recognise that coursebooks empower students, enabling them to review what has been taught and to preview what is to come. They understand the key role that dedicated textbooks can play in preparing students for specific examinations, when students need to practise examination techniques on a regular basis and do many additional exercises for homework. Language teachers also understand the face validity of coursebooks. One teacher reported feeling embarrassed when, on being asked by a student for the name of the coursebook so that they could buy their own copy, she was compelled to reply, 'Sorry, but there isn't one'.

> '[Textbooks] too easily become a convenience that inhibits the imagination. . . . Obviously, there is nothing wrong with using texts and other prepared instructional materials nor with taking advantage of well-designed teaching activities. Total dependence on prefabricated devices, however, prevents the teacher from improvising, making subtle readjustments to the learning situation, and imbuing the lesson with stylistic color.'   Rubin (1985: 75)

Despite recognising the advantages of using commercially produced materials as complete packages, most language teachers make it abundantly clear that wherever possible they avoid doing so. When questioned about how they use coursebooks, or while talking generally about their teaching approaches, language teachers make statements such as, 'I pick the eyes out of textbooks', 'I mix and match', 'I like to dip and dive', or 'I always supplement the book'. Some experienced teachers use coursebooks as overall syllabus frameworks, covering the linguistic structures but replacing the majority of the activities with different ones. Other language teachers select certain chapters from the book, teach them in a jumbled-up sequence – often leaving out some altogether. Teachers often talk in deprecating ways about 'ploughing through the coursebook' 'doing nothing but the book' or 'being coursebook-dependent'.

It is clear that experienced language teachers are usually unwilling to take what would seem to be the easy option: following the coursebook in the prescribed way. Even teachers of examination preparation classes, who are normally required to use coursebooks specifically designed to cover the syllabus, regularly incorporate supplementary activities into their courses. Even in situations when their pedagogic freedom is severely curtailed, many language teachers seem intent on not doing what they are supposed to be doing. One teacher who had taught in Japan, where there was heavy pressure to follow the approved textbook in the prescribed manner, reported having found ingenious ways of doing things differently and of incorporating his own materials into lessons.

The intriguing question is: why do language teachers persist in giving themselves so much extra work? Why do they spend time and effort finding, modifying and photocopying exercises and tasks, when there are plenty in the book to choose from? Why do they bother to search around for authentic materials (materials that have been developed for purposes other than teaching), when the book contains facsimiles of newspaper articles and so on, accompanied by pre-designed activities and exercises? And why, of all things, do they spend valuable leisure time developing their own worksheets, when there is such a wealth of published material readily available (not to mention worksheets developed by colleagues that have somehow entered the public 'pool')? Teachers themselves recognise the irony of the situation, wondering why so many of their colleagues persist in 'reinventing the wheel' (an expression commonly heard in staff rooms), rather than following coursebooks in the designated way.

7.2 Experience-based language teaching

A fundamental reason why language teachers teach so flexibly is that they have a firm experiential foundation upon which to base their decisions about what to do in their classrooms and how to teach the target language. In the words of one teacher, 'You can be cooler about things because you've done it all before'. Language teachers are also aware that they know better than anyone else, including coursebook writers, what the specific needs and interests of their particular classes actually are.

As described in Chapter 2, one of the reasons why training to be a language teacher is so demanding is that trainees have only a flimsy knowledge base upon which to design their lessons. Because they are normally doing everything for the first time, they have little idea how best to make their intentions clear, how best to explain grammar points, or how best to organise things in general. Because they do not yet know which aspects of the target language students will find confusing, it is difficult for them to anticipate problems – let alone address them on the spot. Because they are unsure how much students will be able to absorb in a single lesson, or how long students' concentration spans will be, it is difficult for them to pace their lessons appropriately. And because they plan single, uni-directional lessons (usually with considerable time and effort), they are unlikely to deviate significantly from their plans. They also have limited opportunities to think in terms of sequences of lessons.

The situation of novice teachers contrasts starkly with that of experienced language teachers. While for the former teaching is at first a relatively hit-and-miss affair, for the latter it is a matter of building on knowledge and fine-tuning previously tried-and-tested strategies and techniques. One teacher described this ongoing process in the following way:

> I'm always upgrading my materials and trying to find better ways of doing things. Some things I'm happy with, whereas there are other areas where I'm looking for new and more interesting, entertaining, memorable, effective ways of doing things.

Over the years language teachers develop knowledge bases of the kinds of problems their students are likely to have: the structures they find difficult to master, the words they have difficulty in pronouncing, the expressions they routinely misuse, and so on. They also develop their own preferred ways of presenting new language, of explaining grammar 'rules' and of consolidating student understanding. As one teacher commented:

> I've learnt how to explain some things in what I think is quite a funny and memorable way. Some things I think I do always teach more or less the same way, because I seem to have hit upon some formula that seems to work quite well for me and for the students – and it produces the right results.

When strategies do not work, language teachers either modify them or discard them altogether. When they do work, teachers unconsciously slip them into their memory banks – from where they can be retrieved, dusted off and re-used as required. Gradually teachers' memory banks expand, filled with recollections of strategies that have worked successfully for them in the past. When they later encounter a similar situation, their mind is jogged. They find thoughts flashing across their minds such as, 'That ranking activity would fit in just nicely tomorrow', or, 'Ah yes, I can use that little exercise I made up for that other class to consolidate the understanding of this group'. Often language teachers find themselves responding spontaneously to their perception of students' needs. For example, they may find themselves drawing a timeline on the board to explain the difference between the present perfect and the simple past – without having had any definite plan to do so.

Comment

The flexible ways in which experienced language teachers behave in their classrooms can usefully be explained in terms of schema theory. Cognitive psychologists use the term 'schema' (plural: either 'schemas' or 'schemata') to describe a general knowledge structure used for understanding. According to Medin and Ross (1992: 346), the following points can be made about schemas (italics added):

1. A schema refers to one's knowledge *about* the world (as opposed to information that is *in* the world).
2. It is general, encoding information about a particular *type* of situation, rather than about one particular situation.
3. It is structured, meaning that it includes not only a set of facts, but also how the facts are *related*. This allows *inferences* to be made.

4. Its structure allows it to be used in the comprehension of *types of* situations.

According to Medin and Ross (1992: 347), an additional feature is that they generate expectations about what is likely to happen, help us to understand if something unusual is happening, and enable us to predict what is likely to occur.

The ways that they gradually build up memories of materials, strategies and 'things that work' in their classrooms suggests that language teachers are indeed drawing upon and progressively developing and refining schemas during the course of their everyday teaching.

Livingston and Borko (1989: 36), quoted by Richards (1998: 75), talk about the lessons they observed: 'The success of the experts' improvisation seemed to depend upon their ability to provide examples quickly and to draw connections between students' comments or questions and the lesson's objectives. In terms of cognitive structure, successful improvisational teaching requires that the teachers have an extensive network of interconnected, easily accessible schemata and be able to select particular strategies, routines, and information from these schemata during actual teaching and learning interactions based on specific classroom occurrences.'

Stein (1997) points to the limitations of understanding expertise when studied from a purely cognitive psychological view, suggesting that study of the social context may offer further insights into the nature of expertise. According to Stein, 'An expert is more than the sum of his or her cognitive abilities and skills – he or she is also codefined by context' (1997: 192). The present book supports Stein's position: that it is necessary to understand the expertise of teachers in terms not only of their ability to teach, but also in terms of their ability to function effectively within the social context of the classroom. Subsequent chapters of this book describe some of the ways in which teachers combine both pedagogic and social aspects of the teaching process.

Creating, selecting and adapting teaching materials

Language teachers develop their teaching skills on the job. When they take over a new course they may have the opportunity to chat with the previous teacher of the course, or to look at a course file containing photocopies of the materials that a previous teacher has used. To all intents and purposes, however, they are on their own. In their early days in teaching, most language teachers spend many hours familiarising themselves with the teaching materials currently available in the resource rooms of their language schools. This process of scouring textbooks (both coursebooks and books containing supplementary materials) for clear explanations of grammatical points, exercises for reinforcement and creative ideas for supplementary activities and tasks, enables teachers to expand their repertoires. They glean ideas from these books and progressively try them out, establishing which ones work for them and which do not. For example, one teacher might be captivated by chorus activities such as those in the *Jazz Chants* books, and teach them with great enthusiasm and verve. In contrast, another teacher might try one activity from the book and discover that they do not feel at ease getting their students to engage in chorus work. Gradually teachers develop their personal styles, teaching in ways that feel comfortable to them and recycling the materials that they can find quickly and that they know will work for them.

As far as commercially produced teaching materials are concerned, it is by no means the case that one size fits all. Language teachers develop clear preferences for certain coursebooks and resource books, drawing regularly on certain books and saying of others, 'I just can't use that book'. Although for some teachers being required to use coursebooks whose cultural content is inappropriate for their students is not problematic, for others it is a significant issue. The situation arises relatively often in Australia, where many of the best-selling coursebooks are published in the UK. Some teachers mentally cringe when they come across articles about Princess Diana or the Loch Ness Monster, while others report feeling uncomfortable when requiring their students to read about rural living in the UK. Even having to explain the meaning of words like 'village', 'cottage' or even 'semi-detached house' – when students in Australian language schools will be living in single-storey houses (known simply as 'houses', not 'bungalows') in suburbia – makes some teachers wince. It is relatively easy for language teachers to substitute items in textbooks with others that have more relevance for their students – and this is what many do on a routine basis. For example, a teacher might bring into class a set of tourist maps of the historic port city of Fremantle (a place regularly visited by West Australians) rather than teach students how to give directions by looking at the map of central London provided in the coursebook.

Language teachers regularly find that they like to 'tweak' the materials that they collect from different sources, customising them so that they reflect more accurately their own ideas of what is important for their students to learn. If they are teaching students different ways of apologising or making excuses, for example, they may well include one or two

149

idiomatic expressions that Australians would use. The following comment reflects the experience of many language teachers:

> I find it difficult to use other people's materials. I always feel I have to develop my own – or adapt them or adjust them in some way. Some materials are pretty good and pretty sound – and I certainly haven't got the time and energy to produce all my own materials. But I do produce a fair amount of my own stuff. And the things that I take from elsewhere, I always alter them a bit.

There is a general consensus of opinion that religiously following course-books tends to lead to the development of a flat, single-paced teaching style – as opposed to a more vibrant, ad hoc style of teaching that naturally occurs when students' needs are being responded to.

Focusing on student learning

When they begin their teaching careers language teachers find themselves consciously thinking about what they are doing. Just as learning to drive a car involves listening to the sound of the engine, judging when to change gear, keeping the required distance from the kerb, reading road signs, deciding when to overtake and so on, language teaching involves focusing your attention on many different things at once. Small wonder, then, that just as learner drivers find it difficult to watch out for pedestrians on top of everything else they're doing, so novice language teachers tend to concentrate on the mechanics of teaching rather than on their students' learning. Happily, just as driving a car eventually becomes a fluid, automatic process, so many aspects of language teaching eventually become second nature to language teachers, who no longer have to focus so intently on everything that they are doing. They just know, for example, that they should write new words on the board, rather than simply present them orally – just as they know that explanations must always be given with words that are simpler than the word or concept being explained. Language teachers do not need to remind themselves to behave in these ways: they find themselves doing so automatically.

> Tsui (2003: 19) summarises a core concept of Bereiter and Scardamalia's (1993) theory of expertise, which posits that well-developed routines enable the mental resources of experts to be freed up. These resources can then be 'reinvested' in solving higher-level problems that the expert did not have the capacity to deal with earlier. In this way experts are continually extending the growing edge of their expertise.

> This core concept of Bereiter and Scardamalia's theory of exper-
> tise is reflected by the classroom practices of language teachers who,
> while they may not define themselves as experts, are nevertheless
> able to turn their attention to solving additional problems during the
> course of lessons.

The ability to perform many classroom functions effortlessly and
without conscious deliberation enables language teachers to direct their
attention away from their own teaching and towards their students'
learning. They find themselves increasingly sensitive to subtle indicators
of the degree to which their students have understood, or successfully
mastered, whatever it is they are teaching. One teacher reported no
longer feeling worried when she saw students with their heads down and
frowns on their faces (as she had done in her early days of teaching) –
because experience had taught her that such body language was often an
indicator of concentration rather than dissatisfaction. Rather, she would
probe further, in order to establish the extent to which the students were
really having problems in understanding – either by asking individuals
directly or by more subtle means. In her words:

> I try to find out covertly at first, with indirect questions, trying to
> see how they're getting on with an activity. I try to detect signs of
> whether they're moving towards the aim of the activity, or even
> enjoying the activity, or seeing the point of it.

By focusing on students' responses and overall levels of receptivity language teachers find themselves having ideas about the kinds of topics,
themes and activities that are likely to engage their classes. The fact that
ideas readily spring to mind at unexpected moments outside class time
suggests that the classes they are currently teaching are never far from
their minds. One teacher described the process of identifying the interests
of her classes as 'sussing out your class, through a combination of what
you know about students from that background and what you find out
from them in the course of lessons'. Experience has taught language
teachers that, in the words of one teacher, 'You can only do *some* things
with *some* of your classes *some* of the time'. One high-school teacher of
Japanese reported that one class 'wouldn't let go of the topic of sumo
wrestling', while another displayed no interest in the topic. Similarly, a
teacher of adult migrants reported that playing English songs in class (and
having everyone listen and sing along quietly when they felt ready to do
so) went down extremely well with a class of refugees from El Salvador.
It failed, however, to appeal to a class of students from the former
Yugoslavia, causing the teacher to remark, 'Songs are not for this class'.

> The notion of teaching flexibly is supported by Breen and Littlejohn (2000), who point out that the actual syllabus of the classroom is an unfolding compromise between the original pre-designed syllabus and the individual teacher's alertness to those aspects of learner agendas that may be revealed during classroom work (2000: 9).

Keeping teaching goals in mind

A key distinguishing feature of experienced language teachers is the fact that they have at the back of their minds a clear idea of the overall goals for their courses, in terms of the learning progress that they wish their students to make. This might sound obvious, but it is not. Many less experienced language teachers, while adept at organising classroom tasks and activities, find it difficult to visualise how the discrete parts of lessons relate to overall lesson goals – or how individual lessons relate to overall course goals. For this reason they may be reluctant to let their lessons go off at a tangent, fearing that they may not be able to 'pull the lesson back'. Alternatively, if they are not serious-minded, language teachers may be only too happy to have their lessons go off in unplanned, unexpected directions – particularly if they prepared their lessons in an unfocused way, without really knowing what they wanted to achieve anyway.

In contrast, one of the hallmarks of experienced language teachers is the ability to direct all their teaching efforts towards the achievement of worthwhile learning goals. By so doing their students come to trust them, sensing that every activity has its place in the overall scheme of things, and will benefit their learning in a particular way. When discussing her ability to do what she called 'sidestepping without floundering', one teacher articulated the process in the following way:

> You're able to relax and do these other things, and yet keep the confidence of the class, because there's some sense in which they sense you've got a clear direction and won't let things get out of hand. When you're not so experienced you feel yourself going off track and you might be a bit panic-stricken – and I'm sure the students pick up on that. There's a voice in your head thinking, 'Help! Where am I going? What am I going to do next?' It becomes survival mode – whereas when you're experienced you don't really feel that. You know you're going somewhere worthwhile – you sort of go with the flow, and yet you know it's going where you want it to go.

Ironically, it is the ability to retain in their minds clear learning goals for their classes that enables experienced language teachers to behave

152

flexibly in their classrooms. Just as an experienced yachtsperson keeps their yacht on course by adjusting the direction to take advantage of the wind and the currents, and by tacking in a zig-zag manner whenever necessary, so an experienced language teacher keeps their class on course by being flexible. Without this ability to move indirectly towards the achievement of overall learning goals, language teachers would be compelled to teach in more rigid, formulaic ways. Some language teachers describe this flexible movement towards learning goals in terms of branching lesson plans:

> In my mind I can go in so many different directions at this point in the lesson. I haven't planned it, but because of what's happened, what's been said or thought, it's what you do. You've got to have the main aim of the lesson in mind – but to get to that destination there are many different routes to take. Sometimes when you're in class you think, I was going to take route A, but I could try route B, which might work better with this group.

Some experienced language teachers describe the phenomenon of shifting the goalposts: the practice of having your class achieve something different from what you'd initially intended because you realise that achievement of an alternative linguistic goal is just as valid. Talking about the achievement of specific lesson goals, one teacher said, 'So long as we get to B, or something that's as useful as B in the overall scheme of things, then I'll have taught a successful lesson'. Looking at the broader picture of the achievement of the overall course, as opposed to individual lesson goals, another teacher made the following comment:

> It sort of dawned on me, maybe over one or two courses, that it didn't matter if I didn't achieve those specific objectives, as long as they could do what they were supposed to do at the end of the course. So they didn't have to achieve what I'd set out for them to achieve in that particular lesson.

A common practice, particularly amongst experienced language teachers, is to recap at regular intervals what has been achieved. Some teachers do this by starting each lesson with an activity that requires students to focus on something they learnt yesterday – and then test their peers to see whether they've remembered it too. Teachers whose lessons diverge significantly from the course their students might have expected them to take often not only recap what has been learnt, but also explain precisely how the deviation contributed to their students' learning. They may, for example, explain the circumstances under which students can use the new vocabulary, or remind the class of the specific skill they've just practised and explain how it will benefit them in the future. This retrospective validation is an important way of maintaining student confidence in the overall direction of language courses which, by their open-ended nature, can sometimes appear to lack a sense of coherence and purpose.

Nunan makes the interesting point that in a study of nine ESL teachers teaching in Australia very few lessons began with the teacher's explicitly laying out for the students the objectives of the lesson (1996: 44–5). He believes the reason to be that in the minds of the teachers the notion of individual lessons was not particularly salient for the teachers, who saw the boundaries of lessons dissolving within the larger framework of the course. A further reason may be that, as the teachers in the present section make clear, their goals were generalised ones that enabled them to teach in flexible ways during lessons. The more experienced teachers would then make a point of explaining what had been taught, and justifying its usefulness, in an *ex post facto* manner.

Dörnyei (2001: 79) states that explaining the purpose and utility of whatever a person is being required to do is a key motivational strategy that is regularly used in civilian contexts. Like Nunan, he observes that even experienced teachers sometimes expect students to carry out a task without offering them any real explanation about the purpose of the activity.

Responsiveness to students' needs

Even though they have a clear idea of the general direction in which they wish their lessons to go, experienced language teachers regularly change their minds about the organisation or sequence of activities. These sudden changes of plan are not fanciful whims but rather rapid responses to subtle indicators that their students' learning needs could be better addressed in slightly different ways. One teacher described this process in the following way:

> I changed my mind twice today, sensing that what I'd suggested was too much for the students. I think I must have taken into account their body language, subconsciously almost. I'd been going to get them to fill in the rest of their sheets individually as homework for next week – but then I decided to get the class as a whole to collaborate and pool their knowledge.

Language teachers regularly report how ideas for modifying what they intended to do suddenly flash across their minds – either during lessons, or as they make their way to or from class. One teacher explained how it suddenly came to her during the coffee break that the role-play activity she had planned for after the break (with the students being either 'travel agents' or 'travellers') would be much more dynamic if she ensured that both groups had hidden agendas. She therefore returned to the classroom and immediately added this additional dimension to the activity.

An important aspect of these sudden changes of plan, or adaptations of classroom activities, is that students are not normally aware that they have been made – experienced teachers being able to disguise their adjustments in such a way that their lessons still appear seamless. The process of making adjustments to activities, in order to maintain the illusion that everything has been pre-planned, is described by one teacher in the following way:

> I didn't have enough time for the last task, so on the spot I had to modify how we were going to deal with the worksheet that I'd already distributed. I couldn't do as much with it as I had originally planned, but because I'm reasonably experienced I was able to say, without missing a beat, what we would do – which was a shorter version of what I'd intended. And then I invented a homework activity that would allow them to pull the ends together of what we'd been doing. . . So the structure of the lesson stood – as was intended from the beginning – and they didn't know that the proportions of time were different from what I'd had in my head when I started. But they should have gone away with the impression that they'd done things in an organised way.

The fact that teachers' subtle change of focus or direction go unnoticed by others is supported by an incident when a group of trainees watched a demonstration lesson in which the teacher being observed made considerable adjustments to her lesson, in response to student difficulties. In the feedback session the teacher was amazed to discover that the trainees had no idea that she'd changed her lesson in any way at all.

Capitalising on students' interests

The more self-assured they become, the more likely language teachers are to make significant adjustments to the content and direction of their lessons in direct response to student feedback (provided that they are not tightly constrained by prescribed syllabus frameworks). Again, students are normally unaware that their teacher has changed direction, since teachers tend to keep their intentions to themselves. Sometimes teachers abandon what they intended to do mid-way through lessons, sensing that something dynamic is happening in the form of high levels of student interest and engagement. One teacher described this experience as 'having a sudden insight into what the students are actually experiencing'. When moments such as these occur, teachers are often prepared to surrender temporary control over the direction of their lessons and be guided by their students – sensing that such opportunities are too valuable to let slip. One teacher described how she had planned a grammar lesson based on the structures contained in a particular text. However, after creating interest in the story in a series of pre-reading activities, she allowed the lesson to go in a completely different direction. This is her account of what happened:

> I'd built it up and they were like really excited. Every activity was geared towards the grammar – but the students were really fighting against that. They wanted to read and they wanted to find out everything that was going on in that story. They were just taking so long and reading intensively, and I could feel the atmosphere in the classroom, and I thought to myself, they obviously don't want to do the grammar. And that's the moment when you make that decision, whether to go with that or not – because of course they're taking you somewhere else.

In an interesting chapter in Bailey and Nunan's book *Voices from the language classroom* (1996) Bailey describes a similar incident (reported originally in Allwright and Bailey, 1991) where the grammatical focus of the lesson dissolved when the teacher and the students became engaged in comparing anecdotes about theft. Evidently the conversation then moved to talking generally about 'strange things that happen in Los Angeles', and included discussion of the meaning of the terms 'flasher' and 'streaker'. As Bailey points out, 'In this moment of exuberant conversation, the teacher herself had completely abandoned the very point of the original lesson plan' (1996: 23).

Comment

Bailey's anecdote suggests that it is a regular occurrence for teachers and their students to start speaking spontaneously during lessons about points of common interest. Indeed, teachers who are not over-concerned about achieving specific teaching goals by the end of the lesson are often only too happy to be sidetracked. What is interesting in the teacher's account quoted immediately above is that she reports assessing the situation and making a conscious decision to abandon the grammar focus of the lesson. This is a good example of Schön's 'thinking-in-action' (Schön, 1987).

Language teachers regularly report allowing learning activities to run on, sensing that their students are fully engaged and that the learning opportunity is a valuable one. One teacher reported replaying a song a number of times, when she had fully intended to do something else, 'because the students just seemed so happy and wanting to go along with it'. Language teachers also routinely do the opposite: modifying activities when they see students are finding them too difficult, or cutting them short when they sense that students are getting bored. Again, teachers tend to disguise their subtle changes of plan – unless they choose to abandon the activity altogether.

Many language teachers find that, the more aware they become of their students' learning processes, the stronger their desire becomes to customise their courses to their particular student group and the more reluctant they become to 'deliver' their courses in pre-planned, pre-determined ways. One experienced teacher with a particularly busy schedule decided on one occasion to take the easy option and base her afternoon class around a series of videos about the Australian way of life. She was pleased because the accompanying workbook was colourful and contained a range of interesting-looking interactive tasks. The results were disastrous. The students became bored with the predictable pattern of watching each video and then doing the games and quizzes in the workbook – and attendance dropped significantly. The teacher resolved never again to go against her better judgement – which had been to replace the workbook activities with more 'meaty' follow-up activities as soon as she sensed that the students' interest was waning.

Opportunistic digressions

'Relevant excursions from the central theme . . . help put ideas in context and highlight their utility, thereby increasing learning. Adroit additions add blossoms to the bare limbs of a lesson.'
Rubin (1985: 21)

Just as they deviate in major ways from what they intended to do in their lessons, so language teachers routinely digress in a variety of minor ways during the course of their daily teaching. Teachers talk about 'sidestepping', 'bringing in extra little bits and pieces' or 'dealing with things as they pop up'. They behave in these ways as a matter of course – perhaps as many as 10 or 20 times in any one lesson. Someone who walks into a language classroom at the end of a lesson usually sees ready evidence of this in the form of a whiteboard filled with items. These include isolated words (often with a code letter indicating their part of speech), groups of words bracketed together (to indicate connections), words contrasted because they have opposite meanings, expressions, sentences, arrows, brackets, additional marks (to indicate stressed syllables), ticks, crosses and perhaps little drawings too. All these items are evidence of spontaneous interaction having taken place in the classroom: concepts explained, linkages made, new words supplied, correct usage highlighted, and so on.

Digressions such as these do not normally interrupt the flow of the lesson or set the course of the lesson in a different direction. Rather, they function as little add-ons to the basic lesson, designed either to revise or to reinforce what has already been taught, or to expand or enrich students' knowledge of the target language. For example, a teacher might take a few moments to remind the class of the frequently confused adjectival pairs 'interesting/interested', 'boring/bored' and so on, because they notice a number of students confusing them as they write book reviews. Similarly, a teacher might take the opportunity to teach the class, in passing, an idiom such as 'Better late than never' – because it is applicable to a real-life situation that has suddenly occurred (such as a student arriving late).

Language teachers describe the practice of teaching opportunistically as 'grabbing opportunities', 'seeing a little window of opportunity' or 'striking while the iron is hot'. Such spur-of-the moment decisions are based on a sudden feeling that the moment is right to correct a misconception (described by one teacher as 'doing running repairs'), to expand on something or to teach something extra that students might find interesting or memorable. Teachers do not necessarily check later whether their additional snippets have been absorbed. This is partly because they may not recall all the extra points they have touched upon during the course of their lesson and partly because they sense that some things will be remembered, even though only mentioned in passing. One teacher explained the meaning of the word 'masochistic' to her advanced level class (in the context of discussing people doing exams for the fun of it) – and suddenly found herself teaching the word 'sadistic' as well. In her view the students were ready to appreciate the deep and complex meanings of certain words, and might well remember these two highly specialised words.

Once they have a wealth of experience behind them, language teachers find it easy to stand up at the whiteboard and improvise: they do not need to work out how to present or explain something first. As one teacher remarked: 'I see myself as an instinctive teacher. Perhaps because I've been teaching for a while I just feel that maybe I can think on my feet very quickly now'. Experience also provides language teachers with a basis upon which to decide both what their students need to know, and when they need to know it. Crucially, they develop a sense of when it is worth interrupting a lesson to make a point to the whole class, and when it is not. One teacher with a working knowledge of Chinese decided to stop her lesson to remind the whole class that, whereas in Chinese the same word is used for 'gate' and 'door', in English different words are used. As she explained:

> I suddenly realised that there would always be a chance of putting the wrong one when they were talking about a main door. They know the difference between the door of a room and a garden gate, but they were obviously thinking that if it was a big entrance, then you'd call it a gate. So I thought it was worth stopping and saying that to everybody – because that seemed the kind of error that many of them could make.

The ability to judge when a critical number of students in the room will benefit from a digression is an important one. One teacher reported seeing 'the eyes of everyone else in the class glaze over' when he attempted to address the answer to a very specific question asked by one particular student to the class as a whole. In contrast, another teacher noticed the class suddenly paying attention when she digressed to answer a particular question – sensing that at that particular moment 'the students were clicking because they needed to know'. This teacher explained that her decision to digress was based on the fact that she sensed that there were enough students in the room who would relate to what she wanted to say – and would find the digression (the elucidation of a particular grammar point) worthwhile.

7.3 To thine own self be true

A final reason why language teachers behave in such a wide range of ways in their classrooms is because they are driven by an ongoing desire to satisfy not only the needs and interests of their students, but also their own personal needs for stimulation, fulfilment and creativity. One might have expected language teachers who have been in the profession for a significant length of time to sit back, relax and take the easy option: use the same range of materials, techniques and strategies that they know work for them. Why bother to try anything new? Although some teachers may choose this option, the vast majority consider that by doing so they will be selling themselves short. In the words of one teacher:

> I'd much rather give up my lunch hour putting together a worksheet that I feel excited about and want to use with the students – rather than giving them any old slapdash thing. I just can't do it, because I've got a standard that I've set for myself. I know the easy options, but I just think, 'No, I'm not going to take

the easy road'. I remember saying to one of my other colleagues, 'I plan my lessons, not only for the students, but for myself too' – because I don't want to be bored out of my brain. I prepare stuff that that I believe they as young people will find exciting – and that I find exciting too.

This comment suggests that teachers who have been in the profession for some time feel the need to identify topics and to develop materials and activities that they personally find interesting, engaging and worthwhile. One teacher, required to teach a fill-in lesson for a colleague, chose to reject the textbook-based lesson plan that had been left for her and went into class instead with a set of booklets that she had found in the resource room on how to deal with stress. Her decision to base her lesson on the booklets – and to develop three hours' worth of activities from them once she got inside the room – was influenced by the fact that she had recently learnt that a student in her own class was suffering from stress. It appears that the knowledge of a particular student suffering from stress at that time influenced and validated her decision to focus on the topic of stress with another class. It was as if her awareness had suddenly been raised of the relevance of this particular topic for language learners in general.

It is clear from the ways that they describe getting ready for their lessons that, even though they may not engage in detailed lesson *planning*, language teachers do engage in lesson *preparation*. Apart from assembling materials, lesson preparation involves thinking about the lesson that is about to be taught – sometimes only five minutes before the lesson, or even when walking along the corridor to the classroom. It is different from lesson planning in that it involves teachers preparing themselves mentally to teach their lessons. Teachers report getting themselves 'psyched up' to teach lessons, so that by the time they walk into their classrooms they have got themselves into a state of teaching readiness. In the view of one teacher, 'the key to successful language teaching is feeling in a positive, dynamic frame of mind as you put your hand on the handle of that classroom door'.

When they select materials and devise tasks that they consider interesting and worthwhile, the enthusiasm of language teachers conveys itself readily to the students in their classes. There is a very real sense in which language teachers can make any approach, any materials or any activity work successfully with their classes – provided that they have sufficiently high levels of confidence and enthusiasm, and a strong enough belief in the efficacy and relevance of what they are doing. One teacher regularly required her students to read texts aloud around the class, each student in turn reading one sentence – reporting that her students found this activity stimulating and worthwhile. A fellow teacher decided to try the same technique (not one that she had ever used before) with her own class, curious to see whether it would work equally well for her. Her own students did not respond nearly as positively, and even asked her what the point of the activity was. This teacher came to the conclusion that the activity had not been a success because she did not set up the activity with sufficient conviction that it would benefit the students.

A further reason why language teachers behave so individualistically in their classrooms is that over time they have come to know their personal strengths and weaknesses. Not surprisingly, they choose to do the things that they enjoy doing and can do well – and avoid doing those that they do not. For example, some teachers are highly proficient at using the phonemic alphabet, and write many words on the board in phonemic script to illustrate correct pronunciation while others go to great lengths to avoid ever using the phonemic alphabet. Teachers are also aware that different techniques work for different people and normally avoid using techniques that make them feel uncomfortable in some way. One teacher recalled observing colleagues successfully doing musical-chairs-type activities with classes of adults in which the forfeit for not getting a chair required students to stand in the centre of the circle and make statements about themselves. He said he would never organise such an activity himself, explaining:

> It's just not 'me' somehow. It's something to do with my
> perception of myself and my own character and my own
> personality and the way I relate with adults that just stops me
> from doing things like that.

The desire to teach in accordance with their own personalities, and to seek innovative ways of making language learning come alive in individualistic ways, appears to be a deep-seated one. It is summed up by one teacher, who said: 'I'd hate to teach in a language school that made you follow its own particular method, because it's so controlling, and it seems to rob you of your creativity and autonomy. It would be like teaching in a straightjacket.'

A final reason why language teachers teach in flexible, never-to-be repeated ways in their classrooms is that their behaviour is a product of the dynamic interaction that occurs between themselves and their students. Language teachers develop two-way relationships with their classes, with their own behaviour influencing the responses of their students, and the responses of their students in turn influencing their own behaviour. The notion of language teachers influencing the behaviour of the students in their classes is not surprising. What is less well recognised is the power of classes of language learners either to lift the performance of language teachers, so that they teach in increasingly innovative and creative ways – or conversely to drag their performance down to a more perfunctory level. An example of a teacher and a class raising one another's level of performance was provided by the following teacher, who said at the end of a course:

> I don't think I'll ever have as good a class, ever. And because of that I really put in a good performance these last ten weeks. I wanted to perform better, and they wanted to perform better – it was a reciprocal thing. They made some terrific progress, and I felt it was the best class I'd ever taught. . . It was a big class, but they were always there, and it was just one long positive spin-off all the time. And I thought, 'Well, this is it, I'll actually give them everything I've got.'

Teachers are equally aware of the opposite scenario, when their desire to teach in interesting ways is dampened by their students' lack of enthusiasm. Teachers often report responding to the temptation to slacken off when they feel that their class is not responding to their efforts. When this happens they report spending less time preparing lessons, teaching in more mundane ways and sticking more closely to the book.

The lack of responsiveness on the part of students can also affect how teachers feel about themselves – which in turn affects their classroom behaviour. One teacher reported that he was happy to make a fool of himself in noisy classes – whereas quiet classes made him feel awkward and self-conscious. He gave the example of how, if a class was silent and unresponsive, he would find himself not doing things he would normally do, such as giving a physical demonstration of the meaning of the phrasal verb 'to trip over'. One teacher articulated how language teachers feel when confronted by unresponsive classes, saying, 'There's something quite depressing and almost overwhelming when you face that wall of blankness'.

Teachers report being able to sense when their students are metaphorically sitting back in their chairs with their arms folded, waiting for them to perform. Human nature being what it is, when language teachers sense that their students are unwilling to respond to their initiatives to make their lessons interesting and dynamic, they pull back and think, 'Well, I'm not going to bother to put on a performance for them. Why should I?' As one teacher said, 'If I've done my best to get them involved and they don't respond, then I just get on with it and do the routine old stuff. But if there's more response, I'm more inclined to add things in and run with things and teach in more interesting ways.'

A key to understanding (1) the high levels of individualism demonstrated by language teachers in the ways that they teach, and (2) how
the behaviour of teachers and students influence one another, is to
consider them in terms of the psychological theory of social constructivism. Williams and Burden (1997: 52–3), acknowledging the
work of Salmon (1988), provide an excellent description of a constructivist view of teaching, which accommodates the following
notions:

- Teachers teach the things that are personally meaningful to them,
  rather than a parcel of objective knowledge.
- Teachers teach not only what they know, but their position
  towards it.
- Teachers experience an engagement with their learners. This
  enables both of them to reshape both their ways of understanding and their views of each other.
- No two teachers and no two teaching situations are ever the same.
- The content of any lesson and the way in which it is offered are
  part of the person of each individual teacher.

7.4 Why flexibility does not lead to chaos

This section raises an interesting question: With language teachers
behaving so flexibly in their classrooms, and leading their classes
towards the achievement of learning objectives in such indirect, unpredictable and opportunistic ways, how can their classes possibly continue
to operate as unified communities of learners? Surely they will tend to
become fragmented, with everyone pulling in different directions?

The answer to this question lies in the fact that it is precisely because
experienced language teachers behave so flexibly, routinely adapting
their lessons to the wants and needs of individuals in an ongoing, iterative manner, that their classes, more often than not, do remain united. A
key group dynamics principle is that groups remain cohesive only when
all group members believe that the group is making satisfactory progress
towards the achievement of mutually acceptable common goals.
Although all language classes clearly have the overall, generalised goal
of language learning, individuals within those classes have specific goals
that they want to achieve. By behaving flexibly, and responding to the
language learning needs of individuals in an ongoing way, language
teachers are able to convey the impression that the learning goals of the
class as a whole are an amalgam of individual goals. By responding to
particular students' needs and wants, language teachers are implicitly

acknowledging and validating the contributions that individuals are making (through their questions, problems and difficulties) to the overall learning experience of the whole class. As a result, students find themselves increasingly committed to the class – their own goals having become subsumed, in a sense, under the umbrella goal of the class as a whole. In this way the feeling that the class is learning in a unified, mutually supportive, collaborative way is enhanced.

Dörnyei and Malderez (1999) identify the notion of 'goal-orientedness' as being the extent to which the group is attuned to pursuing its goal. They quote Hadfield (1992: 134), who emphasises that it is fundamental to the successful working of a group to have a sense of direction and common purpose.

Comment

As pointed out in Chapter 4, it is relatively rare for language teachers to negotiate overall learning goals with their classes at the beginning of courses in an open, direct manner. However, the present chapter suggests that it is commonplace for language teachers to adjust their lesson goals in accordance with student needs in a subtle, ongoing way. This strategy increases motivation, since individual students can perceive the value of the activity to them personally (see Williams and Burden, 1997: 125, for a discussion on the notion of the perceived value of activities).

7.5 Conclusion

This chapter has focused on the fact that language teachers routinely behave in highly flexible, individualistic and unanticipated ways in their classrooms. It has advanced a range of reasons why the classroom behaviour of language teachers is so difficult to pin down and describe – all of which have been put forward by practising language teachers themselves as they talk about their work. These reasons go some way to explaining why language teachers behave in ways that appear to border on the perverse: for example not following lesson plans when this seems the most obvious thing to do, or cutting and pasting teaching materials when there seems no good reason for doing so.

The central section of this chapter has suggested that the classroom decision-making of language teachers is based on accumulated classroom experience, obtained at the grass roots level through ongoing exposure to materials and multiple opportunities to experiment. It indicates that language teachers have ever-expanding memory banks, which act as repositories of things they have done successfully (or unsuccessfully) in the past and that can be recycled (or avoided) as appropriate. Once they can perform basic teaching tasks without having to concentrate on them in a conscious manner, language teachers can turn their attention to the responses of the students and begin to behave in even more flexible ways. At this point they find themselves responding more readily and intuitively to the learning needs of their students.

This chapter has also suggested that the deviations and digressions that language teachers routinely make, both during lessons and over the length of their courses as a whole, are a key factor in enabling language classes to progress towards worthwhile learning goals. The process of progressing flexibly towards overall class group goals is represented schematically in the following figure:

Figure 7.1   Progressing flexibly towards group goals

The final section of this chapter has identified the fact that the desire of language teachers to teach in innovative ways is related to an ongoing desire to teach creatively and to obtain personal fulfilment by so doing. It has also articulated the reciprocal nature of language teaching and learning: the fact that the classroom behaviour of language teachers varies according to the response they receive from their students.

Summary

- Contrary to popular belief, language teachers seldom follow lesson plans in a slavish manner, preferring to adjust what and how they teach in line with their perceptions of the needs and interests of the students in their classes.
- Language teachers rarely follow coursebooks in the designated manner, preferring to pick and choose activities from them according to their personal preferences and immediate teaching needs.
- Language teachers become proficient at what they do through increased familiarity with materials available to them, and by ongoing experimentation with teaching techniques.
- Language teachers accumulate personal knowledge banks of materials and techniques with which they feel comfortable, refining and reusing them as required.
- Mastery of increased numbers of teaching techniques enables language teachers to focus their attention more fully on the language learning needs of the students in their classes – and adjust their approaches accordingly.
- Language teachers regularly deviate significantly from what they intended to teach in their lessons in response to ongoing student feedback (even though such deviations may not be apparent to their classes).
- A common classroom practice of language teachers is to make myriad digressions during the course of lessons, in order to teach or re-teach language at opportune moments.
- The ability of language teachers to behave flexibly in their lessons, while at the same time retaining a sense of overall coherence and direction, is related to their ability to keep in mind generalised teaching goals.
- The high level of individualism displayed by language teachers is due in part to their desire to teach creatively, and their need for ongoing stimulation and feedback.
- The high levels of variation in how language teachers teach their lessons is related not only to their personalities and preferred teaching styles, but also to the degree to which they are able to establish dynamic relationships with their classes.
- Experienced language teachers view classroom language teaching and learning as an interactive and collaborative exercise, and have a strong desire to teach flexibly in response to their students' needs.

Comment

The topic of how teachers are so readily able to make classroom decisions 'on the run' has intrigued researchers for a number of years. There is a growing consensus of opinion that the way to understand this phenomenon is to ask what we can learn from a careful examination of artistry in teaching. Schön (1987: 13) defines artistry as 'the competence by which practitioners actually handle indeterminate zones of practice', while Rubin (1985: 4) talks about the 'qualities which undergird teaching virtuosity . . . [being] elusive precisely because they are difficult to analyze and describe'. Some educationalists, including Rubin (1985) and Atkinson and Claxton (2000), consider that teachers are reliant on intuition, which according to Claxton (2000: 50) refers to a loose-knit family of 'ways of knowing' which are less articulate and explicit than normal reasoning and discourse. According to Claxton, the members of this family include the ability to do the following:

- function fluently and flexibly in complex domains without being able to describe or theorise one's expertise;
- extract intricate patterns of information that are embedded in a range of seemingly disparate experiences ('implicit learning');
- make subtle and accurate judgements based on experience without accompanying justification;
- detect and extract the significance of small, incidental details of a situation that others may overlook;
- take time to mull over problems in order to arrive at more insightful or creative solutions; and
- apply this perceptive, ruminative, inquisitive attitude to one's own perceptions and reactions – 'reflection'.

Tsui (2003: 42–66) provides an overview of research in the highly complex area of teacher classroom decision-making. In a recent study Szesztay (2004) uses Schön's twin concepts of knowing-in-action and reflection-in-action (Schön: 1987) to investigate how seven teachers described what she calls 'the immediacy of teaching'. Studies such as these reflect the ongoing resarch interest in this area.

Looking ahead

The following chapter focuses on the many ways in which experienced language teachers vitalise the atmospheres of their classes. These include both superficial techniques and ones that engage the interest and emotions of students at a deeper and more significant level.

8 Vitalising the language class

The previous chapter focused on pedagogic aspects of language classes. It drew attention to the fact that language teachers behave in unique ways because they have developed personal repertoires of tried-and-tested language teaching techniques and activities. It showed that experienced language teachers, attuned to the learning needs of their students, adjust their lessons in line with the ongoing feedback that they receive. It showed how both major deviations and minor digressions are key features of everyday classroom language teaching. The chapter ended by showing how the levels of enthusiasm and engagement of teachers and students in language classes are correlated, with each party able either to lift the performance or, conversely, to sap the energy of the other.

The present chapter continues to focus on the reciprocal relationship between the behaviour of language teachers and the collective behaviour of the students in their classes. It draws particular attention to the overall atmosphere of language classrooms, describing the ways in which both teachers and students vitalise the social atmospheres of their classes in ongoing ways. Section 8.1 describes the relationship between ready responsiveness on the part of students and the effectiveness of communicative tasks. Section 8.2 describes the key role that humour plays in the vitalisation of language classes. Section 8.3 qualifies the previous section by highlighting the danger of confusing fun with learning. In Section 8.4 the chapter describes some of the key ways in which language teachers engage the students in their classes at not only an intellectual but also an emotional level.

8.1 Responsive language classes

In language schools that provide intensive daily tuition it is common for two or more teachers to teach the same class. When teachers share a class they often find themselves chatting informally in the staffroom about the quality of their shared class: comparing initial impressions, discussing individual students and so on. Often the teacher who teaches the first lesson will make a remark to their fellow teacher such as 'They're a good class' or 'They're going to be fine'. Alternatively they might say, 'This group is going to be uphill work'. It is likely that by the end of the first week the teachers will have reached a consensus view about the overall quality of their shared class. Although the level of malleability and responsiveness of classes shifts over time and varies from day to day, often the teacher's initial perception of the innate 'character' of a language class remains unchanged for the duration of the course.

One of the measures that language teachers use to judge the quality of their classes is the overall level of vitality, enthusiasm and responsiveness that they display. Not surprisingly language teachers value classes that contain a high proportion of happy, extroverted, responsive students – and dread teaching classes that contain a critical mass of students who seem dull and reluctant to participate. One teacher described teaching a particularly unresponsive class as being like 'walking into a black hole', with an atmosphere that was 'just dead'. She also reported how demoralising the experience had been, leading her temporarily even to doubt her ability as a teacher. In contrast, teachers find classes with vibrant, bubbly 'personalities' not only easier but also far more exhilarating to teach. One teacher reported not being able to get to sleep at night because of the buzz of excitement of having taught a successful lesson to a highly responsive class. As suggested in the previous chapter, the way that classes of language learners collectively behave affects the levels of energy, enthusiasm and commitment of those who teach them.

The relationship between classroom atmosphere and the success of communicative tasks

All teachers everywhere value students who are alert and keen to learn. However, since the communicative approach requires students to interact with one another, it is particularly crucial for language teachers to have classes that behave collectively in outgoing, responsive and relatively uninhibited ways. A language class characterised by high levels of vitality and enthusiasm provides a social environment within which communicative activities are likely to be successful. Talking about a responsive class, one teacher commented:

> There's just been this positive enthusiastic feeling throughout. . .
> They just spontaneously use the language all the time. If you get a
> discussion going, everyone's talking. It makes my job very easy
> because everything just happens naturally.

The evidence supplied by another teacher, who taught two classes in which she followed the same syllabus and set up many of the same tasks,

169

highlights the relationship between the levels of vitality and enthusiasm of language classes and the success of communicative tasks. By chance, although the classes were similar in terms of size, levels of proficiency (they were both lower-intermediate classes) and demographics (they both contained students from a similar range of linguistic backgrounds), there was a considerable difference in the innate energy levels of the two classes. The second class was far more lively and outgoing than the first. The teacher was struck by the different ways in which the two classes engaged in the same communicative task: an elaborate whole-class role-play demonstrating the relationship between the past continuous and the simple past tenses in English. She had designed the task herself and knew from previous experience that students found it interesting and engaging. She anticipated that it would go down equally well with both classes.

The role-play was a restaurant scenario in which each student assumed a particular role: the chef, the kitchen hand, the wine waiter, waiters/waitresses taking orders and serving the food, customers sitting at tables chatting and giving their orders, a pianist providing background music, and so on. Having revised the language they needed to use, the students were required to act out their parts and improvise conversations – whereupon a 'gunman' (a student who had been primed beforehand) burst into the room and 'shot' the pianist. The teacher, in the role of 'detective', then elicited from the class what they *were doing* when the gunman *shot* the pianist (the two tenses that were the focal point of the activity). The teacher provided the following account of how the second class engaged in the activity:

> This time round I wouldn't have needed to be in the room. The class was just buzzing. I did a similar lead-up, so they all knew that they were going to pretend that they had these roles, and they had to keep talking, but they were just beavering away, and there were all these things happening that they were inventing themselves. They were just putting in that bit extra. . . In the other class I'd had to go round and say, 'Look, on your card it says you want a pay rise – so say something!', whereas with this class it was just happening automatically. They were getting more involved in what was on the role-play cards, and they were doing additional things, and there was just so much noise in the classroom. Everyone was just talking, talking and getting so involved.

It is evident that, just as language classes with positive, friendly, outgoing 'personalities' enhance the quality of communicative language practice, so language classes that exude feelings of reluctance and boredom have a negative impact on the quality of the communication that occurs within them. In classes with atmospheres that lack dynamism teachers report communicative activities being completed in double-quick time, or sometimes fizzling out altogether. They notice students sitting silently waiting to be told what to do next – rather than using their initiative and taking advantage of communicative activities to speak as much as possible. In such classes teachers see students going through the motions of practising the target language – rather than using the target language as a tool for genuine communication of thoughts, observations and views. Even students who might under different circumstances behave in more outgoing ways can be dragged down by the prevailing atmosphere of their class group. Sensing that their initiatives are unlikely to receive a positive response, they find themselves saying less and behaving in less outgoing ways.

Paradoxically the overall levels of vitality and responsiveness of language classes do not appear to be related to the levels of linguistic proficiency or academic ability of the students within the classes. Some beginner-level classes can have much higher levels of vitality than more advanced classes. As will be shown later in this section, limited knowledge of the target language in no way prevents students from vitalising, or being vitalised by, their class groups. The same is true across the board. Classes at whatever level vary considerably in the degree of liveliness and spontaneity that they display. One language school regularly ran a number of six-month intensive pre-university language classes concurrently, all of which followed the same skills-based syllabus. The policy of the program coordinator was to ensure that each class contained as wide a mix of students as possible in terms of linguistic background, future university aspirations and known level of English. The teachers found that, despite the pressurised nature of the program, some classes developed and sustained significantly more lively personalities than did others. The personalities of the more extroverted classes often became evident at the end-of-term award-giving ceremony, when the students would stand up in unison when their class name was called, shouting and cheering wildly. Other classes, meanwhile, behaved in more restrained ways.

Language teachers define classes that are low in vitality and dynamism as being 'bland', 'not having much oomph' or 'having no spice'. Teachers of such classes report the phenomenon of the energy levels of such classes fluctuating: they do not necessarily remain low all the time. When teachers set up communicative activities that are sufficiently engaging for students to forget their inhibitions, their personal agendas, the fact that they are meant to be playing it cool and so on, the atmospheres of their classes can become temporarily vitalised. Everyone is fully involved in the task at hand, and the energy level of the class is correspondingly high. However, it is common in such classes for the feeling of vitality that has permeated the classroom to dissipate quickly – with the class reverting to its normal reduced level of interest and engagement. One teacher described this process as 'seeing the class lapse back into its fairly passive state'. When this happens it is almost as if the energy level of the class has been switched off, like an electric current.

One experienced teacher documented her impressions of the overall 'feel' of one particular class from lesson to lesson. This was a class that the teacher found challenging to teach, because the students within it did not relate readily to one another. Although she considered that the class had low overall energy levels, she found that certain high-interest communicative activities would temporarily vitalise the class. Her comments include the following:

> 'First part dead, second part encouraging.'
> 'Exciting, dynamic.'
> 'A bit flat.'
> 'Enthusiastic and involved.'
> 'First part dynamic, second part slow, students heavy.'
> 'Chugging along.'
> 'Exciting, the students pulling together.'
> 'Sluggish. I was doing too much of the work.'
> 'First part light and fun, second part a bit heavy.'
> 'Seemed to run itself, a relaxed and comfortable feeling.'
> 'Excited, distracted, jovial.'

The final comment indicates that the mood of language classes can also swing in the opposite direction, with students sometimes behaving in hyperactive, frivolous ways. This point will be discussed in more detail in Section 8.3.

When their classes exhibit low levels of vitality, language teachers report having to work much harder and in a much more sustained way to ensure that communicative tasks are successful: they cannot draw on the innate energy level, or latent dynamism, that resides within the class itself. Language teachers describe lethargic classes as 'exhausting' or 'draining' – suggesting that their own energy is sapped by the class.

All teachers, of course, have 'off' lessons, when even normally responsive students behave in lacklustre ways. There can be myriad reasons for this, including the type, level or focus of the activities selected by the teacher. Practical considerations, such as the time of day or the temperature of the room, also enter the equation. In the words of one teacher:

> If it's not a good lesson they just go politely to sleep and you get no response from them at all. They look at you and they vote with their 'nil' response how they're feeling. We've all had lessons like that.

Interestingly, if a teacher gives a lesson that fails to engage the interest of the students in a class that is normally responsive, the teacher tends to forget their one-off 'failure' and move on. However, once they have accepted in their mind that a class is always going to be hard work, yet another lesson that fails to stimulate the students serves to confirm that the teacher's impression is correct: the class is basically a difficult rather than an easy one to 'get going'.

Indicators of responsiveness

Language teachers use a range of behavioural indicators to judge the overall levels of liveliness and responsiveness of the students in their classes. Body language and facial expressions provide important clues. Teachers are quick to notice whether individuals sit forward at their tables looking keen and interested, whether they follow instructions rapidly and easily, whether they interact readily with others and so on. They also notice where students focus their eyes. Do they look directly at the teacher when given explanations and instructions, or do they keep their eyes averted (thereby minimising the risk of catching the teacher's eye and being required to participate more fully in the corporate life of the class group)? Language teachers also notice the expressions on students' faces. Are these bright, animated and alert – or blank and lacklustre? Language teachers from western cultures, accustomed to being looked at in a direct manner and to seeing muscular movement in students' faces, feel unnerved when standing in front of students who are reluctant to engage in eye contact and who maintain bland, impassive expressions on their faces. They have been taught to value directness, openness and forward behaviour – rather than shyness, modesty and circumspection. Because they view classroom language learning as a group endeavour (see Chapter 9), language teachers need to be able to assess the collective mood of each class – in terms of its overall level of interest, engagement and vitality – at any given moment in time. Is there any other way that they readily assess the overall level of alertness and responsiveness of their class?

Fortunately, language teachers who teach classes with informal atmospheres have at their disposal a powerful additional means of gauging the overall level of vitality of their classes: the frequency and alacrity with which their classes burst collectively into whole-class laughter. Anyone who has walked along the corridor of a language school when a number of classes are in progress will normally hear bursts of laughter emanating from behind closed doors. One teacher who taught in a building with particularly thin walls recounted that a colleague in the adjacent room had remarked to her on one occasion that there were always guffaws of laughter coming from her room, saying, 'Don't you ever do any work in there?' This particular teacher, who had taught adult migrants for many years, explained that the bursts of laughter came spontaneously from her students in response to specific catalysts – and had nothing at all to do with her students not working hard.

8.2 The role of humour in the language classroom

Comment

The key role that humour plays in teaching has long been recognised. In a classic book entitled *The art of teaching*, Highet (1963) states that one of the most important qualities of a good teacher is humour. One of the points that he makes is that a teacher who has a sense of humour can build a bridge between youth and maturity. In his view, humour enables both sides to understand each other better, and work together, saying, 'Togetherness is the essence of teaching' (1963: 57).

To date there has been relatively little research into humour in language classrooms, although the fact that it plays a key role is readily recognised by teachers. In a study of nine ESL teachers in Australia that included video-recordings of lessons, Nunan discovered that there were in-jokes shared by the class, which students found amusing and to which they would make contributions on cue (1996: 48).

In one of the few studies that focuses specifically on humour in the ESL classroom, Selleck (1991) recorded and analysed 'humor acts' occurring in nine ESL classes and identified the kinds of humorous initiatives that were most likely to promote laughter in ESL classrooms. Although my own work has not focused specifically on humour, when I examined the social processes occurring in eight classes of adult language learners (the second of the five studies upon which the present book is based), I found it impossible to ignore the bursts of laughter that regularly punctuated the language lessons that I observed. See Senior (2001) for an analysis of the role of humour in the development and maintenance of class cohesion, based on the findings from that particular study.

Humour is a powerful force in any group situation, and most teachers have an intuitive understanding of its coercive power. Educators readily assume that teachers who use humour in their teaching are more effective than those who do not. In a university survey that invited students to evaluate the quality of their instructors, one of the questions required students to assess the degree to which lecturers enhanced their teaching with the use of humour. When they are asked whether they make use of humour during the course of their daily teaching, language teachers make remarks such as 'I couldn't teach without it' or 'It's absolutely vital to my success as a teacher'. They make it clear that they do not view themselves as stand-up comics or tellers of funny stories but, rather, as teachers for whom humour is an integral part of their teaching approach. They have made the assumption – amply supported by the responses of students – that humour in language classrooms is of a universal kind that transcends cultural barriers.

As everyone knows from their own schooldays, humour in the class-room takes many forms and can be used in myriad ways – not all of which are positive. Humour can be used to make people feel relaxed and at ease, thereby encouraging more spontaneity and ready interaction. It can draw people together, enhancing feelings of friendliness, camaraderie and unity. It can make individuals who are singled out for special treat-ment (being gently teased, for example) feel accepted and valued by the group at large. Humour can be used as an indirect means of establishing codes of behaviour, of admonishing people or of drawing them into line. It can also be used for making learning more memorable.

Humour can also operate in negative ways. When there is a burst of collective laughter, anyone who does not understand the cause of the laughter feels excluded and uneasy: there is always an outside chance that they themselves are the focus of the laughter. Individuals who are teased in unsympathetic ways, ridiculed or spoken to in sarcastic tones in front of the class feel demeaned and affronted – while those who unwittingly make an error that causes their classmates to laugh are often distressed and embarrassed by the occurrence. Some students turn the situation around by pretending that they committed the error on purpose. By behaving regularly in these face-saving ways, individuals can develop the reputation of 'class clown': someone who engenders laugh-ter whenever they say or do almost anything.

Laughter can also be an indicator of high levels of excitement (such as when competitive team games are in progress), panic, frustration or con-fusion. When checking the answers to a particularly challenging gap-fill exercise on the use of definite and indefinite articles one class burst out laughing every time yet another student's answer turned out to be wrong. The collective laughter of the students appeared to indicate that the class as a whole found the 'rules' governing the use (or non-use) of articles in English altogether too confusing.

Students can also, of course, laugh and joke amongst themselves in such a way that the teacher feels that they are losing control of the class. Although this behaviour is most commonly demonstrated by adolescents in school situations, adults in language classes occasionally decide to behave in frivolous ways and generate much hilarity and mirth amongst themselves. In one class a group of high-level students from professional backgrounds had fun during a lesson in which their teacher was being observed by a group of trainee teachers. The task required them to work in groups and decide which objects would be of most use to them if they were lost in the jungle. Rather than select objects of practical use for survival they began to call out 'Call for taxi!', 'Cigarettes!', 'Whisky!', 'Mel Gibson!', 'Arnold Schwarzenegger!' and so on.

The ways in which humour most commonly operates in language classrooms are touched upon at various points in the book. Chapter 4 indicated that language teachers make use of humour not only to establish relaxed, informal classroom atmospheres, but also to show that mistakes are an integral part of the process of language learning. By demonstrating that they are prepared to laugh at themselves, and by encouraging students to do likewise, language teachers indicate that they wish to reduce the social distance between themselves and their students. Chapter 6 showed how teachers develop humorous, bantering relationships with certain high-profile students. Chapter 9 will describe how humour is regularly used to enhance class solidarity, allowing students to demonstrate shared knowledge in such a way that the unique culture of the class group is affirmed. It will also show how certain students become focal points for their classes by behaving in humorous ways. The chapter will also point out the dangers of teasing students and of perpetuating clichéd views of individuals and nationality groups.

The present chapter focuses on an additional role played by humour in language classrooms. It outlines how bursts of collective whole-class laughter serve to energise the atmosphere of language classes and reinforce the notion that classroom language learning is a collective endeavour. Spontaneous laughter then becomes an informal device whereby language teachers can monitor the energy levels of their classes.

Laughter: an informal measure of vitality and responsiveness

Some language classes exude feelings of liveliness and receptivity the moment the teacher walks through the door, while others start off in more low-key, restrained ways. Classes containing students who are worried about their abilities, or who are unsure of the level of friendliness of other students in the class, usually take time to settle down. Language teachers are often able to identify a particular moment in the life of a class when a sea change happens: they sense that the students are suddenly starting to behave collectively in a more responsive and unified manner. Teachers use the image of ice cracking, thawing, melting or being broken to describe this phenomenon. The behaviour that enables them to make such pronouncements is nearly always a burst of spontaneous laughter caused by a trivial incident, an unexpected response or a passing remark – made either by themselves or by a particular student. One teacher reported despairing over a class that was composed of particularly reticent, frightened-looking individuals. In one lesson she collected some marker pens from the students and noticed that the lid of one was missing. When she asked if anyone had seen it, the most forward student in the class pointed out that it was on the other end of the pen that she was holding – whereupon the whole class burst into laughter. When this happened the teacher reported breathing a mental sigh of relief: the class had behaved spontaneously at last.

Another teacher described a critical incident in a class that contained groups of both Swiss-German and Swiss-French students who, in her view, were not 'meshing' at all well. One day she set up a 'Who gets the heart?' discussion activity that required students to rank hypothetical patients in order of greatest need for a heart transplant (a young person with their life ahead of them, a parent with a family to support, a person in a key professional job, and so on). Because the students were participating in the activity in a perfunctory manner she decided to personalise the situation and said to the class at large, 'I'm Australian. If I had a heart attack in Switzerland, do you think that they would give me a Swiss heart in the hospital?' At that point a Swiss-German boy called out, 'Forget it!' – a comment that engendered a spontaneous burst of whole-class laughter. The teacher construed the collective response to this single off-the-cuff remark as evidence that the class was 'cracking, melting a bit', and it led her to think to herself, 'Thank goodness! We're getting somewhere at last.' Incidents such as these suggest that laughter in the language classroom functions as a barometer that enables teachers to judge the overall level of responsiveness of their classes. Once their class has demonstrated the ability to laugh collectively, language teachers report feeling more relaxed, comfortable and able to be themselves.

The ways in which teachers respond to untoward events or unexpected remarks that lead to spontaneous outbursts of whole-class laughter can of course vary considerably. It is important to note that neither of the teachers described above interpreted the off-the-cuff response that led to the laughter as cheeky or out-of-line. On the contrary, both laughed along with their students in response to the comment that had been made. By so doing they indicated that they welcomed not only the initiative of the individual who caused the class to laugh, but also the collective response. This point is crucial to an understanding of how humour operates in language classrooms. If teachers adopt a stony-faced, 'I am not amused' demeanour when unexpected classroom events occur (as they inevitably do), then learners quickly get the message that spontaneous humour is not welcomed. This has a two-fold effect. First, the humour is driven underground, with students making jokes quietly (and sometimes not so quietly) amongst themselves. Second, and more crucially, the teacher is deprived of an important informal indicator of the overall level of responsiveness of their class.

Happily, as described in Chapter 4, the majority of language teachers working in western educational settings value informal classroom atmospheres – together with the laughter that is a key manifestation of that informality. By so doing, they have at their disposal a powerful means of receiving ongoing feedback from students about the degree to which their class is attentive, alert and responsive to their efforts to teach in engaging ways. One teacher commented that she always wanted her classes to laugh at her 'silly little jokes' – because then she would know the students understood what she was saying.

Once informal classroom atmospheres have been established and teachers and students feel relaxed and comfortable in one another's company, myriad opportunities present themselves for classes to laugh together. Because they can safely predict a positive response on the part of their teacher (provided that the humour is not out-of-line), students become increasingly confident about making and reacting to humorous initiatives. Since mistakes and misunderstandings are an integral part of learning to communicate in an unfamiliar tongue, the potential for humour in language classrooms is enormous. As the following section will show, language teachers and their classes find countless opportunities to laugh in unison during the course of lessons. Such occurrences do not interrupt the flow of the teaching. Indeed, they are often so fleeting that they go largely unnoticed – like subliminal messages flashed across a TV screen. Even immediately after lessons have finished, language teachers find it difficult to recall the specific incidents that led them and their classes to laugh so readily.

Humorous initiatives and responses

When they are in the mood, language classes will laugh at almost anything: an unexpected noise, someone's file dropping to the floor, a student whose head is nodding as they struggle to stay awake. Students regularly look towards the teacher, seeking a facial expression or off-the-cuff comment to indicate that they are prepared to take the event in their stride. Language teachers who feel confident and relaxed often make a humorous quip when such events occur. One teacher exclaimed, 'There goes another student's leg cut off!', when a pneumatic drill started up outside the window. Indeed, the facility to make passing comments that lubricate the social atmosphere of their classes is one that many language teachers develop over time. As one teacher said:

> I somehow sense when to throw in just a little joke in passing – nothing hilariously funny. For example, yesterday I saw a heavy chain coiled up on the floor by the side of one of the students' desks, so I joked, 'Toru, are you going to murder me?' Of course, it was the chain for locking up his bicycle.

Language teachers who value informal classrooms tend to behave informally themselves, 'hamming things up' to get the atmosphere going, or behaving in ways that confound the conventional view of the teacher as austere and devoid of a light touch. One teacher, who had lent her eraser to a student at the back of the room, was delighted to receive laughter and applause from the class when it was thrown back to her and she 'caught it like a pro'. Within the intimate context of the language classroom students can find spontaneous behaviour such as this surprisingly funny.

In a chapter in an early book on the psychology of humour Martineau (1972) proposes a model of the social functions of humour. Quoting Davis (1961), Martineau states:
'The function of humor is to initiate and facilitate communication and development of social relationships: Through humor, consensus is achieved and social distance is reduced. As an aspect of the socio-emotional role in informal groups, humor serves as a symbol of social approval promoting group solidarity' (1972: 117).

The longer they stay in teaching, the more familiar language teachers become with the kinds of ways in which humour can most readily be used to vitalise the atmospheres of language classes. The easiest way for teachers and students to interact in a mildly joking manner relates to common-or-garden classroom events: late arrivals, the time, homework and so on. When individuals arrive late teachers often say 'Good *eve*ning' in an exaggerated tone of voice. They may even go to more elaborate lengths, such as the teacher who locked her classroom door from the inside and then watched with her students in a conspiratorial fashion as the late arrivals slowly turned the door handle. She then laughed with the class as the quiet, polite knocks became louder and more persistent. If a teacher asks their class for a time check, a bright spark may call out, 'Break time!' or give the wrong time on purpose – while if they mention homework the class may let out a collective groan, or a student call out, 'Oh no!' or 'shopping homework!'

Even students in beginner-level classes are able to give unexpected single-word responses that engender a rapid whole-class response. Often these involve word associations based on cultural knowledge gleaned from advertisements, TV programs, cartoons or western movies. A student might chant an advertising jingle, call out 'Foster's!' in response to a teacher's call for words for all the things you can drink, shout out 'Turkish!' when a teacher mentions the word 'coffee', or exclaim 'Mickey!' when a teacher is teaching the word 'mouse'. Students often unwittingly cause their classes to laugh for the most insignificant of reasons – such as a student who said, 'I can't read my writing' when called upon to give an answer. Teachers themselves often encourage class group laughter through their off-the-cuff comments. They might say, 'Did I wake you?' if they make a student jump, 'Last boarding call!' when they want a student to participate, or, 'You need a new filing system!' when a student is rummaging through an untidy pile of worksheets.

The atmospheres in language classrooms are regularly vitalised through difficulty, confusion or misunderstanding associated with learning the new language. Pronunciation problems often cause classes to laugh – a student struggling to pronounce the consonant cluster in the word 'sixth', for example. (When such problems occur, teachers often capitalise on the moment to give the whole class pronunciation practice – which tends to engender further mirth.) When students misunderstand questions, quirky answers often result – such as the response 'Good morning!' to the teacher's question, 'How are you today?' Students often attribute truth-value to de-contextualised sentences and then laugh at the result – because the sentence either matches or does not match the reality of the situation. For example, a class might laugh at the sentence 'As you eat more so you put on weight' because they have themselves experienced putting on weight in Australia. Conversely, they might find it amusing if a 30-year-old class member reads out the sentence, 'I'm 64 and I'm retiring next year'. Students often give creative explanations or definitions that others find funny. For example, a teacher might elicit the explanation 'fish suicide' for the content of an article about beached whales, 'baby house' (a direct translation from the Korean) as a definition of the word 'womb', or 'roast dead' as the definition of a crematorium.

Misheard or misunderstood words often engender spontaneous laughter in language classrooms, such as a 'porch' being defined as 'a very fast sports car' by a student who thought that the person in the song the class had just listened to was sitting not on his porch, but in a Porsche. Difficulty in communicating can lead both teachers and students to use mime or behave in comic ways. In one class a student talked about going to a farm for the weekend and helping with the 'chip' – which nobody understood until the teacher went 'Baaa!' Many language teachers become highly skilled at conveying meaning through a combination of verbal and physical clues. Students sometimes come to their aid, for example to help explain to someone unfamiliar with dairy produce what precisely yoghurt is. Sometimes the boot is on the other foot, with the teacher not being able to comprehend what a student is trying to say – particularly when the student keeps repeating a single word in isolation. When this occurs the student's compatriots, who normally have little difficulty in understanding what the student is trying to say, will often chip in with their contributions. When the teacher finally understands, the tension is broken and the class bursts out laughing in relief.

Humour in language classrooms is also actively initiated by individuals, with quick-witted students coming into their own with ready responses that energise their classes. To illustrate the meaning of the words 'appropriate' and 'inappropriate', one teacher asked her class how they would feel if she came into class wearing swimwear – whereupon someone immediately quipped, 'It'd be okay if you were our swimming teacher'. Sometimes students ask questions in semi-jest. For example, after being taught the difference between 'needs' and 'wants', a male student said to his teacher, 'I want a wife. Is that a need or a want?' Sexual innuendoes and mildly risqué jokes are commonly made in classes of adult language learners – sometimes generated by teachers and sometimes by students.

In sum, once a spirit of dynamic interaction has been established, classes of language learners and their teachers find themselves bursting into laughter quickly and effortlessly at the widest possible range of stimuli. When these stimuli are analysed they often turn out not to be particularly funny. Even if they are funny, it is unlikely that all individuals appreciate the humour inherent in all the various remarks that engender collective laughter. It is also true that individuals who have unwittingly caused their class to laugh can sometimes feel deeply hurt. Nevertheless, within the charged atmosphere of the vitalised language class, students find themselves swept along by the immediacy of the moment and the powerful influence of the class group: because everyone else is laughing, they find themselves laughing too.

8.3 Activity-based language practice

A person from a country with a relatively traditional educational system who visits a communicative classroom in a western setting might well be surprised, not only at the amount of class time allocated to speaking practice, but also by the animated nature of the interaction that takes place. If they observe an elementary or intermediate-level class, they may well see communication games in progress with students, role-play chits or selected pieces of information in their hands, rushing around the room to interact with others in order to complete the game. They may notice competitive activities, with students cheering their team members on and letting out whoops of delight when their team wins. They may hear a lot of noise, with students chanting or singing, or completing activities such as 'shouting dictations'. They may see students sitting back to back and holding imaginary telephone conversations with one another – becoming increasingly excited as they strive to communicate. They are likely to hear the scraping of desks and chairs as the furniture is moved to clear space for action in the middle of the room. They may then see the class forming a big circle for a pig-in-the-middle-type activity, or interacting in an animated way as they work out how to line themselves up according to a particular criterion (such as height, date of birth within the year – or even shoe size). They may observe students engaging in physical response activities: standing with their hands on their heads prior to an elimination game, or touching their noses or rubbing their tummies in the game 'Simon Says'. They may even see classes move to a different location, where there is more space for physical activity and less chance of the noise generated by the class interfering with other people's lessons.

Classroom observers from more traditional educational systems who for the first time witness language learning activities such as those described above will almost certainly be amazed – such activities being so far removed from everything they have come to associate with teaching and learning in their own cultures.

Although it might seem inappropriate to compel grown adults to engage in activities such as the above in the name of language learning, activities that allow students to have fun are often highly successful. By engaging in activities that generate feelings of involvement, urgency and excitement, language students find themselves forgetting their inhibitions and expressing themselves more readily in the target language. Indeed, it could be said that communication games and tasks, particularly when they incorporate the information-gap principle, are cornerstones of the communicative approach. Provided that games and tasks are selected carefully, set up appropriately and introduced in such a way that their relevance to the overall program can be seen, adult language learners are normally prepared to enter into the spirit of things. Indeed, as mentioned in Chapter 4, students who have been taught in traditional ways often welcome the opportunity to behave in more relaxed, spontaneous and light-hearted ways in their classes.

There is a further reason why games and 'frothy' activities are a useful resource in language classrooms: they enable pent-up tension or energy to be released. As pressure mounts for adult language learners to reach high levels of linguistic proficiency in increasingly reduced lengths of time, so there is less time for language classes to proceed at a pace that allows learning to be thoroughly consolidated. Students in advanced-level classes, and especially those on pathways programs (those that provide eventual access to tertiary education programs conducted in the target language), can feel particularly anxious and pressurised. One language class contained refugees with professional qualifications who were desperate to upgrade their English as quickly as possible. The teacher worked them extremely hard, stretching their cognitive abilities to the full. He also carried around what he called his 'bag of tricks': a file containing photocopied sets of tension-releasing activities such as lists of tongue-twisters that the students could practise just for fun. He would often select such an activity for the last five minutes of a lesson, when he sensed that the students could absorb no more and needed to release their pent-up emotions by messing around in relatively frivolous ways. Other teachers organise the occasional game with high-level classes when they sense that their students need to be 'hyped up' or 'bubbled up a bit'.

At the other end of the spectrum, language teachers in the school system report how important it is to give their students the opportunity to let off steam. Young boys in particular tend to be highly energetic: running instead of walking, throwing rather than passing things round the classroom, giving their neighbour a quick cuff, and so on. Experienced high-school language teachers, particularly female teachers working in boys' schools, have developed strategies that enable their charges to release their energy in ways that are not counter-productive. When everyone has finished their work they might set up a quick language revision game that involves physical activity. For example, they might have students rushing to swap places in a moving queue after providing the correct form of a French verb, or chasing to the front of the room (egged on by shouting team-mates) to be the first to write a Japanese character correctly on the board.

The party games syndrome

Because they have at their disposal such a wide range of tried-and-tested techniques for injecting a feeling of fun into their lessons, it is easy for language teachers to confuse fun with learning. When they see

183

students excited and energised by classroom activities, it is both tempting and convenient to assume that learning is taking place. Why bother to investigate the extent to which students have really learnt anything when a good time is being had by all, and when the students (on the surface at least) seem quite happy? Having set up communicative tasks in which everyone in the room is behaving in animated ways and apparently having lots of fun, some language teachers find themselves sitting back and relaxing. The fact that their students are energised and interacting in lively ways with fellow class members provides them with evidence that language learning is somehow taking place. Reflecting back on classroom activities, language teachers often make approving remarks such as, 'It was a really enjoyable activity', 'They all thoroughly enjoyed it' or 'They were all laughing and clapping and having so much fun'. The fallacious assumptions that underpin such statements run as follows: (1) students learn effectively when their emotions are engaged; (2) when students' emotions are engaged, they are enjoying themselves; and (3) therefore enjoyment is evidence of learning.

Language teachers vary in the degree to which they make the assumption that there is a positive correlation between fun and learning: the more there is of one, the more there is of the other. Some go a step further, viewing enjoyment as an end in itself. Teachers in the latter category are likely to be those who are relatively new to the profession, who have received minimal training and who do not regard language teaching seriously or as a lifelong career. Attaching high value to enjoyment provides a ready justification for selecting fun activities from the resource room, using them as the core content of lessons – and assuming that one has fulfilled one's teaching obligations. In language schools the word often gets around that certain teachers operate primarily as 'entertainers' or 'babysitters': able to generate high levels of energy and excitement in their classes without necessarily delivering the goods. Under such circumstances, students – particularly when they are in a hurry to improve their linguistic skills as quickly as possible – may feel short-changed. Although they may give the superficial impression of being happy with their learning, their inner feelings may be quite different. In the words of one teacher:

> Our students are used to disciplining themselves to learn.
> They're used to it, they expect it, and some of them actually
> believe that if they're having fun they can't possibly be learning
> anything.

> The temptation for teachers to confuse fun with learning is well
> recognised by educationalists. According to Ormrod (2000: 601):
> 'Excitement and entertainment should not be thought of as goals in
> and of themselves. Rather, they are means to a more important goal:
> achieving instructional goals.'

Experienced language teachers make it abundantly clear that they do not
confuse fun with learning. Some teachers distance themselves from language teaching which they consider to be frivolous or 'skin-deep' by
talking in deprecating tones about classes with 'birthday party' or
'happy-clappy Club Med' atmospheres. Most agree, however, that a
feeling of lightness and fun enhances the atmosphere in language classes
– provided that learning is also taking place. As one teacher commented,
'Having fun without learning is a waste of time. A good class is one in
which everyone learns together *and* has fun.'

Other language teachers place fun and enjoyment in separate categories, defining enjoyment as the deep level of emotional satisfaction that
is bound up with the process of learning itself. Reflecting on his personal
experience of completing a higher degree, one teacher explained that it
was the actual process of engaging with others in a challenging and
worthwhile intellectual pursuit that enabled him to say that he had
enjoyed his course. Thinking specifically about language classrooms,
another teacher distinguished between what she called 'frivolous enjoyment' and 'real positive enjoyment', defining the latter as being 'where
everybody feels that they're achieving something and that they're
working cooperatively together'. In her view:

> In a good lesson enjoyment is that feeling that somehow between
> you and the class you've created something positive. You *could*
> enjoy a lesson where you actually don't learn a great deal – but in
> a good lesson enjoyment is where they feel stimulated, where they
> feel they're getting somewhere with their learning.

In sum, experienced language teachers sense that there is a reciprocal
relationship between enjoyment and learning: enjoyment enhances
learning, just as learning enhances enjoyment. They are clear in their
minds that, in the context of the language classroom, enjoyment is
closely related to learning. They are equally sure that enjoyment is not
the same thing at all as the students having a good time together at a
social occasion such as a party: it is of a different order altogether.

Vitalising the language class

8.4 Bringing the pedagogy alive

This chapter has focused so far on the ways in which language teachers strive to inject a feeling of vitality into their lessons by making and valuing humorous initiatives, and by setting up activities that encourage lively interaction. Although of crucial importance, humour is a relatively superficial, 'quick fix' way of injecting a feeling of vitality and spontaneity into language classrooms. The more experienced they become, the more language teachers become aware that there are deeper and more powerful ways in which the atmospheres of language classrooms can be vitalised. These ways involve providing students with opportunities to engage personally with the learning process – not by completing set exercises, but by demonstrating who they are as people through the medium of the target language. Indeed, language classrooms are ideal environments for the engagement of the whole person, since a key function of language is self-expression and the sharing with others of information that is personally meaningful.

Language teachers are readily able to identify moments during lessons when they sense that the atmosphere in the room suddenly 'lifts', somehow becoming more vibrant and alive. This qualitative shift in the atmosphere of language classes is not the result of socially driven classroom behaviour, such as people making jokes or having fun together. Rather, it is evidence of a serious level of student engagement. Students may be listening intently as the teacher, or an individual student, tells the class something of particular interest. They may be collaborating closely with a partner or a small group to complete a demanding task or to solve a tricky problem. They may be sharing and comparing real-life experiences with someone from a cultural background that is different from their own. Alternatively, they may be struggling to communicate ideas, feelings, insights or information to others through the medium of the target language. All of these behaviours suggest high levels of student involvement.

Language teachers value moments when they sense that their students are deeply engaged in the learning process. When this happens they are often reluctant to interrupt the flow, believing that something dynamic and worthwhile is taking place. They report noticing additional kinds of body language, such as students with their heads close together as they converse intensely with others – often using their hands extensively or making sweeping gestures in order to get their point across. During whole-class activities teachers may notice certain individuals leaning forward or jiggling in their seats, making it quite clear that there is something that they want to share with the class. One teacher noticed a student who normally behaved in a withdrawn manner become excited

186

during an information sharing session in which everyone in the class described what they had had for breakfast. This student's urgent desire to communicate an intriguing snippet of information – that the flavour of eggs is enhanced if they are boiled in tea – led him to behave in a particularly animated way.

> There is now growing interest in the notion of 'flow' in language classrooms, when something unplanned and unpredictable leads language teachers to lay aside their lesson plans and literally 'go with the flow'. The concept of flow was first used by the psychologist Csikszentmihalyi to describe the mental state of people at peak moments of experience. Using Csikszentmihalyi's concept of flow (1997), Tardy and Snyder (2004) report on a study in which they conducted open-ended interviews with ten first-year English teachers, inviting them to discuss their flow experiences in their jobs.
>
> The findings of Tardy and Snyder, in terms of practising teachers' descriptions of flow, match closely the personal accounts of the ways in which the teachers in the present book recognised times when the atmospheres in their classes 'lifted' as the communication became more vital, alive and authentic.

Capturing students' interest

Language teachers have at their disposal a range of pedagogic techniques for making lessons more relevant and memorable for their students – and for encouraging students to engage more fully in the learning process. Some of these, such as devising an intriguing departure point for the lesson that captures everyone's interest and attention, are no doubt used by creative-minded teachers in all subjects and across all cultures. One language teacher in China spoke of taking a block of ice into class – the grime that remained on the desk after it had melted providing a lead-in to a text on environmental pollution. Language teachers find myriad ways of creating anticipatory interest in the reading or listening text that they have selected as the focal point of their lesson. One teacher defined this process as 'making students feel curious: getting them to form questions in their minds that the text can then answer'. Prior to giving her class an article on laser surgery to correct short-sightedness, one teacher made a chart that she stuck on the wall next to the whiteboard – enabling students to test their eyesight. While instantly creating interest in the topic of short-sightedness, this five-minute activity had the additional benefit of enabling the teacher to find out who might have difficulty seeing the board.

In his book on motivational strategies in the language classroom Dörnyei (2001: 76) provides a list of the most motivating features of task content. These include 'challenge', 'interesting content', 'the novelty element', 'the intriguing element', 'the exotic element', 'the fantasy element' and 'the personal element'.

Creating anticipatory interest in the content of reading or listening texts means involving students at a personal level: engaging their emotions as well as their intellect. Before having her students read a *New Scientist* article on the so-called 'ice man' (the body of a Bronze Age man found preserved in ice in the Italian Alps), one teacher recounted the true story of how a relative of hers had dug up a body in his garden. She then asked the students to share with one another and the class how they themselves would feel, and what they would do, if they found a body under similar circumstances. Language teachers sense that it is particularly important to give students the opportunity to display personal knowledge, to express personal feelings or to share personal information prior to reading or listening to a text that contains content or concepts that are likely to be unfamiliar. They talk about 'making some kind of a connection for the students', 'trying to touch them in some way' or 'tapping into where they're at as people'. Prior to giving her class a listening comprehension describing the findings of research into differences between male and female discourse patterns, one teacher got her students to share with one another the playground games they had played as children. She then encouraged them to anticipate what the research findings would be – based on how they had communicated in their own playground games.

A technique widely used by language teachers for engaging the interest of students, particularly when starting a lesson or introducing a new topic, is brainstorming. This technique, which requires students to pool prior knowledge (either in small groups or as a whole class), is easy to master and relatively non-threatening for students. At its simplest level all students have to do is think of as many words as they know in certain categories: words beginning with the letter 'B', words for all the different things you can drink, the names of as many sports as they can think of, and so on. Students can also be invited to brainstorm creatively, for example thinking of all the uses of a piece of string or all the things that people can find frightening. At higher levels they can be invited to pool their knowledge of the world, to brainstorm all the causes of or all the solutions to a particular problem or to think of as many words as they can associated with general words such as 'transport' or 'technology'.

The technique of brainstorming is particularly useful in English language classrooms, where virtually every student comes to class with some prior knowledge of the target language – even if only in the form of isolated words gleaned from the media or the Internet. By allowing students to demonstrate what they already know, language teachers are able to achieve a number of objectives. First, they show that they value the contributions made by all individuals (thereby encouraging commitment to the subsequent learning task of all class members). Second, they can establish where the class is at in terms of its overall collective knowledge – and identify those students who have higher levels of prior knowledge and may need 'stretching'. Third, by showing that many heads are better than one, they enhance the feeling that classroom language learning is a collaborative enterprise. The technique of brainstorming quickly becomes integrated into the personal repertoires of many language teachers: they use it regularly, particularly at the start of lessons or when introducing new topics, for the simple reason that it works – and can be used at any level and in virtually any context.

> For a more detailed explanation of the benefits of brainstorming, and for a list of points to remember when using the technique of brainstorming in language classrooms, see Senior (2005).

Creating meaningful statements

Clearly language classrooms vary in the amount of authentic communication in the target language that takes place. Depending on the linguistic level of the students, the nature of the syllabus, the amount of time available and the personal inclination of the teacher, opportunities for individuals to use the target language to make statements that are unique and personally meaningful vary considerably. In some classes such opportunities may be frequent, in others relatively rare. Although language teachers regularly encourage students to make statements about themselves to practise linguistic structures, such statements are often hollow because the focus is on the accuracy of the linguistic form, rather than on the meaning that is conveyed. For example, when teachers ask their students what they did at the weekend, it is unlikely that they are particularly interested in the truth-value of the statements that their students make: their priority is to establish the degree to which their students have mastered the simple past form of various verbs. Students sense when they have been asked a formulaic question, often responding with predictable answers, such as 'I slept' or 'I did homework' or 'I watched TV' when asked to describe their weekend activities. It is not until an individual uses the structure to make an unusual, untoward statement, such as 'I crashed my car', that the collective ears of the class prick up and the atmosphere is instantly vitalised: here is something worth listening to.

Many language teachers are aware, particularly when teaching courses with a heavy focus on grammar (such as those preparing students for examinations run by the University of Cambridge ESOL Examinations), that they can make their lessons more dynamic by relating new language to their students' current lives and circumstances. In the words of one teacher:

> When I do my language focus I ask them to give examples from their daily lives – and it's so much more meaningful than that imaginary person in the book doing something or other. The reality in the book is just meaningless – dead on the page. It's not alive for them. I guess you look at the materials and relate it back to the students' experiences, personalise it for them: get the information, the raw data, coming from them.

One teacher of an examination preparation class made frequent use of this technique when introducing new grammatical forms, sentence structures, functional expressions or idioms. After providing an example that referred to a particular individual in the class, she would invite class members to write down further examples that followed the same linguistic pattern. For example, when teaching reported speech she wrote on the board, 'Marnie has 20 boyfriends' and then said to the class, 'I don't know whether this is true, but I have heard that it's true, so how can I make a sentence?' After students had attempted to use the correct structure, she wrote, 'It is reported that. . .' on the board and everyone wrote down the model sentence about Marnie and her reputed posse of boyfriends. She then got students to use the same structure to create their own 'gossip' sentences about people in the class – which they did with considerable enthusiasm and creativity. Students then shared their sentences with the class, some of which the teacher wrote on the whiteboard. In the view of this teacher, 'When you teach in this way students seem to get it – and the structures have a far better chance of sticking in their minds'.

Comment

The ways in which the teachers in this section create meaningful statements about the students in their classes to illustrate linguistic structures suggest that they are using a modified version of what Thornbury and Meddings (2002) call a Dogme approach. According to Thornbury and Meddings, the first rule of Dogme is that 'teaching should be done using only the resources that teachers and students bring to the classroom – i.e. themselves – and whatever happens to be in the classroom' (2002: 36).

Sharing life experiences

Teachers who find themselves teaching classes composed of adults from a variety of cultural backgrounds are uniquely placed to transform their classrooms into places where genuine information exchange can take place. There is nothing that humans enjoy doing more than talking about themselves – provided that the listener is genuinely interested in what they have to say. Most language teachers are familiar with the information-gap principle: setting up tasks in such a way that students are compelled to converse with one another, since nobody has been given all the relevant information (each student having been given a different part of the jigsaw). However, fewer teachers make full use of the natural information gap that exists in any class that contains students from diverse cultural backgrounds who, naturally, have widely varied life experiences. Language teachers who are aware of the vast potential of the natural information gap that exists in such classes find themselves regularly encouraging their students to exchange information with one another through the medium of the target language. Acknowledging the vitalising effect of such moments, one teacher commented, 'When they share life experiences it gets them all so bright and enthusiastic'.

The flow of information that has such a vitalising effect on the atmospheres of language classrooms does not simply go from student to student. Teachers are aware that students are often keenly interested in themselves and their lives, particularly when the students are living in isolated cultural 'bubbles' and have only superficial contact with citizens of the host country (on public transport, in shops and so on). Students often long to get to know more about life in the host country. Since they may not know how to go about establishing social contact with 'residents', their classroom language teacher often remains their only reference point and source of cultural information. Language teachers can sometimes, of course, go too far – using the language classroom as an opportunity to recount anecdotes from their personal lives to a captive audience, sometimes at considerable length.

The atmospheres of language classes are also vitalised when the information flows in the opposite direction: from students to the teacher. Most language teachers find themselves naturally curious to learn about their students' cultures, and have little difficulty in displaying genuine interest in the information provided – a feeling that readily conveys itself to others in the room.

As mentioned in Chapter 4, Stevick (1980: 28) suggests that good language teachers alternate readily between roles in their classes, a practice he describes as mask changing. In Stevick's view, when teachers show personal interest in what their students are recounting, they are coming out from behind their Teacher masks and putting on their Ordinary Person masks. Stevick notes that this mask change is accompanied by changes in voice, posture and facial expression, saying that, when teachers wear their Ordinary Person masks, they are animated, engaged and apparently intensely interested in the other speaker(s) and in what is being said.

Talking about the importance of learning about students' cultures, one teacher observed:

> It's a reciprocal thing. If they feel you're learning too it makes things more interesting for them and gets them more alert and involved. If they know you're interested in them they warm, they become more interested and more willing to learn. What they're doing is using the target language to teach *you*.

The cultural information that is shared in language classes during genuine information exchange (when the focus is on the meaning of what is said, rather than on the form of the language used) is infinite in variety. Students can share with others details about the size and composition of their families, their experiences of school, memorable places in their countries that they've visited and so on. Teachers can elicit from students information ranging from basic facts to ideas of a more abstract nature. For example, they may ask students to tell the class the age at which people can learn to drive in their home countries, whether smoking is allowed in public places, whether seat belts are compulsory and so on. For advanced-level classes teachers may encourage discussion on culturally embedded concepts such as status symbols or ideals of beauty – comparing those of the students' countries with those of a western country such as Australia. Language teachers find that, when students are asked to share with others information about their countries and cultures, levels of involvement are nearly always high. Teachers who believe that it is particularly important to develop a feeling of inclusivity in their classes make a point of saying that they try to ensure that they ask about the countries represented by all the students in the class. As one teacher commented, 'It's so easy to forget Tuk, because she's the only Thai student in the class. But I know I must ask her the same things as I ask the others – otherwise she'll feel left out.'

In sum, in the words of one teacher, 'We must value the thoughts and ideas of the students – and not treat them as learners all the time. *This* is what engagement is all about.'

Engaging authentically with authentic materials

Authentic materials – which can be defined as any reading or informational materials not specifically designed for classroom use – are now more commonly used by language teachers than they were 20 years ago. One of their greatest advantages – and one increasingly recognised by language teachers – is that students can respond to them in personal ways. Whereas previously it was common for students to fill in missing words on a song sheet while listening to the song, nowadays it is increasingly common for students to sit with their eyes closed letting the words and the music envelop them. They then share their personal responses with their peers. Whereas previously students might have completed mechanistic activities with newspapers such as matching headlines to stories (the teacher having separated the stories from their headlines with a pair of scissors beforehand), nowadays teachers often take to class sets of complete newspapers. They might then ask students to scan a newspaper, select an article of personal interest, read it and then devise a quiz on its content for their friends.

The case is the same with other kinds of authentic materials. One teacher took to class a pile of brochures on how to deal with stress, sensing that her students would find the content particularly pertinent (one of the students having made certain personal revelations in her journal). Although the teacher planned during the course of her three-hour lesson to focus on linguistic aspects of the brochures, she explained that her prime motive for selecting them was because she wanted her students to engage with their content.

A phenomenon regularly reported by language teachers is that, once they have recognised the potential of authentic texts to engage the interests of their students, they find themselves constantly on the alert for materials that might fire the enthusiasm of the class that they are currently teaching. As one teacher explained:

> I find that if you're watching television you'll see a program and think, 'That'll be perfect for them', so you gather that and you work something around it. You're thinking about that particular class and what would be interesting for them, what would help them, and then you think, 'Yes, I can do this with that!'

Another teacher commented that she would find herself reading the newspaper not only from her own point of view, but also from the point of view of the students she was currently teaching – trying to see the

193

world through their eyes. The kinds of authentic materials that teachers select for classroom study reflect their ability to empathise with their students and their current situations. In a class of migrant women struggling to adjust to Australian life while bringing up young families the teacher did not use a coursebook. Rather, she selected as the reading matter for her course a number of articles from women's magazines, all of which provided heart-warming accounts of people overcoming adversity – such as coming to terms with terminal illness, living with a disability, becoming pregnant against the odds or raising a family of quintuplets. Not surprisingly the students in her class displayed a keen level of interest in the stories she selected for them to read.

Identifying potentially engaging topics, themes and issues

Language teachers are increasingly aware that they can vitalise the atmospheres of their classrooms by focusing on topics that are likely to capture the interest and fire the enthusiasm of their students. They select such topics in a number of ways. They may simply follow the textbook and focus on the prescribed topic, assuming that the textbook writers were correct and that the topic will appeal. They may conduct a class survey in order to identify areas of particular interest to the class. They may decide to focus on topics that they know from previous experience go down well with students of certain ages, and for which they have materials readily to hand. Alternatively they may select new topics or themes on the basis of informal feedback received from a single student: something that they believe will resonate with a number of students. Finally, teachers may select topics in which they have a keen personal interest: vegan diets, gay rights, banning logging, and so on. Because they typically enjoy relatively high levels of freedom to select topics and materials for their courses, language teachers are able to pursue personal agendas if they so wish. Some of them take advantage of this opportunity, sometimes even to the extent of propagandising.

A practice increasingly used by language teachers is to select issues for class study: controversial topics about which there are clear differences of opinion, such as premarital sex, surrogate motherhood, euthanasia, foetal stem cell research or the introduction of genetically modified foods. By setting up activities that require students to adopt a particular stance and then argue their case, language teachers find that student emotions can run high. They tend to look on approvingly as students struggle to state their position, formulate and articulate arguments in defence of that position, and refute arguments put forward by the other side – all through the medium of the target language. One teacher who regularly used this technique with advanced-level students recalled with pleasure how students in a previous class had 'been at each others' throats' when discussing the topic of capital punishment, while another commented of a similar activity:

> They were fighting and arguing over who was right and who was wrong. It was great. It turned into huge arguments. It was fantastic – and we finished the day on that point.

Clearly there are good reasons for setting up communicative activities in which students feel compelled to speak: students will have more practice speaking the target language, and may well speak in a more fluent and less inhibited way than normal. However, there is always the risk that individuals will reveal deep-seated attitudes and values that clash with those of others. This is often the case with the topic of crime and punishment, where the views of students from countries with authoritarian political regimes may be very different from those of students from countries with democratic regimes. Experienced teachers usually monitor classroom activities carefully, remaining alert for clues that students are becoming over-involved, and intervening or back-pedalling as required. One teacher cut short a class discussion on the role of the United Nations when two students began to argue in an impassioned way that the United Nations was a nefarious organisation. Realising that these students' arguments were based on personal experience of UN peacekeeping forces operating in their mother country, the teacher judged it inappropriate to continue with the topic, since it had clearly touched a raw nerve.

Most language teachers are aware of the need to tread carefully when discussing in class world affairs or items currently in the news. It may not be prudent, for example, to discuss terrorist attacks in Indonesia with a class containing Indonesian students. On the other hand, such events can provide opportunities for high levels of engagement and the genuine sharing of ideas – and can have a positive effect on intercultural relations within the class. At a time of political tension between China and Taiwan, the Taiwanese and Bosnian students in one particular class became deeply engaged in discussion, identifying similarities in the political situations in their respective countries. One teacher in the Adult Migrant English Program in Australia was affronted when informed at an in-service course that certain topics were not to be mentioned in language classrooms. In her view she was quite capable of deciding for herself how best to deal with issues relating to war, religion, racial vilification and so on, if and when they arose in her class.

An opposite problem can arise when language teachers seek to encourage lively interaction by means of controversial topics: certain students can become more reticent than they were in the first place. There are three main reasons for this. First, individual students may simply not be interested in the topic. When she saw a student doodling and yawning while another gave a presentation on the banning of whaling, one teacher exclaimed to the uninterested student: 'Are you awake? Do you care? Surely the issue of whaling is important to you!' Second, students may be reticent because they do not have sufficient background knowledge to say anything of value. If they have never considered the issue of human rights, they will find it difficult to engage meaningfully in debate about the role of Amnesty International. The idea of animals having rights (a topic dear to the hearts of some teachers) may be even more alien to them. Third, in certain cultures it is inappropriate for young adults to hold strong views, let alone to express them. Accustomed to listening to what older and more experienced people have to say, language students can feel awkward when required to take a stance and persuade their opponent to change their mind, thereby 'winning' the argument. One teacher reported exhorting reluctant students to adopt a position with the words: 'If you don't *have* an opinion, then *invent* one!'

Although many students enter the spirit of things and develop the skill of engaging in lively debate with their peers, for others the prospect of discussing controversial topics remains daunting. One student who was promoted to the top class in a language school, in which discussion on contemporary issues formed a large part of the syllabus, requested to be demoted at the end of term. Although linguistically able, this student evidently felt more comfortable in a class in which the focus was fairly and squarely on grammar.

In sum, with any teaching practice designed to engage not only the intellect but also the emotions, there is always the danger that students will become so personally involved that feelings will run high. Clashes between students' value systems may then occur. There are also issues related to the privacy of the individual. Students may not wish to reveal aspects of themselves or their private lives to others – even for the general good of language learning, and even though the teacher may be encouraging and the atmosphere of the classroom supportive. A final problem with techniques designed to induce students to reveal aspects of themselves in the language classroom is that they do not necessarily work. Students cannot be compelled to speak: they always have the option of remaining silent or minimally responsive, or of creating a mask behind which to hide, if they so wish.

8.5 Conclusion

This chapter has focused on the vitalisation of language classes. It has identified the fact that language teachers value classes in which a critical mass of students respond readily to their initiatives and engage enthusias-tically in communicative tasks. It has identified and described the key role that humour plays in vitalising the atmospheres of communicative classes, showing that humorous initiatives are regularly made both by teachers and students. The chapter has identified the kinds of communicative tasks that teachers regularly use to encourage lively student interaction – while at the same time drawing attention to the fact that less experienced teach-ers can confuse fun and enjoyment with learning. Finally, the chapter has focused on the pedagogic practices of language teachers, showing how those that engage students at both an intellectual and an emotional level are able to create a feeling of vitality and dynamism in language classes.

This chapter has demonstrated that the vitalisation of language classes is a process that is set in motion by the dynamic interaction that occurs between teachers and the students in their classes. This process, which is represented schematically in Figure 8.1, is sustained in an ongoing way by the behaviour of the teacher and certain students, by the collective behaviour of the class group as it reacts to spontaneous events, and by the nature of the tasks themselves.

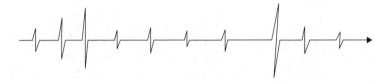

Figure 8.1   The vitalising process: teacher and student impulses

Summary

- In the eyes of language teachers classes differ in their overall levels of responsiveness: students in more responsive classes perform commu-nicative tasks with more energy and enthusiasm than students in less responsive classes.
- Informal language classrooms in which teachers and students feel relaxed with one another are characterised by impromptu bursts of whole-class laughter caused by a range of unexpected events and behaviours.
- Moments when teachers and students laugh in unison serve to vitalise the social atmospheres of language classes and affirm that classroom language learning is a collective experience.
- Energy levels in language classes are reciprocal: teachers energise their classes through the judicial use of humour, and students do likewise (in a range of both witting and unwitting ways).

- Language teachers use bursts of spontaneous whole-class laughter as a means of monitoring the energy levels of their classes.
- Many of the interactive tasks routinely used by language teachers in their classrooms require students to behave in energetic and sometimes hyperactive ways.
- Some language teachers confuse fun with learning, believing that, because students are having fun, worthwhile learning is taking place.
- Experienced language teachers devise tasks in such a way that both the intellect and the emotions are engaged, believing that effective learning occurs when both domains within the human brain are activated.
- Experienced language teachers recognise the potential of multicultural language classrooms to provide opportunities for cultural information exchange through the medium of the target language.
- Because of their desire to have students interact with each other in as lively a manner as possible, language teachers sometimes select discussion topics that are culturally inappropriate for certain students in their classes.

Comment

Foot (1997) provides a useful introduction to theories of humour and laughter, explaining that research on humour has tended to focus on why people find jokes funny (the 'decoding' of humour), rather than on the reasons why people initiate humour (the 'encoding' characteristics of humour). He then provides an overview of the social uses to which humour and laughter can be put, which range from controlling social interaction to coping with embarrassment.

It seems that the function of humour in language classrooms could be a fertile area for further research. According to Foot, 'While there has been a recent explosion of interest in the therapeutic use of humour, its commercial and educational value has continued to receive remarkably little research attention. This is not to say that humour is not widely used in fields such as advertising, political propaganda and teaching, but rather that little empirical evaluation of its effectiveness has been undertaken' (1997: 279).

Looking ahead

The following chapter focuses on how language classes that have been together for some time develop unique cultures, based on shared understandings about how individuals in the class typically behave.

9 Maintaining the classroom community

The previous chapter focused on the different ways in which language teachers vitalise the classroom environment. It drew particular attention to the key role that laughter plays in enabling teachers to judge the overall level of responsiveness of their classes. It also demonstrated how humorous initiatives and responses inject a feeling of vitality into language classes. The central part of the chapter highlighted the danger of confusing enjoyment with language learning, while the final part showed how the atmospheres of language classes are vitalised when students are engaged in learning tasks in ways that are personally meaningful and satisfying. The chapter concluded by highlighting the reciprocal nature of the vitalisation process.

This chapter focuses on how language classes function as communities of learners, with language teachers and their students interacting with one another in dynamic ways to develop the unique cultural environment of each language class. It is divided into three sections. Section 9.1 describes the kinds of shared understandings that routinely develop over time as the individual culture of each language class evolves and becomes readily identifiable. Section 9.2 focuses on group dynamics in the language classroom, showing how the ways in which language classes function as communities of learners can be understood in terms of the construct of cohesiveness. It also draws attention to potential problems associated with perceiving classes of language learners as cohesive. The third section of this chapter, Section 9.3, focuses on the techniques that language teachers commonly use to maintain a sense of community in their classes. It identifies a crucial aspect of the classroom behaviour of language teachers: the fact that much of it is effective at both pedagogic and social levels. The chapter concludes by suggesting that the pedagogically and socially oriented classroom behaviours of language teachers are inextricably entwined.

9.1 Language classes as learning communities

Outside observers, who sit in on language classes and observe single lessons being taught (as opposed to a series or sequence of lessons), tend to focus their attention on teaching and learning behaviour. Typically, they note how effectively the teacher presents new language, sequences activities, explains concepts, sets up tasks and so on. They may also note the learning behaviour of students: the kinds of questions they ask, how effectively they complete learning tasks, how actively they engage in interaction with their peers, and so on. Such teacher and student behaviour can easily be observed and assumptions about effective teaching and learning readily made.

It is far more difficult for outsiders to interpret the significance of any incidental behaviour that occurs concurrently in language classes – for the simple reason that they have no knowledge of the shared history of the class. No first-time visitor to a language classroom can know how well the class has 'gelled', what kind of a relationship the teacher and the class have collaboratively developed, the quality of the interpersonal relationships that exist within the class and so on. Neither can a casual visitor know about the nature or quality of the collective learning experiences that the class has previously had. Take the following sequence of actual events: a student calls out with strong intonation, 'I'm a *bird* and I can *fly*!'; the teacher smiles; someone else exclaims 'I'm a *fish* and I can *swim*!'; the rest of the class laughs knowingly. An outside observer cannot understand the communicative value of the students' words. Little do they know that the students are parodying the 'voices' of animals from a recently viewed language teaching video that everyone agreed was simplistic. At this particular moment the whole class is enjoying a collective joke that serves to affirm that a spirit of camaraderie prevails within the class. The significance of this brief exchange can be understood only with reference to the overall social context and the shared learning history of this particular class.

> 'As a course evolves over days, weeks, and months, a culture emerges through the interaction of personalities and events. Without an understanding of that culture, many of the events which occur in a particular lesson will be meaningless to the outside observer.'
> Nunan (1996: 44)

It is sometimes forgotten that language classes operate as communities, each with its own collection of shared understandings that have been built up over time. The overall character of each language class is created, developed and maintained by everyone in the room. Each class member has a specific role to play, even those with ostensibly low profiles such as 'onlooker' or 'observer' (noticing what is going on), 'knower' (being privy to shared class understandings) and 'follower' (reacting in the same way as everyone else to certain teacher or student initiatives). The unique character of each language class is based on shared understandings about how individuals (including the teacher) typically behave, react and interact with one another within the confines of the communicative classroom.

What everybody knows

By the time any language class has been together for some weeks, there are many things that everyone in the class knows – even if nothing is actually said. First, simply by sitting and observing, students learn a great deal about their teacher. They know whether or not they normally arrive on time, the nature of their wardrobe, and whether they have any particular foibles, mannerisms or idiosyncrasies. They know about their teacher's personality – and have probably made a private decision about whether or not they like and respect them (there are seldom half-measures in this regard). Of crucial importance, students have decided whether or not their teacher treats them in a fair, consistent and considerate manner. Students will be familiar with the teacher's way of teaching, with their class management approach, with their overall expectations and with their general level of expertise. They also know whether or not their teacher remembers to do what they say they will, such as coming back with the answer to a grammar question they could not answer on the spot, or returning written work promptly. Students also register little things, ranging from whether their teacher pronounces their name appropriately (or even remembers it) to how they mark written work. They also know precisely how their teacher uses the whiteboard: whether they write words carefully and legibly or whether they scribble and scrawl – and perhaps make spelling mistakes more often than might be expected. Finally, students know how their teacher deals with inappropriate behaviour – whether they behave in a reasonable manner or whether they lose their temper and make wild threats that they cannot carry out. All this information can be gleaned simply by being a member of a language class for two or three weeks.

During the first few weeks students also learn a great deal about each other. They quickly learn which of their classmates have dominant personalities, who wants to claim more than their fair share of the teacher's attention, who prefers to retain a lower profile, and so on. They soon learn who both the stronger and the weaker students in the class are – even if no formal linguistic proficiency test is given. They will notice, for example, who is always quick to answer, who asks pertinent questions and who always seems to be several paces behind everyone else. Students also absorb a range of seemingly insignificant information about one another, such as who regularly arrives late, who tends to wear unusual clothes, who rushes off to sporting engagements straight after class – and who is romantically involved with whom.

For their part, teachers identify the presence of various personality types in their classes surprisingly quickly (though not necessarily accurately). In a teacher development workshop on student roles in communicative classrooms, language teachers had little difficulty coming up with archetypal terms to describe students, such as 'the scatterbrain', 'the wet blanket', 'the persistent questioner', and so on. The alacrity with which they came up with such labels suggests that language teachers have vivid memories of the presence in their classes of certain student types. However, general impressions are not always correct. One teacher described how mortified she felt on discovering from another teacher that a student whom she had perceived to be 'an arrogant creep' was in fact lacking in confidence and, with a history of performing badly under exam conditions, was desperately worried about the upcoming exam.

Who sits where

Another form of understanding quickly developed by classes of language learners – usually with very little said – relates to which seats in the room 'belong' to whom. Although high-school language teachers may tell their students where to sit – perhaps pairing boys with girls to avoid the formation of groups of potential troublemakers – teachers of adult language learners tend to let students sit where they wish. As a result classroom groupings can quickly become apparent, with cultural cliques often forming and solidifying for the duration of the course. In one class of migrant women the Indonesians, who had made a special point of not sitting together, were disapproving of a group of Chinese women who always sat in the same corner of the open 'U' and conferred closely with one another. In this particular case the teacher had made the decision not to break up the groups, judging that the benefits the women gained from remaining within their cultural and linguistic comfort zones outweighed the opportunities lost for interaction with a wider range of class members. A strong sense of community existed within this class anyway, since the students had access to a kitchen where they chatted to one another as they prepared their morning tea and cleaned up afterwards.

It is natural for students to gravitate towards the same seats when they enter the room for each new lesson. Out of the corner of their eyes teachers notice latecomers making straight for their accustomed seats. If a student hesitates at the door, or if their seat is taken, teachers have a golden opportunity (provided they are quick enough) to suggest that the student sit next to someone else. New relationships can develop in this way, with students choosing to remain sitting next to new-found companions. One teacher, who believed that allowing students' seating positions to become fixed was detrimental to the development of a feeling of community within her class, had developed a system of random allocation of seats. At the beginning of each week the sixteen students in her writing class knew that they would be required to sit somewhere different and work closely with whomever they happened to be sitting next to for the next five sessions. There was no question about the procedure: this was the teacher's expectation for the class.

Directors of studies in language schools are familiar with the phenomenon of students not wanting to be shifted to another class after the first week of term (unless they feel they have been wrongly placed). There may be compelling reasons for moving students around, such as parallel classes being unbalanced in terms of student numbers. The fact that it is difficult to persuade students to move suggests that within a surprisingly short space of time students have started to feel part of their classroom communities. Not surprisingly, having learnt what their class is like, they are reluctant to join an alternative classroom community in which the customs and practices will be subtly different.

The notion of classroom culture

Although 'culture' is a tricky term whose definition is hotly debated, the term 'classroom culture' is a useful one to describe the body of understandings that are developed, shared and maintained by both teachers and students for the duration of each language class. One teacher found herself teaching the highest level class in a language school under particularly difficult circumstances: small numbers of students either joined or left the class at the end of each week, making the whole class a movable feast. This particular teacher, keenly aware of the need to establish a sense of corporate identity within the class and to maintain a sense of continuity, talked regularly about the techniques that she used to achieve these twin goals. She used terms including Durkheim's 'collective consciousness' and the social-psychological term 'collective memory' to describe the shared understandings that she constantly fostered in her class:

> You develop some sense of shared history, some collective
> consciousness, and you constantly build on that. For instance, you
> develop a class history of topics they're interested in – which you
> can then revisit later on in the course. You also build up

203

> knowledge of what particular students have said or done in the
> class. And you talk about those regularly too.

This teacher had developed a number of techniques for maintaining a
sense of community in her classroom. A simple one involved keeping a
list of student names currently enrolled in the class permanently on the
whiteboard – so that with the shifting student population students would
always remember who the current class members actually were. Another
technique she developed was so effective for maintaining a collegiate
feeling in her classes that it became part of her regular repertoire (even
when teaching classes with stable student populations). It involved
holding a regular 'news' session at the beginning of each lesson, during
which time she would gather information about the interests, concerns
and out-of-class activities of the students. She would then ensure that the
information was shared with the class, discussed by everyone, stored in
the collegiate class 'memory' and referred to on a regular basis. For
example, if she knew that a student had purchased a bicycle she would
ask them where they had been and what they had found interesting. If
other students then purchased bicycles she would ask them about their
experiences too. The sharing of information about cycle paths and good
places to visit then became a regular topic of conversation for that particular class. This teacher, with her genuine interest in the personal
growth and development of young adults, created a strong sense of community within her classes by employing this single technique. By the end
of term she knew so much about individual class members that she was
able to construct class quizzes with questions such as, 'Who has a birthday right at the end of the year?' or 'Who recently passed their driving
test?'

Affirming the classroom culture

The beginnings of lessons are times when a sense of community is re-
established, when behavioural expectations are reinforced and when the
individual culture of the particular language class is reaffirmed. The first
few minutes of each lesson are especially important in high schools,
where the culture of the language class may be significantly different
from the prevailing culture of the school as a whole. Talking about the
beginnings of lessons, a teacher of Indonesian said:

> They're a time for focusing, because the students may have come
> from classes where they were throwing spit balls. So the
> impression I give is, 'Hi, how are you going? We're back together
> again!' Even a quick game is good because it gives me a chance to
> 'get the goss', to judge the mood of the class, to help the students

let go – and, by simply giving instructions in Indonesian, to switch their Indonesian back on again.

One teacher talked about how much her students enjoyed the ritualised beginnings of their Japanese lessons: standing behind their chairs waiting for her to bow and speak, whereupon they would bow and respond and be given permission to sit down. Evidently the students loved having people visit the class because it gave them the opportunity to perform the ritual all over again. Clearly teachers have individual ways of establishing their classroom environments. One high-school teacher of English as a second language would have Baroque music playing as the students entered the room, and would routinely make quick little jokes in order to 'clear the slate' (clear the students' minds of their experiences in their mainstream classes before proceeding with the lesson).

Students have long memories. One teacher always started each lesson with a ball-throwing activity that required students to catch and throw a ball around the class – asking a question in French as they threw it and answering the question as they caught it. She would constantly remind her students of the pedagogic goal of the game: to 'open up the drawers in their brains' and get their language going again. At one point this particular teacher went overseas for six months. On her return she resumed her teaching duties, including teaching a class of 17-year-olds preparing for their final exams. She did not take the ball to this particular class, judging that the students would not want to resume the activity since they were now older and exam-focused. She was wrong. The first thing the students said as she walked in the room was, 'Where's the ball?'

Not all language teachers have the luxury of teaching in the same classroom every day and, even if they do, may not be permitted to decorate their rooms or even to pin things up on the noticeboard. High-school language teachers in particular crave their own dedicated classrooms in which they can create learning environments that reflect the cultures of the languages they are teaching. Language teachers are adept at transforming the most unprepossessing classrooms into veritable Aladdin's caves – filling them with the widest possible range of cultural artefacts: kites, dolls, posters, calendars, charts, paper models, flags, maps and so on. Language teachers tend not to mind the physical state of their classrooms – provided they contain spaces that can be used flexibly for communicative activities: room for everyone to stand in a circle, open spaces for mingling activities, a carpet so that everyone can sit on the floor, and so on. One teacher was thrilled to be allocated a redundant science lab with a gas point and a sink because she could cook Japanese noodles for the class at the end of term.

High-school language teachers sometimes describe their classrooms as 'havens' or 'oases' – places away from the razzmatazz of normal school life where students can behave differently from how they might normally behave. One teacher pointed out that in language classes boys were able to display the gentler, more female sides of their characters, saying:

> The Australian playground defines a male narrowly: kicking a ball, hanging out with their mates, drinking and so on. Language classes have things in common with art and music classes. There's lots of creativity because of role-play activities, where you can be expressive and show your feelings. You can even enjoy quietly reading together and not saying anything at all.

It seems, then, that language teachers – and particularly those involved in teaching minority languages in high schools – are aware that their classrooms can function as both social environments in which behavioural norms can be established and physical environments in which the culture of the target language can be promoted.

Institutionalised rewards

In order to function effectively communities must have codes of behaviour that are known by everyone and enforced by those in authority. The situation is no different in high-school language classes. Having established behavioural parameters, experienced language teachers report that wherever possible they try to deal with discipline problems themselves rather than sending their students out of the class to be punished through the official school system. The systems of rewards and punishments that individual language teachers establish often become part of the shared classroom culture or folklore: part of what 'everybody knows will happen' if students behave appropriately or, conversely, step out of line. Talking about rewards, one teacher said:

> They know if they've worked really hard they'll be able to play a game – but only if *everyone* has worked hard – so they can get really ratty with a person who hasn't pulled their weight. They know which games they can play, so they often ask for particular ones that they like. They know which ones I've got in my cupboard.

Sometimes rewards systems put in place by imaginative language teachers become classroom institutions that are known and cherished by successive classes of students. One teacher established a system of dishing out what she called 'Bertie coupons': little slips of paper that she'd unexpectedly give to individuals who did anything commendable, ranging from holding open a door to pronouncing a word correctly. The students would put their coupons in a specially labelled tissue box, which would sit on the top of the cupboard and gradually fill with more and more coupons. The attraction of the system was that the teacher had a twinkle in her eye and would often give coupons to the most unlikely students for the smallest thing that they had done right. When the time came for the prize draw the whole class was keenly interested, since even a student with one coupon in the box had some chance of winning. The draw would take place in a ritualised way, with the students doing a ceremonial drum roll on their desks as the teacher prepared to plunge her hand into the box and draw out three winners – each of whom would receive a small prize. By instituting a system of rewards that students found both democratic and fun, this teacher encouraged the development of a strong sense of fellowship and community within her class.

9.2 Group dynamics in the language classroom

'Making one's classroom a learning community is one of the most important things a teacher can do, even more important perhaps than the practices used in the more formal aspects of instruction. The classroom learning community influences student engagement and achievement, and it determines how a teacher's class will evolve from a collection of individuals into a cohesive group characterised by high expectations, caring relationships, and productive inquiry.'

Arends (2004: 137)

Classes that function effectively as communities of learners display many of the features of cohesive groups in the social-psychological sense. Researchers in the area of group dynamics – the branch of social psychology that deals with how people behave in groups – have found out a great deal about how small groups develop and function. These include the effect of different leadership styles on group behaviour, the different roles that can be played by group members, the development of group norms, the notion of peer pressure, the relationship between individual and group goals, and so on. Successful small groups reach high levels of cohesiveness, at which point they can be defined as mature work groups – groups that demonstrate high levels of solidarity and are capable of maximum productivity.

There are many definitions of cohesiveness in the group dynamics literature, all of which focus on the notion of groups having an overall feeling of togetherness or a collective sense of unity. The following definition by Vaughan and Hogg identifies some of the properties of cohesive groups:

> One of the most basic properties of a group is its cohesiveness
> (solidarity, esprit de corps, team spirit, morale) – the way it 'hangs
> together' as a tightly knit, self-contained entity characterised by
> uniformity of conduct and mutual support among members.
>
> Vaughan and Hogg (1995: 151)

When asked to describe classes they consider cohesive, the terms that
language teachers give are surprisingly similar to those used by
researchers. They use words such as 'team spirit', 'unity within the class',
'a sense of ensemble', 'a warm sea of people', 'no isolated islands', 'no
friction', 'camaraderie within the group', 'a feeling of oneness' and so on.
The properties of cohesive classes that teachers identify, such as 'being
helpful towards others', 'being willing to work with everyone' and 'identifying with the class', are also similar to those identified in the research
literature.

Studies have shown that cohesiveness is related to both the quality and
the quantity of group interaction (Shaw, 1981: 218) – members of cohesive groups interact more with one another, and in more meaningful and
productive ways, than do members of less cohesive groups. Again, the
impressions of language teachers seem to match the findings of
researchers. Experience has taught them that communicative tasks are
completed more eagerly and in a more sustained way by classes in which
an overall feeling of cohesiveness prevails. Quite independently of
research findings, they appear to have identified a relationship between
class cohesion and the effectiveness of communicative tasks.

It has long been recognised by educationalists that principles of
group behaviour can usefully be applied to classrooms of all kinds.
In their book *Group processes in the classroom*, now in its eighth
edition, Schmuck and Schmuck (2001) show how a range of facets
of group development (from leadership styles to the development of
group norms) can be applied to educational contexts.

Only now is the relevance of group dynamics for teaching classes
of language learners becoming fully recognised. In 1991 Hadfield
wrote a resource book for teachers containing activities encouraging
classes of language learners to 'gel'. It was based on feedback from
teachers that a central concern for them was whether or not their
classes developed into cohesive groups. In a recent book Dörnyei
and Murphey (2003) show how group dynamics principles can usefully be applied to language classrooms. They offer practical advice
on how to manage classes of language learners in such a way that
they develop into cohesive and productive groups.

Many experienced language teachers have an understanding of certain key group dynamics principles, which they apply intuitively as they go about their daily teaching. A teacher who says, 'Often the other students will pull someone into line – it doesn't always have to be me', has an understanding of the power of the group to exert a normative influence over the behaviour of the individual. Similarly, a teacher who remarks, 'She plays an important leadership role in the class', has an understanding of the fact that leadership is not the sole prerogative of the teacher.

A note of caution

The notion of class cohesion, however, is a tricky one that needs to be treated with care. It is tempting to jump to the conclusions (1) that class cohesion actually exists, and (2) that it is automatically highly desirable. Who is to say whether any language class is ever truly cohesive? Even in the apparently most cohesive class, full of lively students who seem to relate well to one another, might there not be undercurrents of antagonism of which the teacher is sublimely unaware? Is class cohesion something that, once attained, remains constant for the remainder of the course – or do levels of cohesion fluctuate from day to day? Finally, is there not a sense in which cohesive classes operate as coercive forces, compelling students through the power of group processes to conform and to behave in ways that they might otherwise not do? This being the case, might there be occasions on which high levels of class cohesion could conceivably be detrimental to the wellbeing of individuals?

A further problem with the notion of class cohesion is that it exists essentially in the mind of the beholder – rather than in reality. Like other abstract concepts, such as beauty, love or happiness, we all know what they are, yet all define them differently. A class that functions in a highly cohesive manner in the view of one teacher may appear far less cohesive to another. Equally, a class that appears highly cohesive to its teacher might be something quite different in the eyes of its student membership. Some researchers have devised elaborate ways of measuring levels of cohesiveness within groups, using specific criteria. In the hustle and bustle of communicative classrooms the best that language teachers can do is assess levels of class cohesion in an impressionistic manner. This they do on a regular basis, using external indicators such as facial expressions and body language. However, who is to say that their impressions are accurate?

A final comment needs to be made about the construct of cohesiveness: why is it that language teachers value cohesive classes so highly? There are both pedagogic and personal reasons why this is the case. From a teaching point of view, classes that operate in a cohesive manner are easier to teach than non-cohesive classes. The students within cohesive classes respond collectively rather than individually, interact readily with their peers, are quick to follow instructions and engage fully in communicative tasks. They make the teacher's task far easier and more pleasant – and provide them with welcome feedback that they are good at their jobs. From a personal point of view, teaching cohesive classes is exciting and rewarding. There is nothing more exhilarating than coming out of a classroom with the feeling that your class has been 'eating out of your hand': responding to your every whim, hanging on your every word, laughing at all your jokes – and generally giving the impression that you are quite marvellous. It can give you a real emotional buzz – and a considerable feeling of power. This leads to another important question: Do language teachers ever abuse the positions of power they wield in language classrooms through the subtle manipulation of group processes – albeit for genuine pedagogic ends?

Once in motion, group processes operate as powerful forces in language classrooms. Sometimes teachers can find themselves sucked in by the very processes they themselves have set in motion – becoming increasingly involved with and committed to classes that demonstrate high levels of cohesiveness. Interestingly, teachers only define as cohesive those classes of which they themselves feel an integral part.

Dörnyei and Murphey (2003: 70) issue a note of caution about classes that display high levels of cohesiveness without strong goal-oriented norms. They cite Wilson (2002), who points out that it is possible for a task group to be too cohesive. As they say, 'In such cases members begin to enjoy one another's company so much that they focus on their relationships rather than on their task. Soon the group becomes a *social group* and productivity will fall.'

The unique developmental pattern of each class group

Previous chapters have drawn attention to the infinite number of variables that can influence the social development of each class group. All language classes are unique entities composed of a particular combination of individuals. Each class takes place in a specific context and under a particular set of circumstances that can never be repeated. As a result each language class follows a unique developmental pattern that can never be predicted.

Some classes exude a strong group feeling from the very first day, giving the message to latecomers of, 'Come in, come in! Welcome to our class!' Classes can develop a feeling of unity surprisingly quickly – even when the students are complete strangers to one another and hail from a range of linguistic and cultural backgrounds. (Indeed, circumstantial evidence suggests that, the more heterogeneous the student mix within language classes, the more likely the class is to 'gel' – provided that the goals of the students are broadly similar.) Other classes remain collections of isolated individuals or disparate groups for the duration of their courses – despite the best efforts of their teachers to meld the disparate elements into a cohesive learning group. Some classes start off well and then 'go off the boil', while others plod on in a pedestrian way and gradually metamorphose into dynamic learning groups. Sometimes a single occurrence, such as a particularly difficult student leaving the class, can lead everyone in the class to utter what one teacher termed 'a collective sigh of relief' and feel instantly more unified and comfortable. Conversely, a single occurrence, such as two influential class members having a clash of views or values during a learning task, can upset the social equilibrium of the class group for the remainder of the course.

> For a description of teachers' impressions of the unique developmental patterns of eight classes of adult language learners see Senior (1999: 330–67).

It should also be noted that teachers' impressions of the levels of cohesiveness 'achieved' by their classes shift over time. In the immediate afterglow of having successfully completed teaching a particular course (and wishing to show the researcher that they have done a good job), teachers tend to assess the cohesion levels of their classes highly. However, in hindsight teachers often admit that their immediate impressions were optimistic – particularly if they have just finished teaching a subsequent class that turned out to be more cohesive than the previous one. In teachers' minds the experience of teaching language classes is a cumulative one, with memories of previous classes being subtly influenced by the experience of teaching subsequent ones. Eventually teachers' recollections meld and fade – although memories of the overall feel of certain classes remain forever etched on their minds, as do memories of certain critical incidents and the behaviour or words of certain individuals. The memories that remain most clearly in teachers' minds are those that have affected their feelings – either giving them a boost or touching a raw nerve. One teacher never forgot the words 'English is a barbaric language', hissed by a student in a way that was critical of her as she struggled to explain a grammar point in her early days of teaching.

Despite the unique and unpredictable evolutionary patterns of classes of language learners in terms of the development of cohesiveness, it is

211

nevertheless the case that experienced language teachers have a higher proportion of classes that function as effective learning communities than do less experienced teachers. What is it that these teachers are doing, and that others less experienced than themselves are not doing, that enable language classes to develop into and then reamain as communities of learners with a strong sense of individual identity and common purpose? As the following section will show, there are certain strategies that successful teachers employ, sometimes consciously and sometimes unconsciously, which encourage the maintenance of a spirit of community within their class groups.

9.3 Community maintenance techniques

Students in most communicative classrooms are required to work with different partners, to form different groupings for different tasks, to engage in mingling activities, and so on. With so many opportunities to get to know one another, one might have expected students in communicative classes to develop a strong sense of community without any additional effort on the teacher's part. This, however, is not the case. Providing students with regular opportunities to interact with one another is not of itself sufficient to develop a spirit of community within language classes. Indeed, if students decide that they dislike each other, being compelled to work together can have quite the opposite effect. In one advanced class in which students were expected to work collaboratively, relationships became so strained that it was mutually agreed that for the remainder of the term the class would no longer function as a learning community at all. Instead, the students would study independently, with the teacher acting as a resource person, helping students on an individual basis but not teaching the class as a group.

Most language teachers have had the opportunity to teach language classes in rooms with different seating arrangements: open 'U's, pairs of desks or rows of tables facing the front, blocks of tables where four or more students sit together, and so on. Some language teachers believe that certain configurations are more conducive to the development of a feeling of community than others – and sometimes go to their classrooms early in order to rearrange the furniture. However, even though the ways that language classrooms are set up may make it either easier or more difficult for a sense of community to develop, the physical environment of the language classroom is by no means the most important factor.

Learning collectively

From their training language teachers often gain the impression that teaching in teacher-centred ways (with the teacher addressing the class from the front of the room) is undesirable, and that teaching in student-centred ways (with the focus of lessons being on students doing things for themselves) is clearly preferable. In one sense this belief holds good. There is nothing more demotivating for students than sitting for extended periods of time listening to the drone of the teacher's voice. Teachers sometimes report feeling angry with themselves when they know they have engaged in too much 'TTT' (teacher talking time) in a particular lesson.

Ironically, in order to build a sense of community in their classrooms it is essential for language teachers to behave in teacher-centred ways at regular intervals during their lessons. If they allow students to work in groups for extended periods of time their classes can become fragmented, with little sense of unity. Experienced teachers routinely focus the attention of their class on themselves at both the beginning and the end of lessons – when they make opening statements about the focus of the lesson and when they draw the lesson to a close by giving homework and so on. They also request everyone's attention when introducing new linguistic items, explaining the meaning of unfamiliar words or issuing instructions. Experienced teachers also focus the collective attention of their classes on what they have to say at regular points during lessons. For example, they may interrupt a communicative task to ensure that everyone is completing it correctly, to provide additional vocabulary or to remind the class of how a particular structure is used (when it becomes clear that a number of individuals are unsure). They sense that it is important to give ongoing support and subtle reminders to their classes at large during the course of individual or small-group tasks.

While talking too much is clearly undesirable, being teacher-centred for genuine pedagogic purposes helps to keep language classes focused and 'together'. By addressing their classes at large, teachers convey the impression that their explanations are for the benefit of everyone, that their humorous asides are for everyone to appreciate and that the answers they provide in response to specific questions are useful for everyone in the room. One teacher, aware that other students kept their ears pricked for nuggets of information whenever she went round the class helping individuals, purposely gave her explanations in a louder voice – so that the class as a whole could benefit from what she was saying. Another teacher made a point of writing on the board all the words requested by individual students during in-class writing tasks so that the rest of the class did not feel that they were missing out. One of the factors that contributes towards classes operating as effective learning communities is students knowing that the teacher will provide opportunities for everyone in the room to have equal access to their knowledge and expertise.

Techniques that are effective both pedagogically and socially

A significant number of teaching techniques favoured by experienced language teachers perform more than one function. They not only provide suitable opportunities for individuals within the class to learn, but also promote a feeling of social unity within the class. By enhancing both the learning and the social atmosphere of the class, such techniques are doubly effective.

As mentioned in Chapter 8, a well-known technique that is widely used by many language teachers is that of 'brainstorming': requiring students to work in groups in order to pool prior linguistic knowledge, general cultural and world knowledge, personal insights and interpretations, creative ideas and so on. Some teachers routinely do quick whole-class information sharing sessions that have the effect of what one teacher described as 'drawing individuals into the fold'. Prior to giving her class a listening comprehension exercise on the processes involved in manufacturing different types of tea, one teacher asked her students to share with the class what they had eaten and drunk for breakfast that morning. The wide array of foods and drinks consumed by the class generated considerable interest, some humorous comments and an overall feeling of 'togetherness' within the class group. After completing the listening task the students readily passed around the room the notes they had taken – for scrutiny and comment by their peers.

Brainstorming is powerful pedagogically because it enables teachers to establish what students already know. Increasing numbers of students are joining English classes with some prior knowledge of individual words and phrases – from the Internet, television, movies, advertising and so on. One beginner-level class was able to produce an average of 20 English words for each letter of the alphabet: 'start', 'stop', 'save', 'slow', 'singer', 'star', 'sandwich', 'sex', 'Simpsons', 'Startrek' and so on for the letter 'S' – before the teacher had formally taught any of those words at all.

Increasing numbers of English language classes contain false beginners: students with some previous experience of learning the language from previous stints of studying. By eliciting from students what they already know (or think they know), language teachers are encouraging students who might consider themselves superior in terms of their prior knowledge to view themselves as both valuable and valued contributors to whole-class learning.

Brainstorming is also powerful socially because it draws classes together – giving individuals or groups of students the opportunity to share with the class words or ideas that they have generated. The pooling of words or ideas with the class as a whole reinforces the notion that many heads are better than one: that the class can collectively achieve more than it can when individuals or groups work independently of one another.

A further technique that can be highly effective in language classrooms is chorus work: having students chant words, phrases, dialogues or songs in unison. Apart from being an effective way of helping linguistic patterns to become embedded through regular repetition, collective chanting enables all the students in a class, regardless of their linguistic ability, to feel that they are integral members of their class group. Chorus work has the added advantage of providing diffident students with a high degree of protection: they can participate fully in the classroom action without anyone noticing whether or not their pronunciation is correct. Because of its connotations of behaviourism, chorus work (otherwise known as 'drilling') is currently unfashionable and is seldom promoted by teacher trainers. One teacher who regularly incorporated chorus work into her lessons whispered in an almost guilty tone that she did so, while another commented that she knew drilling was 'a dirty word'. Some teachers say that under no circumstances would they submit their classes to such a mechanical procedure as drilling. However, language teachers who have experimented with chorus work regularly extol its virtues.

> Van Lier (1988: 226) argues for maintaining a ritual element in language classrooms, suggesting that, regardless of other possible developmental benefits, rituals such as chorus sequences may serve to 'create a sense of collaborative achievement which is important for creating social cohesion and a positive ambiance'.

Chorus work is most commonly used in primary or secondary school language classes where students, initially at least, are studying the target language at a basic level (learning how to use stock phrases and say numbers, colours, dates and so on). Some teachers report regularly using chorus work with adult learners, particularly at elementary and intermediate levels. One teacher who had taught Japanese right across the age spectrum – from seven-year-old children to middle-aged businessmen – was emphatic

215

that chorus work was a universally effective technique for breaking down barriers and establishing a feeling of rapport within her classes.

There are many variations of chorus work: doing 'string repetitions' round the class (with students having to memorise and repeat longer and longer strings of information), having students say new words out loud several times over, having students chant rhymes, poems, dialogues and so on in a choral fashion. One teacher, familiar with chorus work from a training course completed many years previously, tentatively began using the technique with advanced-level classes. To her surprise, students grasped opportunities to repeat words, phrases and whole sentences out loud with considerable alacrity and enthusiasm. As a result she found herself using the technique increasingly frequently with such classes – having students repeat linguistic forms chorally first, and then with a partner or to themselves.

In sum, techniques such as brainstorming and chorus work can be effective, not only in terms of student learning but also in terms of maintaining a sense of community within language classes. A host of other language-teaching techniques, when used in certain ways, can function on two levels: they can be effective both pedagogically and socially.

> For examples of further ways in which language-teaching techniques can fulfil both pedagogic and social functions in language classes see Senior (2002). Techniques that can fulfil these dual functions range from whole-class information-gathering tasks to individual oral presentations. The article explains how even having students working independently in classrooms can enhance a feeling of community and common purpose, provided that the activity is set up appropriately.

Following the lead set by Hadfield's groundbreaking resource book *Classroom dynamics*, published in 1992, increasing numbers of resource books for language teachers contain selected classroom activities that have as a sub-goal the enhancement of class cohesion. Experienced language teachers do not appear to rely overmuch on such books to develop a spirit of cohesion within their classes, perhaps because the general teaching techniques that they already use have the same effect. Interpersonal relationships in language classes being so complex and unpredictable, the group-building language-practice activities contained within resource books may not have the desired result anyway. The processes whereby language classes maintain a sense of community and social equilibrium are complex and dynamic – and cannot be forced.

Maintaining a feeling of friendly intimacy

A further way in which language teachers maintain a sense of community in their classrooms is by emphasising that their class is a social unit, composed of a collection of unique individuals, each with their own personality and personal set of foibles. Just as family members get to know one another extremely well – and are aware of the strengths and weaknesses of each member – so it is the same in language classes: the teacher and students become intimately acquainted with one another as the course progresses. Particularly with intensive language courses, where students and their teachers spend many class hours in one another's company, there is ample opportunity for self-revelation. In communicative classrooms it is virtually impossible to 'hide'. Sooner or later, like it or not, each student develops a unique reputation for themselves, based on what everyone knows about their typical classroom behaviour, their mode of dress, their interests, their personal relationships and the things they feel strongly about.

One of the techniques used by experienced language teachers to maintain a sense of community in their classes in an ongoing way is to exploit this shared class knowledge in ways that give a quick 'lift' or 'boost' to the classroom community's sense of self. If they remark, 'Ah, I see Kanari has painted her famous fingernails green today!' or 'Don't say Alice has overslept yet *again*!', the class can laugh knowingly to itself. Everyone knows that Kanari is proud of her long fingernails (and that she paints them regularly) – just as they know that Alice is nearly always late for class. A wide variety of remarks of this kind are routinely made by language teachers. The role of comments such as these is to lubricate the social atmosphere within the class group and to reaffirm that a feeling of friendly intimacy prevails.

> 'When a class and its teacher all laugh together, they cease for a time to be separated by individuality, authority, and age. They become a unit, feeling pleasure and enjoying the shared experience.'
>
> Highet (1963: 56)

One way in which language teachers develop a sense of intimacy in their classrooms is by finding out how their students wish to be addressed, and always calling them by their class name – which is often some kind of a pet name, or anglicised version of their formal name. Sometimes a joking comment made by a teacher or another student can lead to the development of a nickname that attaches itself to a student for the duration of the course. One student, who announced that his name was Clark, was pleased to be dubbed 'Superman' by his teacher (with reference to Clark Kent, the hero of the Superman series) – and regularly reminded the class of his Superman status for the duration of the course. Occasionally students feel comfortable enough with their teachers to create nicknames for them. One teacher was amused to be dubbed 'Mrs Thesis Statement' by her writing class – construing it as a term of endearment that would only be used by a group of students who knew her well and accepted her as an integral member of the class community.

> 'Classes often develop their own humor and in-group identification. Nicknames, group history and gags help to promote cohesiveness and directly affect task productivity and learner satisfaction.'
>
> Korobkin (1988: 157)

One language teacher with a sense of fun and a creative turn of phrase made it part of his regular classroom practice to create amusing sobriquets for up to five students in each class. These included names such as Señor Incognito for the South American guy with the dark glasses, Count Mondeo for the squarely built guy with a passion for Ford cars and Mr Mobile for the student who regularly forgot to switch off his mobile phone. This teacher described the snowballing effect of giving students names in the following way:

> If I start to call someone by a special name, after a while the other students will start to call them by that name too. Immediately the others start to do that, there's this incredible effect on the class. It's transformed. It becomes intimate, like a family, like a peer group.

Experience had taught this teacher that transforming individuals into class personalities through this simple technique not only developed a sense of community, but also made the 'names' less critical and more committed to the class and to learning. However, this teacher had also had failures, admitting that he sometimes teased too much and that on occasions he had upset certain students. In his words, 'The nickname thing is a great mechanism, but if you pick the wrong person, the wrong nickname and the wrong time, you have to double back very quickly'.

As language courses progress, increasing numbers of students within class groups develop what one teacher termed 'heightened visibility'. They might assume one of a variety of roles for themselves, ranging from the furniture remover (the student who always arranges the tables at the start of the class) to the class artist (the student who will always do quick drawings on the board at the behest of the teacher). It is relatively common for confident individuals in language classes to assume the role of the teacher's foil: someone who is prepared to engage in humorous banter with the teacher while the rest of the class listens in. In one class a bantering relationship developed between the cricket-loving teacher and a soccer-loving student. The standing joke (the fact that the teacher repeatedly said that he loved cricket – which would then draw a cheeky riposte from the student) became part of the social 'glue' that bound that particular classroom community together.

Often the roles that students play in their classes gradually evolve. Many teachers are familiar with the notion of the class clown: the student who messes around and plays the fool to disguise feelings of inadequacy. Once it became evident that he was progressing at a slower rate than other members of his class, one student regularly engendered whole-class laughter by hitting himself on the side of the head and exclaiming 'Stupid Yugoslav!' whenever he made a mistake. On one occasion the student and his friend defaced a picture of an Australian family having a barbecue in the bush – drawing storm clouds and rain, and having the family barbecue a small lizard that was in the corner of the picture – much to the amusement of the class. As the course progressed this student and his friend started to play the fool with increasing frequency (eventually starting to do so in their own language, which made the teacher feel excluded from the evolving in-jokes shared by the class).

Sometimes students unwittingly develop roles and reputations for themselves. In one class a student developed a reputation for falling asleep, after dropping off on a hot afternoon and having the whole class (including the teacher) creep out on tiptoe, leaving him to sleep through recess. In another class a student developed a reputation for asking the same questions week after week. The students sitting behind her, evidently finding the questions unnecessary and time-wasting, would convey their feelings to the teacher by rolling their eyes and putting their hands over their mouths to cover mock yawns. In these cases the teachers conspired with students who were 'in the know' against students who did not know that they were the butt of the class joke. Students in situations such as these can feel upset when they find out what has been happening: laughter at their expense.

Clearly there are many occasions when individual students may feel angered or upset by the reputations they have earned, particularly when they feel that these are unwarranted and unfair. The Korean students in one class took offence at their reputation for being accident prone – after a student purchased a car and had a minor accident on the very same day. Once reputations become attached to individuals, they are difficult to dislodge. Experienced language teachers are aware that they need to balance the benefit to the class at large of sustaining reputations for individuals, against the detrimental effect that ongoing reputations may have on the self-esteem of the person concerned.

> See Senior (2004) for a more detailed description of the kinds of roles that students can play in the development of a spirit of cohesion in their classes.

A further way in which language teachers can develop and sustain a feeling of friendly intimacy in their classrooms is by teasing individuals in front of the class. All teachers are in positions of power in their classrooms, by virtue of their assigned status as teachers. Teachers whose job is to teach language are in even more powerful positions than teachers of other subjects since they are the only person in the room to have mastery of the key means of communication. They can use words more incisively than anyone else, react more quickly, be more amusing, use words more appropriately, be more cutting and so on.

Teasing is a particularly powerful tool in the hands of language teachers, and is used by countless teachers in appropriate and judicious ways. However, as teachers themselves are aware, there is the ever-present danger of 'overstepping that line of familiarity' or 'going that bit too far'. Most teachers admit to having offended students at some point in their teaching lives – and of having had to 'back off', 'backtrack' or make amends as quickly as they can. It is difficult, of course, to judge how students will react to being the focal point of class attention. In one class intense interest developed in the budding romance between two students, who appeared after recess one day with grass on their backs – to the amusement of the teacher and the class, who made knowing remarks that made the couple laugh. In another class two students reacted very differently to being the focal point of class attention. The teacher's repeated references to their ongoing romance, and to the fact that they held hands and rubbed knees under the desk, were eventually too much for the girl, who got up and rushed from the room in tears, her boyfriend close on her heels.

Maintaining a feeling of friendly intimacy in language classes is always a matter of balance: what works under one set of circumstances may not work under another. For the most part language teachers are alert to the reactions of individuals as they make jokes and subtle innuendoes in their classrooms. Sometimes, of course, they may be sublimely unaware of having caused offence.

Foot (1997: 268) observes that it is within a group context that in-group jokes – often barely understood by others outside the group – can thrive. He quotes LaGaipa (1977: 421), who says, 'Jocular gripes require some common experiences. Teasing requires knowledge about the butt of the joke and an acceptance and accurate perception of intent. Hostile wit is often not expressed unless the group has achieved a level of cohesiveness able to tolerate it. . . Situational jokes are likely to reflect the dynamics underlying the social interactions at any given point in time.'

Maintaining momentum

Often language classes that have been together for prolonged periods of time can begin to feel jaded. Everyone knows everyone else just that bit too well – and everyone is fully attuned to the teacher's personality, teaching approach and repertoire of tasks. When they sense that their class has lapsed into a comfortable routine that is perhaps too familiar and predictable, language teachers may boost the social atmosphere of the class by providing opportunities for students to see one another in fresh ways. This often involves a social event of some kind: a picnic in the park, a meal at a restaurant or even a weekend away. In one language school several teachers routinely took their exam preparation classes to a holiday island where the students stayed in self-catering accommodation and rode around the island on bicycles, swimming and snorkelling at the various beaches. According to the teachers, this group experience had a highly positive effect on class morale, reinvigorating the class atmosphere and enabling the students to prepare for the forthcoming exam with renewed energy and commitment. It also gave the students much to talk about in terms of shared memories of their collective experience: getting sunburnt, eating mounds of spaghetti, singing songs round the campfire and so on.

Many language teachers have had the experience of their classes suddenly starting to 'run out of steam' or 'go off the boil', with the collective energy level of the class somehow being sapped. Approximately two-thirds of the way through courses it is common for classes to start to lose momentum, with students suddenly finding the going almost impossibly hard. With only a few weeks remaining students often realise that they are unlikely to achieve all they had hoped: they are not going to become proficient users of the target language within such a tight timeframe. Students often gain the impression that their rate of learning is slowing down or levelling out – a phenomenon commonly described by teachers as 'plateauing out'. When they sense that their classes are slowing down, experienced teachers often interrupt their teaching to give their classes pep talks. They may urge their students to keep going by emphasising how much they have already achieved, or by telling them that those who have gone before have felt exactly the same – but have nearly always succeeded in the end.

When they sense that the students in their class are feeling overwhelmed, experienced language teachers may slot in a lesson of a completely different kind, which gives the class a temporary breathing space. This usually takes the form of a learning task that serves not only to reinforce what has been learnt, but also to boost the social atmosphere of the class group. One teacher replaced a 'heavy' academic listening and note-taking lesson with a 'light' lesson on Australian slang. The latter required students to listen to a tape of a pub conversation between an Aussie guy and an Aussie girl, practise pronouncing the expressions used, and then role-play the conversation with a partner. This one-off lesson, in which the students participated with considerable gusto, was enough to brighten the collective mood of the class. The teacher reported that the students completed the scheduled listening and note-taking task the following week with renewed vigour.

Students studying within access programs (programs that grant entry to further courses of study) can start to feel particularly dragged down as their courses progress. Not only their careers but also the whole future direction of their lives can depend on reaching the required grade in the end-of-term exams. Students can become haunted by the very real possibility of failure – and find themselves lying awake at night worrying (and then not being able to concentrate in class the next day). The situation is particularly stressful for scholarship students, for whom failure to reach the required linguistic standard in their access course can mean returning the scholarship money to the funding agency and returning shamefully home.

Experienced language teachers often sense when a significant proportion of students in their classes are so downcast and worried that they are unlikely to absorb what is being taught. Rather than pressing on regardless with their planned teaching programs, teachers occasionally abandon teaching altogether, giving their students instead the opportunity to express their worries and share their concerns with the class group. When they do this their class is temporarily transformed into a therapy group, whose goal is to address the psychological wellbeing of its membership (rather than its learning needs). A teacher who had taken this step on more than one occasion reported that the process invariably had a positive effect on class morale. She reported that the 'time out' was far from wasted, since it enabled her class to recharge its

collective batteries and move forward with renewed vigour and determination.

In sum, experienced language teachers are sensitive to the social needs
of their class groups. In order to maintain a feeling of forward momentum they sometimes set up outside activities, classroom tasks or even
'time out' during lessons when the social needs of their classes take priority over their learning needs. Aware of the relationship between class
morale and learning, they sense that time spent attending to the social
wellbeing of their class groups is time well spent.

Letting go

As language courses draw to a close the students within them begin to
look ahead. Perhaps they will be progressing to a higher-level class,
perhaps returning home, perhaps going travelling or perhaps entering a
different kind of course or program. Whatever their future path, the class
community of which they have been a member will cease to exist. Even
if a core group of students progresses to a higher level, the chances are
that a different teacher will teach them and that new students will join
the class. The shared understandings that were an integral part of the
culture of the previous class will disappear.

Ritualised endings are important for language classes, particularly
when groups of students have been together for many weeks in the
hothouse environments of intensive language courses. They provide
opportunities for classes to celebrate a collective sense of achievement. One student who pulled out of the exam for which his class
had been preparing at the last minute confided to his teacher that he
felt 'sad' and 'left out of the good feeling' at the end-of-class party.
End-of-term ceremonies enable students symbolically to let go of their
current teacher and develop a working relationship with their new
one. In one instance a language class petered out in the middle of a
teaching week, with no goodbyes said and no formal sense of closure.
In the following week the teacher was surprised to be approached by
a student who wanted permission to continue to ask him for linguistic advice. This student appeared unable to let go of the proverbial
apron strings.

Ritualised endings of language classes can take many forms, which
often involve the sharing of food. Classes might decide to bring food to
the classroom, go to a restaurant, have a picnic in the park, hold a
musical session – or the teacher might offer to have a party in their home.
Often the ease and enthusiasm with which classes go about negotiating
end-of-term events are indicative of the degree to which they have come
to function as unified learning communities. In one class that had

223

operated in a fragmented manner for the duration of the course, arguments developed about which restaurant would be suitable for the end-of-term class lunch. On the final day of term, when the class was to have its final lesson and then go on to lunch, certain students were notably absent.

As with adventure holidays, when language classes come to an end there is often a feeling of collective euphoria – tinged by an element of sadness. There is a sense in which each class has collectively gone through – and survived – a unique group experience. At events that mark the formal endings of courses it is common for students to exchange telephone numbers or email addresses and vow to keep in touch – as if wishing to retain the bonds that they formed during their collective group experience. On such occasions extended photographic sessions are the order of the day, with classes posing for a succession of group photos as individuals rush back and forth swapping cameras. It is as if each student wishes to preserve digitally or on celluloid the unique learning community of which they were a part.

9.4 Conclusion

The present chapter has focused on the myriad ways in which classes of language learners function as individual communities, each with its own unique culture and set of accepted norms. It has shown that, although many shared understandings develop naturally as courses progress, certain language teachers consciously foster the sharing of information about individuals in order to affirm the existence of a class community with its unique identity. The established classroom practices of individual language teachers – provided that the teacher is liked and valued – create understandings in students' minds about what can and should happen in their classes.

The second section of the chapter showed how knowledge derived from research into how human beings function in groups informs our understanding of how communities of language learners typically behave. It emphasised the fact that, although language teachers readily recognise and value classes that operate cohesively, the notion of class cohesion needs to be treated with care: it can mean different things to different people, and seldom remains constant. Language classes do not progress through developmental stages in the formulaic ways suggested by group dynamicists: sometimes classes appear to function cohesively from the very first day.

The third section of the chapter drew attention to the ways in which language teachers, both through their routine pedagogic practices and their socially driven classroom behaviour, are able to maintain a sense of community in their classrooms. It highlighted in particular the fact that many commonly used teaching techniques function on two levels: the pedagogic and the social. It also focused on the fact that, in teachers' minds, the social wellbeing of their classes is of crucial importance. In order to boost the morale of their class groups, and hence their ability to learn, language teachers occasionally cater purely to the social needs of their class groups. The relationship between the pedagogically oriented and socially oriented behaviours of language teachers may be represented as follows:

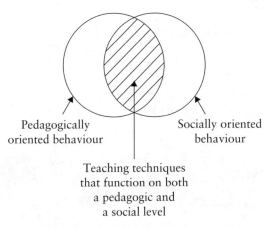

Pedagogically
oriented behaviour

Socially oriented
behaviour

Teaching techniques
that function on both
a pedagogic and
a social level

Figure 9.1   The relationship between pedagogically oriented and socially oriented behaviours

The clear sections of the circles represent either the wholly pedagogically or the wholly socially oriented classroom behaviour of language teachers. The shaded section where the circles overlap represents all those times during lessons when the behaviour of language teachers or students not only facilitates learning, but also reinforces a feeling of community within the classroom. These processes often occur concurrently.

Summary

- Every language class develops a unique culture, composed of understandings shared by all class members about how individuals within the classroom community typically behave.
- Many of the classroom practices routinely used by experienced teachers serve to foster the development of unique classroom cultures, thereby maintaining a sense of collective identity within each class group.

- Findings from research into group dynamics provide a useful way of understanding how language classes function as communities of learners.
- Language teachers value classes that appear to them to function in cohesive ways.
- The notion of class cohesion is a tricky one, since the degree to which it exists is always open to question.
- Being influenced by multiple factors, the developmental pattern of each language class is unique.
- Teacher-centred behaviour helps to maintain a feeling of community within language classes.
- Many of the teaching techniques routinely used by language teachers function on two levels: they are effective both pedagogically and socially.
- Teasing is widely used in language classes as a means of maintaining a sense of friendly intimacy in language classes. Sometimes teachers tease in ways that are hurtful to individuals.
- Experienced language teachers attend to the social and sometimes the psychological needs of their class groups, thereby boosting morale and giving their classes a sense of forward momentum.
- End-of-term rituals mark the disbanding of classroom communities that existed in unique ways for a set period of time.

For further reading
Arends' comprehensive book on learning to teach (sixth edition, 2004) contains a useful chapter on classrooms as learning communities. In it Arends provides both theoretical and empirical support for regarding classrooms as learning communities, citing in particular work by Doyle (1986) and by Schmuck and Schmuck (2001). He describes how Doyle takes an ecological perspective of classrooms, while the Schmucks propose a slightly different framework that highlights the importance of interpersonal and group processes (2004: 149).

Note
As described in Chapter 1, the overall framework selected for the present book was a social-psychological one that reflects the perspective of Schmuck and Schmuck. However, the properties of classrooms identified by Doyle are also amply displayed within the pages of the present book. They are as follows: multidimensionality, simultaneity, immediacy, unpredictability, publicness and history (2004: 147–9).

Looking ahead

The next chapter shows how the feelings that language teachers have about their profession are related to the broader educational contexts within which they work.

10   Frustrations and rewards

The previous chapter focused on how language classes function as learning communities, with all class members privy to shared understandings about how their particular class typically functions – understandings that cannot be accessed by outsiders who observe classes on a one-off basis. The chapter showed how each language class is a unique social environment with an individual culture that, by definition, can never be repeated. It then illustrated the kinds of steps that language teachers typically take, and the kinds of classroom interactions that subsequently occur, which help to foster and maintain a spirit of friendly intimacy within each class. The chapter concluded by showing the kind of ritualised behaviour that often occurs as language classes draw to a close and the students within them prepare to go their separate ways.

The present chapter has a wider focus, showing how teachers' feelings about language teaching are related to the broader educational contexts within which they work. The chapter demonstrates that, even though language teachers teach in individualistic ways, their feelings about the experience of language teaching are surprisingly similar. Section 10.1 describes the kinds of situations in which language teachers in English-speaking countries typically find themselves working. Section 10.2 identifies those aspects of language teaching that language teachers find most frustrating, showing that the causes of their negative feelings most commonly stem from constraints on their teaching resulting from financially driven management decisions. The third section of the chapter, Section 10.3, describes the many ways in which language teachers find their jobs satisfying and rewarding. It highlights the fact that for many language teachers the intrinsic rewards of teaching well and receiving positive feedback in their classrooms frequently compensate for the lack of extrinsic rewards.

10.1 The English language boom

It is now widely accepted that the English language, originally an obscure Germanic dialect spoken by the inhabitants of a cold, rainy island in the north-west of Europe, has in recent years gained an unassailable position as the lingua franca of the world. As the preferred language of electronic communication, its predominance can readily be seen in areas ranging from business and trade to medicine, education, sport and entertainment. The advantages of being able to communicate through the medium of English are becoming increasingly recognised, with interest in learning English increasing at an exponential rate in countries around the globe. Governments everywhere recognise the potential of English, with the education departments of increasing numbers of countries making English a compulsory school subject for all children. Parents want their children to learn English too, and may have them sent in school groups to the British Isles during their summer holidays for quick bursts of English language tuition. Adult students around the world, keen to enhance their job prospects by improving their English language proficiency, are flooding to English-speaking countries at an unprecedented rate to enrol in intensive English language courses.

The kinds of English language courses currently available in Australia for adult language learners fall into three main categories. First are short intensive English language courses offered to overseas students on short-term visas either by private language schools or public institutions such as universities or colleges of further education. Second are government-subsidised intensive English language courses available for recently arrived migrants from non-English-speaking countries. The third type of courses are pathway programs that offer intensive English language tuition for students from overseas countries who intend to study in Australian tertiary institutions.

Although there are seasonal fluctuations in the demand for English language courses, and longer-term fluctuations because of events with world-wide implications such as September 11 or the London bombings, the demand for the provision of English language tuition continues to increase. On the surface this situation appears to suit all interested parties. It suits students, because of the range of courses available, it suits institutions because of the overseas revenue it generates, and it suits teachers because of the high number of teaching positions that need to be filled. The situation is not, however, equally satisfactory for all parties. As the next section will show, language teachers find themselves subjected to increasingly heavy demands as the institutions for which they work compete with one another to enrol more students by cutting costs and reducing fees.

The big squeeze

There are considerable opportunities for entrepreneurs around the world to open up independent language schools. It is also becoming increasingly common for international chains of language schools to take over smaller language schools in several countries. These profit-driven enterprises are often owned by big business with associated interests in casinos or hotel chains. Although the language-teaching industry in Australia is regulated (with the national accrediting body placing a ceiling on class sizes and so on), this is not necessarily the case in other countries. Many language schools prefer not to become members of national associations because quality-control restrictions may limit their freedom to take short cuts. When profit-driven language schools need teachers in a hurry, they take on whomever they can find – a practice described by sceptics as 'grabbing native speakers off the street'.

> The profit-driven nature of English language teaching is reported regularly in the British press. Articles with colourful titles, such as 'The slavery of teaching English' (Cresswell-Turner, 2004) or 'Running after the gravy train' (Meddings, 2004), capture the sentiment with which English language teaching is popularly regarded.

It is not only private institutions that are driven by economic imperatives. Like their counterparts in Britain, Australian universities are increasingly under-funded by central government and must find ways of making good the shortfall between the government subsidy they receive and their high operating costs. International students provide the golden answer. They are prepared to pay for a product (the opportunity to study for and obtain a degree from a 'western' university), while the university is only too pleased to supply the goods (doing all they can to ensure that students pass their courses) in exchange for a substantial fee. Unfortunately, even after completing intensive courses in English before entering their undergraduate or postgraduate degree programs, significant numbers of students from non-English-speaking backgrounds continue to be hampered by restricted levels of English language proficiency throughout their studies. This puts pressure not only on themselves, but also on their lecturers, who often find themselves struggling to maintain standards.

Prior to enrolling in university courses, students from non-English-speaking backgrounds often need intensive English language tuition in order to reach a particular band score in an English language proficiency test. Even after attaining the minimum score required for university entry they may need ongoing language and/or study skills support. Tuition is normally supplied by specialist language teachers who often have postgraduate diplomas or masters degrees. These teachers, even though they work in universities, are usually employed by language centres that have been set up as commercial offshoots of the universities. Such teachers, commonly called tutors or instructors, tend to be employed casually or to be given contracts that stipulate different conditions from those of university academics. Their position is therefore an anomalous one. Even though the work they do with international students is necessary for the ongoing economic survival of their universities, language specialists are seldom considered part of mainstream academic life. A common perception amongst language teachers is that the centres that employ them are cash cows, whose profits can be milked by the university to which they are attached.

Teachers who have been in language teaching for a number of years believe that opportunistic management decisions made for short-term financial gain are responsible for an overall decline in standards. In the words of one teacher:

> There's a general feeling that things are declining, things are deteriorating, because of the need for short-term profit, and short-term profit is at the expense of the longer-term growth of the department. There's the idea that you've just got to hang in there in the market, because it's so competitive, and there's a very short-sighted attitude where people are not thinking ahead, they're just thinking, right, make a profit this week. . . There's this feeling that if there's any short cut that can be taken, it must be taken.

Bums on seats

For language schools the difference between profit and loss depends on enrolments. The unexpected arrival of an additional group of students – or even a single student – is a financial bonus. Students are seldom turned away – even when existing classes are full. When sufficient new students arrive to open up a new class, this will be done, and a new teacher quickly found. If it is not economically viable to open a new class, students must be added to existing classes – even if those classes are in full swing. Many schools have specific enrolment dates, for example at monthly, five-weekly or ten-weekly intervals. However, in order not to lose students who might go elsewhere, increasing numbers of language schools are enrolling new students whenever they arrive and placing them directly into existing classes, irrespective of whether those classes have already begun or what stage they have reached. Some classes roll on like educational conveyor belts, never starting up afresh and never coming fully to an end. Teachers involved in teaching such classes describe the experience as 'like teaching on a moving bus, or in the middle of a railway station, with people coming and going all the time'.

For language teachers the problem with having new students join their classes partway through courses is that the new students tend to upset the equilibrium of their existing class groups. As seen in Chapter 4, teachers work hard at the start of each new course to gain the confidence of their students and to develop a feeling of direction and purpose for the class as a whole. Although new students may sometimes slot into existing classes in a seamless way, on many occasions they do not. The situation is particularly difficult when an attempt is made to slot students with particular sets of learning needs and goals into an existing class that has already made significant progress towards the achievement of those same goals. The class teacher faces a dilemma. Do they continue to follow the program for the sake of their existing students (and risk not satisfying the needs of the new students), or do they modify their program and risk alienating their existing students? Language teachers become adept at reaching compromise solutions, but sometimes the gap is too wide for this to be possible.

The casualisation of the workforce

As described in Chapter 3, it is common practice for English language teachers to be employed initially on a casual basis. If they are lucky, they may receive a three-month or even a year's contract. If they fit in well, and if the director of studies has not received any negative feedback through the informal grapevine, a teacher can expect to be employed on a continuous basis with the status of what the head of one language school called 'a permanent temporary'. This informal system typically operates on a 'last-in, first-out' basis, with new teachers being told that their services are no longer required if there is a downturn in student numbers. An additional dimension, however, must be taken into account: qualifications and experience. The Australian regulatory board stipulates that teachers with higher qualifications and more experience are paid at a higher hourly rate. The backlash effect of this is that language schools that are driven by the profit motive often prefer to employ less able, less experienced teachers – because they are cheaper. As one teacher explained:

> There's less emphasis now on getting people who are very qualified and experienced. There tends to be a feeling that, if the students are vaguely happy – happy in as much as they don't complain, then everything is okay. So you can take staff who can be paid low salaries, as long as they can just about keep the students happy.

The fact that they are in temporary positions leaves many teachers feeling vulnerable and uneasy. They are often reluctant to voice their concerns or make practical suggestions for fear of losing their jobs. One teacher described the financial uncertainty pervading the profession as follows:

> There's this huge financial thing that's really hanging over the whole industry. Constant threat – not spoken threat – but teachers know that their jobs are very, very insecure, which leads to certain sessional staff not being able to say that things are not right. Not being able to ask for things. There's very much a feeling that you've got to be totally flexible, you have to be totally accepting, and if you speak out in any way, even if it's because you want to improve the lot of students, then you're likely not to be employed the next month. At the moment there are quite a lot of teachers around, so that's another unspoken threat – if you won't do this, if you voice dissatisfaction, there's always someone else who can come in and take your place.

Most language schools recognise that they need a core of committed regulars who know the system and who can be relied upon to induct new teachers. Such teachers tend to guard their positions jealously, and consider themselves highly fortunate if they are offered a permanent position. Many sessional language teachers become part of stable workforces that remain loyal to particular language schools for many years – even though they are not permanent and do not receive holiday pay, sickness benefits or superannuation contributions. Such teachers become accustomed to finishing one class on a Friday and starting a new one with a new group of students on the following Monday. Typically they teach classes of up to 18 students for 23 hours a week, 48 weeks of the year. They know that if they are laid off because of a temporary downturn in student numbers, they will be the first to receive a phone call from the director of studies when numbers pick up again.

A further cause of frustration for language teachers is that, for those who wish to continue working within the same institution, there are likely to be relatively few opportunities for promotion to positions of responsibility. Typically, in any one institution, there will be one director of studies and, if a CELTA program is run, two or perhaps three teacher trainers. Such people tend to remain in their positions for many years, since the career ladder does not extend any higher. Unless they are prepared to relocate to other towns or cities, or to move overseas, lower-rung teachers are unlikely to find many opportunities for carving out a career.

A core of language teachers who entered the Australian Adult

Migrant English Program some years ago have enjoyed permanent positions for some time. The Federal Department of Immigration and Multicultural and Indigenous Affairs, which originally both owned and ran the service, made the decision in 1997 to invite competitive tenders from other institutions to run the service on its behalf. As a result the teaching of migrants is now contracted out to both public and private providers. For some time there was uncertainty about which teachers who worked for the public and private providers would be offered permanent positions, and which teachers would not. This uncertainty caused considerable anxiety, frustration and ill-feeling, with teachers who were not offered permanent positions being compelled to seek work elsewhere (their jobs having been reallocated to the newly appointed permanent staff). One such teacher, who had recently received a merit award for teaching and who believed that she had missed out on permanency because of a timing issue, eventually found an institution that offered her nine hours' teaching a week – which was subsequently reduced to six. On receiving an email on a Friday afternoon to tell her that her services were no longer required (her class having been merged with another one for logistical reasons), this teacher resolved to leave teaching and return to her previous job as a salesperson.

> The problem of the casualisation of the workforce is not limited to Australia. Reporting on the situation of part-time employment in TESOL in the USA, Graf (2003) states: 'The problem with flexible employment is not that it is available to those who want it, but that it is all that is available to many educators who would prefer secure, full-time contracts.' She proceeds to cite 'the proliferation of inferior part-time and temporary TESOL positions, especially in adult and higher education'.

The knock-on effect: teaching languages in primary and high schools

Ironically, the dominant position that the English language now enjoys has had a negative effect on the teaching of minority languages in Australian schools. Because of its isolated geographical position and its British-based language and culture, many Australians have developed insular attitudes. They have seen little reason to look beyond the shores of their island continent or to embrace other cultures or languages. Although the official government line is that Australia is a multicultural country that is unified in its diversity, the reality of the situation is somewhat different. Many Australians define themselves in terms of being 'ocker', a word that implies not only desirable qualities such as mateship, resourcefulness and good humour, but also less desirable attitudes such as intolerance, boorishness and chauvinism. Significant numbers of Australians have never travelled overseas (apart, perhaps, from a package holiday to Bali) and see little practical reason for their children to learn foreign languages. Occasionally parents even object to their children being given language homework. One father questioned the need for his son to do French homework, telling the teacher that it was interfering with his son's after-school sporting commitments.

Over the past few years the Western Australian government has sought to introduce compulsory foreign language learning for all children in the state (including those living in remote communities) between Years 3 and 10. Since there was a shortage of suitably qualified and experienced teachers, training courses were set up for people interested in training as language specialists. Some trainees had high levels of fluency in a foreign language but little experience of managing classes, while others had excellent class management skills but only a restricted (and often rusty) knowledge of the language they were being trained to teach. The languages that could be taught in schools were not stipulated. In Western Australia the most common languages taught in primary and high schools are Indonesian, French, Italian, Japanese and German. The language that any student learns depends on the school they attend, and on the availability of a teacher. Children in isolated communities, such as those living in remote Aboriginal settlements or on isolated farms or cattle stations, are taught languages through the School of Isolated and Distance Education. In Australia foreign languages or minority languages are known as 'LOTES' (Languages other than English), a term that is faintly derogatory since it defines all languages apart from English as 'other'.

While admirable in its intention, the decision to provide every Australian child with the opportunity to study a language other than English poses enormous logistical problems. In Year 3 (the year they turn eight) children typically learn a LOTE for 30 minutes a week, often from an itinerant teacher who must teach every child in the school and then move on and teach in other schools as well. When children from a number of feeder schools enter high school they regularly face one of two scenarios: either they must start the language that they have already been learning all over again (because their year intake includes children from feeder schools where other LOTES were taught), or they must start to learn a completely different language (because the one that they have previously studied is not on offer). Schools have devised a range of ingenious solutions to address this and the many other practical problems associated with compulsory LOTE teaching. In effect many schools in Western

Australia are as yet unable to provide LOTE tuition to all students beyond Year 8 (the first year of high school) – although additional federal funding has been promised. At the present time, because of timetabling problems, many LOTES are placed on options grid-lines in Years 9 and 10 (the second and third years of high school). This means that a student can only continue with a LOTE by rejecting a range of softer options such as dance, photography, jewellery-making or personal grooming.

Although different in detail, the situation regarding the teaching of modern foreign languages in schools is, broadly speaking, similar in Britain. The emergence of English as the lingua franca of international communication has resulted in a similar decline in the status of modern foreign languages within the school curriculum. Watts (2004: 64) reports that a sample of teachers in Britain identified a general climate of negativity towards foreign language learning, believing that this was dictated largely by the negative portrayal of 'Europe', 'foreigners' and 'all things foreign' in all parts of the British media and particularly in the popular press. Despite the support of professional organisations, it is likely that foreign-language teachers working in schools in the UK must at times feel as their Australian counterparts do – that teaching minority languages in schools is an uphill struggle.

Since 2004 it has no longer been a statutory requirement for school children in the UK to learn a modern foreign language after the age of 14 (Qualifications and Curriculum Authority: 2004). Ward (2005) reports findings from an Association for Language Learning survey which suggests that the opportunities to learn a foreign language at school are now also diminishing for pupils below the age of 14. These trends are occurring in the face of recommendations by the Nuffield Languages Inquiry (2000) for expanding language teaching in schools.

10.2 Major causes of frustration for language teachers

Apart from situational factors that can place excessive demands on language teachers, there are certain other aspects of language teaching that make experienced teachers feel particularly aggravated.

Public misconceptions

In the eyes of the general public the perception exists that English language teaching is something that anyone who speaks English can easily do: a quick certificate is all you need. Language teachers who view themselves as professionals know that nothing could be further from the truth. Having gained experience over many years and obtained postgraduate diplomas or master's degrees in applied linguistics, career language teachers find it particularly galling to be placed in the same category as fresh-faced young people straight off the CELTA course. They are keenly aware that there is an enormous qualitative difference between themselves and some of their colleagues. As one teacher complained, 'I sweated blood over my master's degree, and now here I am lumped together with all those youngsters who don't even know what a preposition is.' Some seasoned language teachers report that they no longer say what they do at social occasions because they are so fed up with the stock response along the lines of, 'Oh yes, that's what my neighbour's daughter does!' Everyone, it seems, knows someone in language teaching – just as everyone has something derogatory to say about declining linguistic standards.

> The low status of teaching in general, and of English language teaching in particular, coupled with the ease with which people can train as teachers and find jobs, is reflected in the ongoing debate about whether or not English language teaching can be described as a profession. The overwhelming consensus of opinion is that it cannot. See Clandfield and Kerr (2004) for a discussion on this issue.

Language teachers who work in the school system have learnt to cope as best they can with intractable problems relating to timetabling, class composition, class sizes and so on. The single most disappointing aspect of their jobs is the fact that their subject is so often undervalued by those who surround them: school principals, school administrators and fellow teachers. In the words of one teacher, 'LOTES are still marginalised in every school. No school considers them as important or valuable as science or maths or English.' When placed in a new school language teachers routinely have to fight for conditions under which they can teach their language effectively. One teacher with a good reputation – and therefore bargaining power – refused to teach until she was given a dedicated classroom in which she could display posters and other realia relating to her language, and which had enough space for students to move around and engage in communicative activities. Language teachers complain that students are more frequently withdrawn from their classes for extra-curricular activities, such as cricket training, than they are from other core subjects. They also complain bitterly about not being invited to senior staff meetings (where key timetabling decisions affecting them are made), even though they teach in a designated key curriculum area and are required to do budgets and other head-of-department duties. When she asked to be included in one such meeting, one language teacher recalled being brushed off by the school principal with the words, 'There's no need for you to be there – the head of maths will fill you in.'

Language teachers make huge efforts to raise the profile of their particular LOTE within their school. For example, some ensure that piles of publicity brochures, such as *Why learn Japanese,* are always available on the front desk of their schools, some write regular columns for their school newsletters with catchy titles such as *French is Fun!* while others ensure that language students are regularly presented with merit awards in assemblies. Time and again language teachers talk about the importance of 'winning the school principal over' or 'getting them on side'. They are acutely aware that the attitude of the principal towards language learning is crucial to their success in raising the status of their subject, because the principal's attitude can permeate the culture of the entire school. If they have a principal who sees their presence in the school as an irritant rather than an asset, their teaching lives are made even more difficult than they already are. Summing up the situation in high schools one language teacher said:

> If you weren't passionate about what you did you wouldn't bother to be a language teacher. It's so tiring. You need energy to keep up the fight, to keep the flag flying, to stop your LOTE (already an endangered species) from becoming extinct.

Being professionally stretched

A major cause of frustration for teachers engaged in teaching on intensive language courses for adults lies in the fact that, because the language schools for which they work are under increased economic pressure, they are expected to do more with less. They increasingly find themselves with less paid preparation time, larger classes, more limited resources, fewer teaching hours within which to achieve the same outcomes, reduced opportunities for professional development or liaison with colleagues – and students who expect to achieve more in a shorter period of time. These factors combine to make increasing numbers of language teachers feel that their professionalism is being stretched almost to breaking point. They cannot help feeling that their goodwill and desire to do their best for the students in their classes are being exploited for the benefit of others. In the words of one teacher:

> The main thing that makes you feel satisfied as a teacher is when you have a group of students and you know what they need and you have time and resources to design and deliver a course, to the best of your ability, that meets their needs. And it's when you can't do that – when you know you haven't put in enough time, for

example in planning and preparation, because of time constraints – all things like that mean that you come out of a class frustrated because you haven't been able to meet the needs that you can see are there. And the frustrating thing is, you know that you could – under the right circumstances.

Keeping up appearances

Language teachers find it much easier to teach adult students who have confidence in their teaching ability and in their overall level of competence. Experienced language teachers are particularly keen to preserve their professional integrity. Since they operate at the interface between the institutions for whom they work and the students who have paid for a service, it makes sense for them to convey the impression that the institution is as professional as they are. Unfortunately this is frequently not the case. Growing numbers of language teachers make remarks such as 'We seem to lurch from one week to another throwing resources together and pulling something out of the bag' or 'I feel a fraud, having to hold the whole thing together when it's chaos behind the scenes'. Remarks such as these suggest that teachers frequently see themselves as in the firing line, having to defend the inadequacies of their institutions against student criticism that may often be quite justified. Language teachers sometimes find themselves having to apologise for inadequate facilities: classrooms that do not have enough tables and chairs, overhead projectors that do not work, and so on. They find this embarrassing. Even though there are many institutions that have excellent facilities for students, there are many that do not. Tension builds up in the minds of language teachers when they find themselves struggling to behave professionally in environments that they regard as increasingly unprofessional. In the words of one teacher:

> There's a tension between your own conscience and what you're expected to do. You're trying to maintain old values in a new structure, and that leads to unhappiness. You try to talk about values and quality and the bosses look at you as if you've got horns.

Leaving the profession

Language teachers can easily become burnt out by what one teacher called 'the sheer relentlessness of it' and another termed 'the stress and tiredness from being constantly on display'. Increasing numbers of language teachers, especially women who are the secondary breadwinners

239

in their households, are making the decision to work part-time rather than full time – even when full-time work is available. Significant numbers of talented teachers are leaving the profession, their positions filled by people less well-qualified and experienced than themselves. A key reason for seeking alternative career paths is that language teaching offers few pathways for promotion, and makes it difficult for teachers without permanent positions to secure mortgages or be confident that they can support their families in the long term. When asked whether they would advise a young person today to go into English language teaching with a view to making it a lifelong career, many language teachers say that they would not, using expressions such as, 'Definitely not!' or 'No way! The job is far too fickle!'

10.3 The rewards of language teaching

> The feelings of the teachers described in this section are surprisingly similar to those expressed by the teachers in the 'Career and work rewards' chapter of Lortie's (1975) classic book *School teacher: A sociological study* – written 30 years ago.
>
> Of the three kinds of rewards to be gained from teaching, Lortie identifies 'psychic rewards' as being by far the most important. These psychic rewards, which he describes as consisting entirely of subjective valuations made in the course of work engagement (1975: 101), correspond to the intrinsic rewards described by language teachers in this section.

The contexts that have been described in the above sections suggest that language teachers have ample reasons to feel frustrated about their jobs. With all its disadvantages, why do language teachers continue in the profession? This section shows that for some teachers the low status, low pay, lack of permanency or any of the other generic aspects of designated career paths are outweighed by the ongoing personal rewards that can be reaped from the experience of classroom language teaching. This is particularly the case for married women with young families, who recognise the benefits of flexible teaching hours, and who welcome the opportunity to do a job that pays for childcare facilities and enables them to get out of the home and feel that they are part of the workforce.

> Lortie describes how teaching suits women, facilitating what he calls their 'in and out' plans. In his words, 'The energies and interests of women teachers flow back and forth between family and work claims in discernible, regular rhythms.' (1975: 94)

Intrinsic rewards

Seeing anybody learn anything, whether it is a toddler taking her or his first staggering steps or a flabby, adult non-swimmer developing into a sleek, proficient swimmer, is a heart-warming experience. It is particularly satisfying when you yourself have been instrumental in that person's development. Not surprisingly, language teachers feel a warm glow of satisfaction when they see individuals making sound linguistic progress within their classrooms. They make statements such as 'I love seeing their eyes light up', 'It's wonderful to see the penny drop' or 'I get great satisfaction when a student who has struggled with a concept or grammatical problem finally clicks. It's great to see their reactions – it's almost joyful.' Teachers also take pleasure in observing the personal development of students as they become more self-assured and outgoing. One teacher described her feelings in the following way:

> Watching our students graduate, that's absolutely brilliant. It makes me want to cry. Seeing them change from very immature, shy people into mature, confident, capable international people – that's very satisfying indeed.

It is clear that for many language teachers the intrinsic rewards of seeing students develop and grow both linguistically and personally more than compensate for the limited extrinsic rewards. As one teacher who had rejected a lucrative career in favour of language teaching explained, 'I'm not doing this job for the money. I'm doing it because it gives me satisfaction. For me the satisfaction takes the place of the higher salary I'd get in a better paid job.'

> 'It is of great importance to teachers to feel they have "reached" their students – their core rewards are tied to that perception. Other sources of satisfaction (e.g., private scholarly activities, relationships with adults) pale in comparison with teachers' exchanges with students and the feeling that students have learned.' Lortie (1975: 106)

Being your own boss

Within the confines of their classrooms, language teachers enjoy a high degree of autonomy. They value this freedom, making comments such as

Frustrations and rewards

'I love being my own boss in the classroom' or 'Once the door's closed behind you, you're in your little kingdom'. As demonstrated in previous chapters, although they normally have a syllabus outline to follow, an examination to prepare their students for or a set of competencies to work towards, once they are inside their classrooms all language teachers do their own thing to a greater or lesser extent. Many discover latent talents in creative areas such as acting, writing, drawing or music, and find it exhilarating to energise their classes through their own enthusiasms. One teacher with a love of Shakespeare regularly had students declaiming parts of Shakespeare's best-known speeches. Another with a passion for writing poetry had classes of migrant women writing moving poems about their life experiences, which she then 'published' in a series of books, properly bound and complete with illustrations. Language teachers with an ability to draw on the whiteboard are fortunate, as are those who can get their classes to sing along as they strum on their guitars on Friday afternoons.

Professional satisfaction

Language learning is never straightforward or predictable. Students regularly misunderstand things, fail to learn things, find easy things difficult and difficult things easy, do not respond to tried-and-tested techniques, are not interested in planned topics and so on. Because of their relative pedagogic freedom, described by one teacher as 'controlled freedom to do whatever you want in the name of learning', language teachers are able to devise ways of overcoming these pedagogic hurdles – a process that, if successful, is deeply satisfying. Teachers feel rewarded after explaining something in a simpler way so that more students understand, or coming across a reading passage that is a perfect vehicle for consolidating something previously taught. 'It links in perfectly', they say to themselves as they make a beeline for the photocopier. Pedagogic challenges provide language teachers with the opportunity to exercise their professional judgement – a process that is inherently satisfying.

Language teachers are also rewarded when their lessons go well: when there is a buzz of productive activity in the classroom as students interact with one another to complete a task. When this happens teachers tend to sit back for a few moments and observe their class with pride. This is *their* class, and the students in it are *their* students, and here they are busily doing the prescribed task and taking responsibility for their learning. One teacher used the term 'presiding over the class' to describe how she saw herself when she was taking a back seat and allowing her students to interact naturally with one another, with minimal interference on her part. Moments such as these are some of the most rewarding ones for language teachers: in their minds, they are observing the process of learning actually happening.

Intercultural satisfaction

Many people who move into the area of English language teaching do so because they are deeply interested in other people and other cultures. For them it is a privilege to teach classes containing students from a range of ethnic, linguistic and cultural backgrounds. In the words of one teacher:

> I just love the people, just meeting new people all the time and their personalities and their sense of humour and their cultures, their cultural perspectives, and I think it's the best job in the world from that point of view.

Other teachers love teaching multicultural classes because of the opportunity it provides for their own personal growth:

> I'm forever learning off my students, learning about them, and I think that's what I love as well. There's such variety. I'll turn up at the beginning of term and I've got someone from a country that I really don't know that much about and I think, Wow! I just want to learn from them. . . I feel like I'm working overseas in my own country.

Many language teachers are also motivated by a desire to do something worthwhile and to be of service to the community. Those involved in teaching migrants feel particularly gratified in this regard. As one teacher said:

> They desperately need English, so you're feeling like a kind of saint. You're giving them this tool, language, with which to survive in their adopted country. It's terribly good for your self-esteem – it can give you a real buzz.

Teachers of migrants are amply rewarded at the end of their courses by receiving tokens of gratitude in the form of cards containing heartfelt expressions of thanks, flowers and a wide variety of small and not-so-small presents. Teachers of fee-paying students also receive plenty of 'warm fuzzies' at the end term, particularly when their classes have been together for many hours a week for lengthy periods of time (as is the case with exam-preparation classes). Cards are frequently signed by everyone in the class, and a communal present purchased. One teacher explained the personal rewards that she received from teaching adult migrants in the following way:

> You give such a lot, but you get so much back. They really end up caring for you as a person. It's incredible. So that's why, when

243

people say, 'Why are you still teaching migrants?' That's why. Where else would you get that?

Language classrooms as microcosms of society

One of the greatest sources of gratification for language teachers is seeing students from widely differing countries and cultures relating well to one another in their class: a Swiss boy developing a friendship with a Japanese girl, a Bosnian woman becoming close friends with an Indonesian woman, and so on. It gives language teachers deep feelings of pleasure to watch students in their classes sharing experiences and coming to the realisation that the commonalities between their cultures are more profound than their differences. Talking about a class activity in which she had got her students to focus on cross-cultural problems within the class, one teacher commented:

> It broke down so many barriers – but it was the camaraderie while it was going on. . . They were so sympathetic to one another and it was so nice and, oh, it was just lovely, it almost brought tears to your eyes – the friendships, the bonds.

It is particularly heart-warming for teachers when they see a rapprochement occurring within their classroom between students from countries that have had a long history of antagonism – or have actively been at war with one another. One teacher was impressed to learn from a Korean student that the first time in his life that he had ever spoken to a Japanese person was in her classroom in Australia. A migrant class with few European students contained one student from Serbia and another from Bosnia. On the last day of term the teacher gave a small present to each student, inviting them to come one by one to the front of the class. When the Serbian student received his present he ceremonially handed it to the Bosnian with the words, 'This is to show that Bosnians and Serbians can be friends' – a symbolic gesture that the teacher found particularly moving. Language teachers, it seems, view their classrooms as microcosms of society. In the words of one teacher, 'When I see all those good intercultural things happening in my class, I feel that there's hope for the world'.

10.4 Conclusion

Teaching is a service profession and for language teachers the service itself is the reward. Language teachers recognise that there are limited extrinsic rewards in terms of pay, status, career structure and so on. But many are prepared to accept this – provided that they are able to reap the intrinsic rewards of being able to teach effectively and, as a result, to earn the respect and gratitude of their students. What causes language teachers high levels of anxiety and frustration is when circumstances make it increasingly difficult and sometimes impossible for them to reap the intrinsic rewards of teaching in professional ways.

Summary

- English language teaching is an enormous growth area, with language teaching institutions of variable quality opening up around the world at an exponential rate.
- In recent years the overall context within which language teachers find themselves working has become increasingly market-driven, with new language schools with aggressive marketing strategies putting pressure on established institutions to reduce fees in order to remain competitive.
- The extrinsic rewards of language teaching are limited. Generally speaking, language teachers have low status, low pay, low rates of permanency and limited opportunities for career advancement.
- Language teachers, many of whom went into language teaching for idealistic reasons, increasingly find themselves struggling to maintain pedagogic standards within organisations that are increasingly driven by financial imperatives.
- This situation places teachers under considerable pressure: the institutions for which they work are being financially squeezed, while they themselves are being pedagogically stretched in terms of what they are expected to achieve.
- The exponential growth of English has had a negative effect on the status of language teaching in schools.
- The practical problems involved in supplying effective foreign language tuition to primary and high-school children have placed language teachers in schools in an almost untenable position.
- Despite their poor conditions of service, English language teachers reap enormous intrinsic rewards from teaching adult learners from a range of ethnic, cultural and linguistic backgrounds.
- For language teachers the rewards of teaching involve having the freedom to teach creatively, feeling that they are of service to the community, and seeing cross-cultural synergies occur in their classrooms.

Looking ahead

The following chapter focuses on the motivational factors that underpin the classroom behaviour of language teachers, and which lead them to behave in the ways that they do in their classrooms.

245

11   What drives language teachers

The previous chapter described the range of contexts in which language teachers in English-speaking countries typically work. It focused on both the frustrations and the rewards of language teaching – showing how the frustrations of being a language teacher often relate to factors beyond the teacher's control, while the rewards are personal ones that result from interacting with responsive students and teaching in personally satisfying ways. The chapter demonstrated that for language teachers the intrinsic rewards of teaching far outweigh extrinsic rewards such as status or money. It showed that frustration and dissatisfaction occur when opportunities to reap the intrinsic rewards of teaching are reduced.

The present chapter outlines the key assumptions, beliefs and values of experienced language teachers. Section 11.1 points out why it is necessary to tread cautiously when seeking to investigate the assumptions and beliefs of language teachers – and the motivational forces that appear to drive their classroom actions. Section 11.2 outlines the assumptions and beliefs about language learning that underpin communicative language teaching as it is implemented in western educational contexts. It also describes how language teachers teach pragmatic versions of CLT that are in line with their preferred practices and personal assumptions about classroom language learning. Section 11.3 describes the values shared by language teachers, showing that their classroom behaviour is driven by a desire to keep their classes functioning as unified groups and maintain rapport with individuals.

11.1 Standing back: a note of caution on assumptions and beliefs

In this chapter I stand back from the detailed data that forms the basis of this book, identify the shortcomings of interview-based research, and provide a critical interpretation of the teachers' words. In particular, I draw attention to certain inconsistencies in the assumptions and beliefs about language teaching provided by practising teachers working within the communicative tradition. I advance a number of reasons why language teachers make the assumptions, articulate the beliefs and hold the values that they do about classroom language teaching.

The limitations of evidence supplied by teachers

Language teachers vary enormously in the extent to which they articulate why they teach in the ways they do, and why they behave in certain ways in their classrooms. For many of them language teaching involves getting on with the daily business of teaching – getting the job done as efficiently and as effectively as possible – and then moving on to think about tomorrow's lesson without much further reflection. For some language teachers, teaching certain classes may be a matter of survival: making pragmatic classroom decisions based not on deep- seated beliefs about quality teaching, but on how to keep control of the class and survive till the end of the lesson.

Most language teachers, even when fully in control, seldom have the time to think too deeply or to agonise too much about whether or not they did the right thing or whether a different approach might have been more effective. Many do not have the inclination to sit down and reflect on the reasons that underlie their classroom decision-making. Indeed, on many occasions there may not be any conscious reasoning behind teachers' classroom actions: they simply do things on the spur of the moment, in the way that seems best at the time. Comments such as 'I just found myself doing it' or 'It seemed like the right thing to do at the time' suggest that for much of the time language teachers rely on their gut feeling or intuitive sense of what is appropriate for their class at any given moment.

> Brown (2000: 292–3) provides an outline of intuition from a cognitive psychological perspective, pointing out that one of the important characteristics of intuition is its nonverbalisability. By this he means that people are not able to give much verbal explanation of why they have made a particular decision or solution.

Why formal research can produce misleading results

Language teachers who agree to participate in research projects fall into a different category. For them the opportunity to talk to a researcher is often a welcome one, especially if they have an interest in a particular aspect of teaching, are considering further study, or are teaching in an innovative way of which they are proud and for which they seek recognition. Some language teachers are naturally keen to grasp opportunities to share with others their reflections on their professional practice. Once they are participants in a research project, teacher informants normally try to provide the researcher with the information they think is required: if the researcher wants them to describe the factors that underpin their classroom decision-making, they normally do their best to oblige. If they know they are to be observed, they may go out of their way to prepare more innovative lessons than they might do otherwise. Personal pride is at stake: nobody wants to be observed teaching a boring lesson.

Any information provided by informants who are describing their thoughts and actions in naturalistic settings must be treated with caution for a number of reasons. First, teachers who agree to participate in research are typically articulate individuals who are outgoing and confident of their abilities as teachers. Not surprisingly they tend to be happy to share their beliefs and insights with a researcher. They will be keen to talk about their successes rather than their failures – about the things they are proud of, rather than the things that they are not. Such teachers cannot be regarded as representative of language teachers in general.

Second, when asked to provide reasons for specific classroom actions after the event, it is tempting for language teachers to be economical with the truth. They may invent a reason for doing something – a reason that they did not have at the time, having perhaps acted purely on a whim. They may provide a different reason for doing something because they do not care to admit the real reason – such as getting students to complete a worksheet because they wanted to keep the class quiet. Alternatively, they may provide a new reason for a classroom action because they have forgotten what the original one actually was.

The third problem associated with collecting, categorising and describing the thoughts and impressions of language teachers is that these are constantly shifting. The pedagogic world view of a teacher on any given day may differ significantly from the one they held on the previous day because of a seminal experience with a particular class or student. The views of language teachers are constantly developing and evolving as insights gained from new teaching experiences are fed into their personal frameworks of understanding of what language teaching is all about.

The flexible nature of teachers' thoughts, views and impressions, which are so often bound up with how they feel at the time they are interviewed, make life extremely difficult for researchers. Those who wish to investigate the belief systems of practising language teachers naturally want to pin down the views, categorise them to provide a semblance of order and structure, and present them to the reader in the form of descriptions of 'what is'. The trouble is that, like the weather, teachers' views are changeable.

Nevertheless, despite the limitations of the research approach outlined above, it was possible to identify a number of common assumptions and beliefs about language learning in communicative classrooms from the studies upon which this book is based. These commonalities emerge from what the teachers were collectively saying and doing in their classrooms – commonalities that appear to transcend the fact that every teacher who provided the data for this book taught in an individualistic way.

11.2 Assumptions and beliefs underpinning the communicative approach

When invited to provide personal definitions of communicative language teaching, language teachers are sometimes hesitant to do so, as if sensing that there is a 'correct' response that they should give. Those who readily supply definitions tend, as might be expected, to focus on the interactive aspects of the approach. To one teacher CLT was 'the meaningful exchange of information' while to another it was 'teaching what they want to talk about and what they need to know and what they want to communicate'. These views reflect the central precept of the communicative approach: that a second language is not a body of knowledge that can be learnt in a systematic, cumulative way. Rather, it is a set of interactive skills that can be developed through practice gained by an ongoing, sustained effort to communicate with others.

Key features of the communicative approach

According to Lightbown and Spada (1999: 95), in communicative instructional settings:

- 'There is a limited amount of error correction, and meaning is emphasised over form.
- Input is simplified and made comprehensible by the use of contextual cues, props and gestures, rather than through *structural grading*.
- Learners usually have only limited time for learning. Sometimes, however, subject-matter courses taught through the second language can add time for language learning (. . .)
- Contact with proficient or native speakers of the language is limited. As with traditional instruction, it is often only the teacher who is a proficient speaker. Learners have considerable exposure to the interlanguage of other learners. This naturally contains

---

> errors which would not be heard in an environment where the interlocutors are native speakers.
> - A variety of discourse types are introduced through stories, role-playing and the use of 'real-life' materials such as newspapers, television broadcasts and field trips.
> - There is little pressure to perform at high levels of accuracy, and there is often a greater emphasis on comprehension than on production, especially in the early stages of learning.
> - Modified input is a defining feature of this approach to instruction. The teacher in these classes makes every effort to speak to students at a level of language they can understand. In addition, other students speak a simplified language.'
>
> For alternative definitions of the communicative approach see Richards and Rodgers' five principles that reflect a communicative view of language and language learning (2001: 172), or Brown's four interconnected characteristics of CLT (2000: 266).

Relatively few language teachers spontaneously articulate the central tenets of the communicative approach during the course of interviews. An exception is the following teacher, who said:

> Sometimes you think, 'My god, are they learning anything?' But gradually they are, and their speaking becomes a little bit more accurate. You look at their faces and you see them correcting themselves. . . It's a gradually expanding thing. It's not building blocks. I see it more like a set of stairs, where everything increases through use, through hearing things again and again, through having to speak and having to say the same things – or different variations of the same thing, again and again.

In the view of another teacher, 'You have to trigger off the students in order to lift the language out', while a third commented, 'You can't teach people English. You structure the situation so that they learn.' Comments such as these suggest that these particular teachers regard language learning as an ongoing developmental process – seeing themselves as facilitators whose role is to aid, rather than to direct, the learning process.

While being interviewed language teachers regularly reveal their attitudes and values, together with a range of assumptions about language learning. Particularly if the interviews are wide-ranging ones in which they are encouraged to talk about the things that are important to them, teachers become increasingly relaxed and expansive. As a result they find themselves revealing their assumptions in a natural, unforced way.

During the course of such interviews teachers can be asked to explain the reasoning behind their classroom actions. The following kinds of questions are likely to lead to the articulation of assumptions about the nature of language teaching and learning:

- 'That's interesting. Why did you decide to do that?'
- 'Do you do this kind of thing regularly? Why?'
- 'You said you think it's important to do that. Can you explain why?'

During interviews teachers tend to reveal their assumptions about language learning in a relatively low-key manner, beginning their sentences with words such as 'I think' or simply 'Because'. Occasionally certain individuals use stronger language. One teacher, recalling a negative experience of teaching in a school in Africa and being criticised for not finishing the coursebook by the end of term, said, 'My philosophy – my conviction – is that what is important is not how much you cover, but how much the students learn'. Teachers also articulate their beliefs strongly when describing the driving forces that underpin their classroom behaviour (see Section 11.3). In the main, however, it is unusual for language teachers to state their beliefs in forceful ways.

Language teachers also reveal their assumptions about language learning through their classroom talk. Experienced language teachers regularly exhort their students to do certain things – such as speaking in a sustained way without worrying overmuch about making errors – providing, as they do so, the rationale behind the advice that they are giving. To convey his assumption that successful language learning requires active engagement, one teacher would routinely draw a picture on the board of a student's head with the top hinged back, with a jug next to it, and say to the class:

> You can't sit there passively and expect me to pour English into your heads. It won't work – it can't work. I can't do it, and you just wouldn't learn anything that way. You have to participate in the process.

Classroom homilies of this kind provide evidence of teachers' beliefs about how students are most likely to succeed as language learners.

Pragmatic approaches to CLT

Alongside assumptions relating to the communicative approach, language teachers hold individual sets of assumptions and beliefs about classroom language learning that are informed by many factors. These include: school-based memories of both good and bad learning experiences; personal language-learning experiences (both inside and outside the classroom); the quality, extent and focus of teacher training programs; past and current experiences of language teaching; in-service teacher development programs; the influence of respected colleagues.

> 'As the teacher gains experience and knowledge, he or she will begin to develop an individual approach or personal method of teaching, one that draws on an established approach or method but that also uniquely reflects the teacher's individual beliefs, values, principles and experiences.' Richards and Rodgers (2001: 251)

Often memories of particular learning or teaching events remain strongly etched on teachers' minds, reinforcing their beliefs and practices. One high-school second-language teacher expressed a firm belief in chorus work, because it gave nervous individuals the option of mouthing words silently. She explained that this belief was the result of her childhood experience of playing in a youth band on an old trumpet with valves that tended to stick. Terrified of creating a sound that would be out of tune with the notes played by the other trumpeters, this teacher reported 'playing' in the band for an extended period of time by doing the correct fingering but never creating any sound at all.

Teachers report many other events, large and small, that have influenced their classroom practices. With some, such events appear to have resonated so strongly that they have never been forgotten. One teacher reported that she always wrote her objectives for each lesson on the board – ticking each one off as it was achieved. She explained that her belief in the importance of doing this was based on the memory of a high-school teacher who had always used this technique, thereby letting the class know the direction of each lesson (something that, as a student, she had greatly valued). Another teacher resolved never to jump to conclusions too quickly – having given a student 'zero' for a test, because she thought she had cheated, and seen a tear roll down the girl's cheek. A third always asked questions generally to the class before selecting someone to answer, rather than pouncing unexpectedly on individuals – explaining that she remembered how it felt 'to be that child sitting there in a pool of sweat, dreading being picked upon by the teacher'.

Teachers also remember the words of wisdom of experienced teachers who have made a particular impression on them – either during their initial training, their early days of teaching or in professional development workshops. Often what remains firmly imprinted on teachers' minds is nothing more than an isolated remark. One teacher recalled a teacher telling her many years ago that humour could be used to judge whether or not you had your class 'with you'. Another teacher commented:

> One of the first things I was told when I came here, by one quite wise teacher, was that they'd learn despite me, so not to worry too much about it, that they would learn anyway, no matter what I did.

When statements such as these resonate strongly with teachers they are not easily forgotten – but go into their memory banks, from where it is likely they will continue to influence classroom decisions for many years to come.

Hybrid versions of CLT

A key feature of communicative language teaching is that it is an approach rather than a method. Methods dictate in relatively narrow, prescriptive ways how teachers should teach, whereas approaches are broad frameworks that are flexible enough to accommodate a wide range of individual beliefs and practices. One of the strengths of the communicative approach is that it can mean different things to different people. Even teachers working with parallel classes within the same institution implement the approach in strikingly different ways. Indeed, it would be no exaggeration to say that there are as many individual versions of the communicative approach as there are teachers.

> Lightbown and Spada (1999: 95) provide the following definition: 'The communicative approach is based on innatist and interactionist theories of language learning and emphasizes the communication of meaning both between teacher and students and among the students themselves in group or pair work. Grammatical forms are focused on *only* in order to clarify meaning. The assumption is that learners *can* and *must* do the grammatical development *on their own*.' [italics added]

It is now widely accepted that it is impractical to adopt the communicative approach in its 'pure' form as defined by Lightbown and Spada (above): setting up learning tasks and then only focusing on grammar or other technical aspects of the language in passing, as the need arises. In effect most language teachers adopt a pragmatic approach. They design their lessons and courses so that, while there is a strong communicative element in each lesson, there is also room for specific linguistic input. For example, teachers normally pre-teach key items of vocabulary prior to having their class read a text – or focus on specific grammatical structures prior to having their students undertake a piece of writing in which those structures are to be incorporated. As one teacher remarked, 'You can't teach communicatively all the time. You've got to feed in the language too.'

> Thompson (1996) believes that a practical form of CLT has emerged that represents good contemporary practice. According to this consensus view of CLT, Thompson states that it is now fully accepted that an appropriate amount of class time should be devoted to grammar. However, he points out that this has not meant a simple return to a traditional treatment of grammar rules.

Although current orthodoxy suggests that it may be more appropriate to have students engage in communicative tasks before focusing on linguistic forms (see the box below), many teachers prefer to 'feed in' the language before rather than after students complete tasks. According to one teacher, 'Whatever grammar I teach I try to apply it to a communicative context and try to see how they can relate it to things that they are doing in their own field and their own life here, their own experience'. For another teacher, 'Being communicative is when you're actually using the grammar or whatever it is in a situation that they can relate to and want to talk about'. For both these teachers, focus on the form of the language occurs prior to focus on the meaning.

> **Comment**
>
> Common sense dictates that, when teaching beginner-level classes, it is appropriate for teachers to focus on form, feeding in a range of appropriate words and phrases that will enable students to interact with their peers. However, when teaching students who already have some knowledge of the target language, teachers have more flexibility: they can focus on form either before or after they provide opportunities for the class to focus on meaning.
>
> For a description of various frameworks that teachers can use for designing their lessons see Harmer (2001: 78). These frameworks, which are commonly used for training purposes, enable trainees to conceptualise the focus of learning activities and tasks. Nowadays fewer trainers promote the traditional 'PPP' (Presentation, Practice and Production) framework because it is considered to be out of

keeping with humanistic, learner-centred approaches. It is increasingly common for trainers to promote either the flexible 'ARC' framework (Authentic use, Restricted use and Clarification) proposed by Scrivener (1994) or the 'TBL' (Task-Based Learning) framework proposed by Willis (1996). The latter advocates having students complete tasks using their existing linguistic resources (thereby focusing on meaning) and only later study the language that fluent or native speakers typically use in the task situation (thereby focusing on form).

In reality, many teachers working within the communicative tradition, and particularly those who have been teaching for a number of years, continue to follow the more traditional 'PPP' format.

The specific ways in which teachers provide linguistic input are extremely varied, and reflect their individual beliefs about how language can most effectively be learnt. These beliefs in turn reflect the educational backgrounds and/or the ways in which teachers were trained. One teacher who had trained as a language teacher some 25 years ago, and who had a good knowledge of both classical Latin and two European languages, regularly gave his students written structural drills and sentence transformation exercises so that the students could 'get the solid structures right'. This teacher did not expect students to read any meaning into the de-contextualised sentences that he had them create and then read aloud to be checked for grammatical accuracy. However, he firmly believed that his students' language would improve as a result of focusing consciously on the structure of the language, saying on one occasion, 'She can now use the inverted form ('Had I had a compass I wouldn't have got lost') that she couldn't use before'.

In the view of Harmer (2003: 289), modern coursebooks are not significantly more communicative than they used to be. While acknowledging that such books provide opportunities for discussion and other forms of speaking and writing tasks, Harmer states: 'Almost all of them are still based on a grammatical syllabus largely unchanged from the structural-situational pattern books of the 1950s, or the 1960/70s coursebooks of Louis Alexander.'

If Harmer's statement is correct, it is not surprising that some language teachers teach in ways that are out of keeping with the key assumptions underlying the communicative approach.

The beliefs of the above teacher contrast strongly with those of other teachers regarding the value of grammar exercises. Some teachers state openly that they believe grammar exercises to be a waste of time – because they can see little evidence of transfer when their students actually come to communicate. Such teachers regularly report that, as soon as their students focus on what they are saying or writing (that is, on the meaning rather than the form), accuracy goes out of the window. Interestingly, many teachers report continuing to give their students grammar exercises – not because they believe that these will do them any good, but because they believe that completing them will give their students (provided they get the answers right) the feeling that they have achieved something concrete.

> In the words of Karavas-Doukas (1996: 187), 'Despite the widespread adoption of the communicative approach by textbooks and curricula around the world, research suggests that communicative language teaching principles in classrooms are rare, with most teachers professing commitment to the communicative approach but following more structural approaches in their classrooms.'
>
> Sato (2002: 45) cites a number of studies that support the findings of Karavas-Doukas. Sato's study of the beliefs of ten teachers of Japanese in Australia (Sato and Kleinsasser, 1999) yielded similar results. Not only did the beliefs of the teachers have little in common with CLT as conceptualised in the theoretical literature, but the teachers also claimed to make relatively little use of CLT in class.

Some teachers hold parallel sets of beliefs about language learning that might seem self-contradictory. For example, one teacher stated categorically that in her view language learning was habit formation, and had her students imitate models of correct language in the classroom. However, she also encouraged her students to read newspapers and to share with the class interesting things that they'd read or heard. Describing how she exhorted her students, this teacher said:

> I go on to them about reading books and learning the language unconsciously. I say to them, 'You don't know you're doing it, but you're absorbing the structures, just learning how we say things, in a natural way'.

This teacher held a behaviourist view of language learning (seeing language learning as a matter of being trained to speak correctly) when it came to classwork. However, when it came to advising her students how best to develop their linguistic skills outside class time, she held a language-acquisition view of language learning (seeing linguistic development as something that would happen naturally when students had the need to communicate in the real world). This teacher's pragmatic approach was based on her desire to cater for all the students in her class. Experience had taught her that different students had different learning styles – and that not all students would respond to her exhortations.

> In a study of teacher decision-making in the adult ESL classroom Smith (1996) found that experienced teachers first select from a range of theoretical ideas those aspects which correlate with their personal beliefs and use the surface features (the techniques) they have found to be effective from experience to meet their practical needs (1996: 208). She also found that, while teacher decisions were guided by a coherent set of personal beliefs, these teachers' use of theory was eclectic. This enabled them to teach in ways that accommodated opposing theoretical perspectives: the product view of language as a product to be mastered, and the process view of teaching language as a communicative process. The findings of Smith support the notion of language teachers practising hybrid versions of CLT.

The fact that they routinely focus on structural aspects of the language – thereby implicitly acknowledging that classroom language learning is as much about inputting linguistic forms as it is about providing students with opportunities to develop linguistic proficiency through interaction – shows that experienced language teachers are pragmatic. They are prepared to cater not only for their students' needs, but also for their wants. Aware that their students need to develop oral proficiency, they provide multiple opportunities for oral interaction. However, conscious of their students' desire to be taught in more time-honoured ways, they also provide 'building block'-type activities that focus on discrete aspects of the language. As one teacher of a beginner-level class of adult migrants from the former Yugoslavia commented:

> The students in my class need very structured stuff. They're good when you give them something definite to do. They get their heads down and they do it.

Language teachers are often quite open about the fact that they have grafted the communicative approach onto their own preferred teaching approach. One teacher claimed to have taught in exactly the same way for fourteen years – simply calling his approach whatever the current name happened to be. Most teachers, however, believe that it is appropriate to teach in an eclectic way – selecting from a range of techniques that they have mastered whichever seems most appropriate for the class they are currently teaching. Describing this approach, one teacher said:

> To be quite honest, I think what happens is, you learn a new method and so you incorporate that, and then another one comes in, and you incorporate that a bit, and then another one comes in and you incorporate that too. So you end up doing a bit of a smorgasbord – like we're doing competency-based teaching now. But we still teach grammar, we still teach functions, and we still try and work in the communicative vein, so in a way we do lots of different methods.

The specific ways in which individual teachers implement the various 'methods' are strikingly different – reflecting personal beliefs about how language is best taught. One teacher who had his students read aloud on a regular basis made the following comment:

> A lot of teachers think it's taboo to get students reading aloud, so they don't do it. Well, that's a load of rubbish! How else are you going to check their pronunciation? I don't like to check their pronunciation when they're speaking spontaneously, otherwise you're going to make them stutter, stammer, get a complex. But they know now that when I get them to read aloud – that's when I'm going to check their pronunciation. And they appreciate that.

In contrast, another teacher did the exact opposite. She explained that she would never dream of having students in her class read aloud in front of everyone because the students would feel too intimidated – recalling her own school experiences of feeling terrified when required to stand up in front of the class and read aloud. This particular teacher did, however, correct students' pronunciation as they were speaking – pointing out that she did it in a low-key manner intended not to interrupt the overall flow of what the students were saying. It is likely that the approaches of both these teachers were equally effective, since they both taught in line with their beliefs and were consistent and purposeful in their classroom practices.

In conclusion, for pragmatic reasons many language teachers adopt a 'belt-and-braces' approach in the way they teach. They not only provide their students with opportunities to acquire the target language by communicating freely with one another, but also focus consciously on 'inputting' new linguistic forms. By so doing they are accommodating two quite different sets of assumptions. On the one hand they hold conventional assumptions that underpin the communicative approach. These are embedded in the view of language acquisition as an ongoing developmental process that occurs naturally as students struggle to express themselves in the target language. On the other hand they harbour personal, individualised assumptions about how language learning is most effectively acquired in language class-rooms. These reflect the view that classroom language learning involves the constant expansion of linguistic knowledge and the development of skills in a series of incremental steps.

Comment

To some extent the compromise between focusing on content and focusing on form is textbook-driven. Popular language textbooks such as *Headway* are multi-layered, following a structural sequence and focusing on grammar, vocabulary, phonology and skills, while other more recent textbooks, such as the *Cutting Edge* series, include extended tasks in which skills are integrated. Communicative language teaching is therefore presented as a comprehensive package of what one trainer called 'linguistic bits and pieces'. The format of textbooks such as these negates the idea of second language acquisition being solely a natural developmental process.

Shifting beliefs: a minority perspective

The above evidence suggests that the personal belief systems of the majority of language teachers are remarkably stable and resistant to change. While they have the capacity to expand and develop their personal repertoires of teaching techniques, the evidence suggests that language teachers adopt strategies and techniques selectively, adapt them in subtle ways and slot them into pre-existing belief systems. It seems that language teachers are able to integrate ideas that are congruent with their beliefs into their pre-existing belief systems – and to reject or ignore others.

Pajares (1992: 324) states that a recurring theme to have emerged from research into teacher beliefs is the resistant-to-change nature of educational beliefs. He cites a number of studies that have found that beliefs are formed early and tend to self-perpetuate, persevering even against contradictions caused by reason, time, schooling or experience.

Although the majority of language teachers make no mention of their beliefs having shifted over time, a minority make a point of saying that their beliefs have indeed changed and that they now no longer hold the same beliefs as they did in the past. One teacher explained that for years she had been 'utterly convinced' that it was the layout of the classroom that led to the development of a positive group atmosphere in her classes. Based on this assumption she had always made sure that she got to class early on the first day of each course so that she could arrange the tables into a semi-circle, or open 'U', facing the front of the room. After teaching in a cramped room in which the tables could not be arranged into an open 'U' – and finding that just such a positive atmosphere developed – she reported that her belief had now changed.

Shifts in teachers' belief systems often occur with regard to teaching writing. One teacher, who had been a firm believer in having students learn to write through copying models, reported her conversion in the following way:

> A few years ago I became a convert to process writing. I believe it's by far the best way to learn to write, because I've seen students learn so much by it. I remember a high-level Swiss student writing out instructions for how to make an apple pie, and struggling as she did so to come to grips with the use of the definite and indefinite articles. It might have seemed an easy task, but it wasn't at all – and she herself said how much she'd learnt from the experience. Now that I've seen with my own eyes how much students learn from a process approach I find teaching by showing students models and getting them to copy them artificial and formulaic – like painting by numbers. I just *know* that they learn more by writing and rewriting their stuff – because I've seen it with my own eyes.

All things are relative. Another teacher reported having gone a step further in her thinking, saying, 'I don't think you teach people that there are cycles, and that you draft and redraft. That's too artificial. I think you just redraft as you go along.' This teacher put her beliefs into practice, explaining that she routinely had her class (a small class of advanced-level students) gradually build up a text in a collaborative manner, which she would write up on the whiteboard.

Comment

Teachers whose beliefs have shifted may find that circumstances prevent them from continuing to teach in line with their recently refined beliefs. Tsui (1996: 97–119) reports an interesting case study of a young Chinese ESL teacher who adopted a process approach to the teaching of writing, but was subsequently compelled to revert to a modified version of the product approach because of time constraints and the need to prepare students for examinations. This teacher was evidently satisfied with the compromise solution that she was able to reach.

The strength of the relationship between teachers' beliefs and their class-room practices is illustrated by the angst that is expressed by certain teachers when they find themselves in a position of having to teach in ways that run contrary to their personal beliefs. One teacher complained of regularly feeling 'like a round peg in a square hole' when teaching on a course that was tightly constraining and which prevented her from teaching in ways that were in tune with her personal beliefs. She described her feelings in the following way:

> I don't find myself at one with the teaching philosophy of the course, which is essentially a product one. You input specific techniques and then the students churn out work. I find it difficult because I'm more of an organic teacher. I see myself helping the students develop their skills for themselves. I see myself essentially in the position of a facilitator and helper, rather than as an authoritarian teacher in control of everything they do. This means that I'm in a constant state of tension because the course, with its huge amount of material to cover and the vast amount of marking, doesn't allow me to be the kind of teacher I want to be – it's always 'push, push, push'. Everything is set in stone and there isn't room for personal creativity – and I feel straightjacketed by the endless stream of assessments.

Another teacher explained that, if put in such a situation, she would subvert the system and continue to teach in the way she believed was right. A third teacher remarked that she could no longer teach from coursebooks because she no longer believed that simply following the designated coursebook was the best way of meeting the needs of any class. As mentioned in Chapter 10, being compelled to teach in ways that are out of keeping with personal beliefs is one of the major causes of teacher dissatisfaction.

In sum, only a small proportion of teachers draw attention to the fact that their beliefs have shifted over time. When they recount shifts in their beliefs about what they consider important in language teaching and learning, the shifts are typically away from a step-by-step, incremental view of language learning and towards a more organic, developmental view of the process. The direction of these shifts suggests that the personal beliefs of these particular teachers are becoming more closely aligned to the assumptions that underpin the communicative approach.

> **Comment**
>
> An interesting issue currently being debated is the degree to which CLT can, and should, be adapted to local contexts (see articles by both Bax and Harmer, 2003). Bax argues that CLT has been applied to many situations without regard to the local context. Harmer, meanwhile, argues that it is unreasonable to expect teachers, who are the product of their culture, their training, their learning and their experiences, to teach in ways that may not harmonise with their belief in the essentially humanistic and communicative nature of language.

11.3 Values shared by experienced language teachers

> I think the classroom has to be a happy place, with a non-threatening environment. Intrinsic to their learning, which is communication-based, is the fact that they're happy to be there. I can't teach them a lot unless they're interacting with each other and with me.

The above comment by an experienced teacher encapsulates what language teachers within the communicative tradition believe to be of value: the overall atmosphere of the classroom. This belief permeates the present book: language teachers universally value classes that function as happy, responsive, cohesive groups. The following summary of the core chapters demonstrates that the ongoing efforts of experienced language teachers to keep their classes functioning as unified communities of learners reflects their shared belief in the importance of class cohesion.

Chapter 4 showed how language teachers strive to establish warm, friendly, protective classroom environments within which students will feel comfortable enough to experiment with the target language. It showed how they wish their classes to function as protective, non-judgemental support groups within which students can feel secure in the knowledge that they are not going to be ridiculed by their peers as they struggle to express themselves in the target language.

Chapters 5 and 6 demonstrated that language teachers are unhappy with classes that function in fragmented ways. It showed that they go to considerable lengths to manage students in such a way that their classes continue to function as unified groups, rather than as assemblies of individuals or cliques. Chapter 7 showed that, by keeping in mind that classroom language learning is a group experience that involves progress towards overall group goals, language teachers are able to teach in flexible ways. Chapter 8 demonstrated that language teachers value classes that are collectively responsive to their teaching initiatives. It also showed that they value classes that function in a cohesive manner, experience having taught them that students in classes that function cohesively engage in communicative tasks more readily and in a more sustained way than do students in less cohesive classes.

Chapter 9 described how language classes function as communities of learners, each with its individual culture and set of shared understandings. It demonstrated how the classroom behaviour of language teachers – so tantalisingly difficult to predict – can be understood in terms of the high value that language teachers place on their classes functioning effectively as groups. Experienced teachers, it seems, behave in the ways that they do because they have an intuitive understanding of group dynamics principles – and sense that to keep their classes 'together' they must engage in both pedagogically and socially driven classroom behaviour.

There is of course a sense in which all teachers, regardless of the subject they teach, value classes that function in a unified manner. All teachers value classes that are collectively alert and attentive, that respond readily to their teaching initiatives and their humour, and that engage in learning tasks with energy and enthusiasm. However, what distinguishes language teachers from teachers of other subjects is that for language teachers classroom interaction is central to the learning process. Not only is it a means of developing understanding of particular concepts: it is a goal in itself (the assumption being that, the more students practise language through interaction with their peers, the more proficient they will become). It is perhaps because classroom interaction is such an integral part of the learning process that the quality of the class group is valued so highly by language teachers.

According to Dörnyei and Murphey (2003: 64), past research has consistently revealed a positive relationship between group cohesiveness and performance. Interestingly, however, the empirical research upon which this statement is based has nearly always focused on cooperative learning – when students (usually of primary school age) complete tasks in small groups within the class (see Ehrman and Dörnyei, 1998, for an analysis of cooperative learning and productivity). To date there is a paucity of empirical research into the relationship between the overall levels of cohesiveness of language classes and the quality of learning outcomes.

Language learners, too, are readily able to identify the quality of their class groups, defining classes that they value across a similar range of dimensions to those used by their teachers. Some of their comments are presented below.

Students' views

'Everybody in this class is friendly. No-one is aggressive. If I don't understand I feel comfortable to ask. I am not afraid to make mistakes. Everyone understands. Nobody laughs at me.'

'I never feel lonely because we have a good teacher and friendly classmates. We study together and share happiness and pride.'

'We all have a total different mentality, yet we get on well. Everyone is open for the other one [*sic*]. I am positively surprised that there is no problem.'

'I always feel comfortable because there is a good atmosphere in our class between the students and between the students and the teacher.'

'We have a good teacher – but this is a bad class. Half of the people don't have good discipline and they speak their own language loudly in class, even in small groups. They are very rude.'

However, while their teachers consider the quality of the class group to be related to the quality of the learning that occurs, students are not so sure. In their eyes, warm and friendly class atmospheres, while a welcome bonus, are not essential to the learning process. For students who are in a hurry to learn, the quality of the teaching – which they measure in terms of how much they believe they are learning – assumes far greater importance.

Establishing rapport

As they talk about their teaching practices it becomes evident that experienced language teachers are keen to identify and describe certain imperatives that underpin their classroom behaviour. When they talk about these imperatives language teachers tend to speak with confidence and vigour, using expressions such as, 'I strongly believe that . . .' or 'I'm absolutely convinced that . . .' or 'It's my personal conviction that . . .'. When talking in this way language teachers often lean forward in their seats and use hand movements to emphasise the points they make. Language teachers make it clear that personal codes of behaviour govern their individual 'ways of being' in their classrooms, reminding them of how to behave. Codes such as these relate to interpersonal behaviour rather than to pedagogic practice.

Language teachers express what drives them in a range of different ways. Talking about the temptation to treat every language class in the same way, one teacher commented:

> Every ten weeks you get a different group and sometimes the temptation is to treat it as an assembly line, you know, 'Here's another class'. But I can't do that because I like to build a special relationship with each group.

One teacher explained that she considered the relationship that she developed with her class to be 'foundational' to her teaching, saying, 'It's my primary goal – when I walk into class – to establish rapport with individuals and with the class: the teaching is secondary'. This particular teacher made a regular practice of having her students keep personal journals in which they documented their experiences, thoughts and feelings. When she collected these she would write comments which showed that she empathised with their situations. She also explained how she treated individuals in the class:

> If someone is looking at me as if I'm from outer space and plainly not understanding what I'm saying, I'll go over and establish contact with them. If they know I like them, that transcends the language barrier. Even if they can't understand, there's still that contact there.

Another teacher, expressing the view that how language teachers actually teach is immaterial provided that they show genuine concern for their students, said:

> It doesn't matter what you do as long as they feel that they are valued and that you care about them individually. . . The students are like children: they sense straight away if you care.

Teachers use a variety of expressions to describe the relationships they consider valuable to establish with their classes. One teacher said, 'You really need to reach out to them in a lot of ways', while another said, 'I show that I enjoy the uniqueness of whoever I've got in my class'. The following teacher's description of 'connecting authentically' with his classes is another way of articulating this shared belief:

> My theory has always been that the teacher is the critical factor in the language classroom. . . The most important thing is to establish intimacy – but this doesn't mean you have to be like an entertainer. You establish intimacy through connecting

> authentically. That's the critical factor in all human relationships: to connect authentically. . . Even a teacher who's a fairly reserved, quiet sort of person, they can still get that intimacy. You don't have to be a comedian or anything like that. . . People accept anything if you're real. For instance, they wouldn't worry about stuff like you being a chain smoker, providing that you are real and authentic and don't pretend to be what you're not. . . People will admire you if you're real, and they won't if you're not. You've got to be really yourself, with no masks and no pretentiousness.

Another teacher described her personal style of teaching as 'person-centred teaching', explaining that she had a strong belief in connecting personally to each student in the class. The way that this teacher put her beliefs into practice was by making a point of doing whatever it was that she asked her students to do alongside everyone else. For example, if she required her class to do a piece of creative writing, she would sit down and do a piece of writing as well. When the students compared their work, and shared with others their thoughts and concerns about the writing process, she would offer her own work for critical comment and share with the class her own feelings about the writing process. Other teachers, too, point out that connecting to a class is not a one-way, but a two-way process. Explaining why she thought language teachers should offer something of themselves to their classes, one teacher said:

> Why on earth should they pour their hearts out to you if you're not going to let them into a little bit of your life? The power relationship's a bit 'iffy' – if they do all the sharing and you just sit back and listen.

In sum, it seems that general humanistic principles underpin the classroom behaviour of experienced language teachers. What is of paramount importance for them is the unique relationship that they establish with both individuals and their classes as wholes. Indeed, it seems that in teachers' minds the rapport that they develop with their classes is as important as the pedagogy itself. They have assumed that, without the vital links or threads that bind them to their classes in unique, personal ways, the essentially human process of classroom language learning is a soulless endeavour.

Dörnyei and Murphey (2003: 93) summarise the attributes of a good facilitator identified by the humanistic psychologist Rogers (1961) as being 'empathy', 'acceptance' and 'being congruent'. The following are aspects of the definitions:

- Empathy: the teacher getting on the same wavelength as the students and being sensitive to the group atmosphere, motivated by an interest in the welfare of the students.
- Acceptance: the teacher having a non-judgemental, positive attitude towards the students as complex human beings with both virtues and shortcomings.
- Being congruent: the teacher having the ability to live, to be and to communicate according to their true self, and to be in a state of 'realness' and 'authenticity'.

Dörnyei and Murphey elaborate further on the notion of congruence, quoting Hook and Vass (2000: 46), who state that 'personal congruence is your ability to have your verbal and non-verbal language fully supported by your beliefs and values'.

11.4 Conclusion

The core chapters of the book (Chapters 2 to 10) focused on the classroom actions of experienced language teachers, together with their interpretations of classroom events. The present chapter has delved a little deeper, focusing on the assumptions, beliefs and values that underpin the classroom decision-making of experienced language teachers. Although the interviews on which this book is based did not focus specifically on teacher cognition, a wealth of assumptions, beliefs and values emerged as the teachers talked about aspects of their work. These cognitive aspects of classroom language teaching formed the basis of the present chapter.

The chapter began by explaining why research based on qualitative interviews must be treated with caution, since it always has the potential to produce misleading results. The following section introduced the notion of a pragmatic approach to communicative language teaching, suggesting that experienced language teachers seldom teach solely in ways that reflect the assumptions that underpin the communicative approach. Rather, their personalised teaching approaches and practices, which include inputting language in conventional ways, reflect individual beliefs about language learning that have been informed by their own teaching and learning experiences. The section showed that such beliefs,

267

which are not easily dislodged, exist in teachers' minds alongside the widely accepted assumptions that underpin the communicative approach. It then drew attention to those language teachers – a minority – who report that their beliefs do shift over time, usually towards a more organic view of linguistic development that reflects more fully the tenets of the communicative approach.

A picture has emerged from this chapter of the communicative approach to language teaching as implemented by CELTA-trained or influenced language teachers working in western teaching contexts. It seems that, while most language teachers embrace the central tenets of the communicative approach and provide the students in their classes with multiple opportunities to interact with each other, they also teach in pragmatic ways that are consistent with their beliefs about how they can best meet the needs of their students. These ways involve consciously teaching the structure of the language using teaching techniques with which they are familiar. This hybrid approach can be described as a pragmatic version of communicative language teaching.

The chapter then identified the values that are shared by experienced language teachers, showing that language teachers universally value classes that function as happy, responsive, cohesive groups. In summarising the themes of the core chapters, the chapter demonstrated that the ongoing efforts of experienced language teachers to keep their classes functioning as unified communities of learners reflect their shared belief in the importance of class cohesion.

The final section of the chapter showed how the classroom behaviour of experienced language teachers is strongly driven by personal codes of behaviour. It demonstrated that for language teachers the rapport that they develop with their classes assumes as much importance as the pedagogy itself.

Summary

- Research into teachers' accounts of their classroom practices, and their assumptions and beliefs about communicative language teaching, has a number of potential pitfalls that need to be acknowledged.
- Language teachers hold in their minds a range of assumptions about language teaching and learning which they seldom fully articulate (although they may do so indirectly, through their classroom talk and actions).
- The beliefs held by individual language teachers which are embedded in personal experience are remarkably stable and resilient to change.
- For pragmatic reasons language teachers commonly teach hybridised versions of CLT in which they graft their preferred approaches for

inputting new language onto well-established ways of encouraging classroom interaction.

- The techniques that language teachers use to provide their students with linguistic input accord with their personal beliefs about how language is most effectively learned in language classrooms.
- In teachers' minds contradictory sets of assumptions about the nature of language teaching and learning (those based on language acquisition as a developmental process, and those based on language learning as mastery of a skill involving specific linguistic input) can coexist.
- A small number of language teachers report a shift in their beliefs from an incremental to a more organic view of the language-learning process.
- Experienced language teachers universally value classes that function in a cohesive manner. Their classroom actions reflect a sustained effort to develop and maintain a feeling of community within their classes.
- For language teachers the establishment of rapport with individuals and their class groups is central to their teaching.

For further reading

For a useful introduction to teacher beliefs and decision-making see Chapter 4 of Richards' book *Beyond training: perspectives on language teacher education* (1998).

Looking ahead

The following chapter, the final chapter of the book, draws together the threads of the book and proposes a socio-pedagogic theory of classroom practice.

12 Towards a teacher-generated theory of classroom practice

The previous chapter described the assumptions, beliefs and values that underpin the classroom practices of language teachers teaching within the communicative tradition in western educational settings. It showed that, although they embrace the basic tenets of the communicative approach, experienced language teachers rarely follow 'pure' versions of the approach. Rather, they develop personal, hybridised versions of CLT – teaching in pragmatic ways according to their personal beliefs (developed from experience) about how best to teach language in classroom situations. The chapter also demonstrated that language teachers universally value classes that function in a cohesive manner, and are driven by a desire to develop and maintain rapport both with individuals and with their class groups.

The present chapter draws together the threads of the previous chapters, showing how the classroom experiences of practising teachers may be integrated into a teacher-generated theory of classroom practice. It is divided into two sections: Section 12.1 shows that the on-the-spot decisions of experienced language teachers are guided by a desire to keep their language classes in a state of harmony and balance. A biological metaphor is used to encapsulate the notion of teachers constantly adjusting their behaviour in line with the ongoing feedback they receive. Section 12.2 presents the central thesis of the book: that the classroom behaviour of language teachers is both pedagogically and socially driven. A second biological metaphor is used to represent the notion that pedagogic and social processes in language classrooms are intertwined and inextricably linked. A socio-pedagogic theory of classroom practice is then formulated. The chapter ends by locating the theory within its historical context, suggesting that the class-centred approach favoured by language teachers who teach communicatively represents a post-authoritarian style of classroom leadership.

12.1 Harmony and balance

By listening to what practising teachers have to say about their day-to-day experiences, their classroom practices and their beliefs about

270

language teaching and learning, it has been possible to develop a composite picture of what language teachers are collectively saying. Despite the diversity of the situations within which they work, the classroom experiences of language teachers who teach in western contexts are surprisingly similar. Clearly all teachers are unique, with no two teachers ever teaching in the same way – and certainly not responding to the hundred-and-one events that occur in their classrooms in identical ways. Nevertheless, similar driving-forces appear to underlie much of their classroom behaviour.

The core chapters of this book have progressively revealed the complex, inter-related nature of the behaviour of experienced language teachers and their students as they engage collaboratively in the twin processes of teaching and learning. The defining feature of the classroom behaviour of language teachers is that of flexibility: not delivering lessons in predetermined ways, but rather responding to the immediacy of the moment. Much of what they say about their teaching suggests that experienced language teachers are prepared to adopt a flexible approach. They continually evaluate the ever-changing situation in their classrooms from moment to moment and, in the light of the feedback they receive, make on-the-spot decisions and small adjustments to how they teach and manage their classes. Is it possible to discern any general principle that underpins their classroom decision-making?

The principle of balance

Language teachers constantly seek to balance what they do. At the pedagogic level they ensure that they provide their classes with a balance of learning activities. Typically they provide students with the opportunity to engage in a variety of learning tasks during the course of a single lesson, some of which will focus on meaning and others on form. They normally ensure that at least two of the four macro-skills (listening, speaking, reading and writing) are practised in any one lesson, and that those that are not are practised in subsequent lessons. Language teachers regularly vary the interaction patterns within their classes. They balance teacher-fronted activities, when the focus of the whole class group is on themselves, with activities in which students work individually, in pairs, in small groups, or collectively as a whole class. Alert to the need to vary the intensity of learning tasks, they regularly intersperse demanding tasks with ones that are lighter and less challenging. They also vary the pace of their lessons, sometimes slowing things down and sometimes speeding things up.

Sometimes language teachers require students to move around the room in mingling activities, while at other times they require them to stay put. At times during their lessons they may give students a fair degree of freedom, while at other times they exercise tight control. While they sometimes allow lessons to go in unexpected directions, at other times they keep their lessons running down a predetermined track. Sometimes language teachers let activities run over time, and sometimes they cut them short. Sometimes they correct students' errors on the spot, and sometimes they do not. They sense when to intervene during communicative tasks, and when to let things run. Sometimes they allow the students in their classes to let off steam and behave in noisy ways, while at other times they insist on quiet activity. Although normally they behave in relatively predictable ways, language teachers sometimes introduce an element of surprise – behaving in unusual ways themselves, or getting their students to do something unexpected. Everyday classroom decisions such as these, which are normally made speedily and without much conscious deliberation, suggest that language teachers have an intuitive understanding of the need for variety and balance in their pedagogic practice.

The ways that experienced language teachers interact with both individuals and their classes as wholes are governed by a desire to maintain social harmony within their class groups. Sometimes language teachers pay particular attention to certain students, while at other times they direct their attention elsewhere, choosing not to favour the same students with their attention. Sometimes they show their disapproval of undesirable behaviour, while at other times they choose to turn a blind eye. Sometimes they foreground quiet students, while at other times they allow such students to maintain a low profile. Sometimes they laugh and joke with their classes, encouraging individuals to contribute to the social dynamics of the class group, while at other times they pull the class back and ensure that students have their heads down so that group processes are less evident.

As a general rule language teachers ensure that the social atmosphere of the classroom is neither too serious nor too light-hearted, neither too heavy nor too frothy – sensing that a balance between these two extremes is desirable. Language teachers regularly try to ensure that as many students as possible have the opportunity to contribute to the emerging culture of the language classroom. Wherever possible they try to draw students who appear marginalised for whatever reason (shyness, lack of confidence, sense of superiority, feelings of alienation or whatever) into the sphere of influence of the overall class group. Although they may allow certain individuals to adopt higher-profile roles than others, they constantly seek to show that they value all class members equally.

A key skill of experienced language teachers is the ability to switch readily between two quite different roles. The first is that of class group leader: the person who is not only in authority, because they are the teacher, but also an authority, because of their knowledge of the target language. The second is that of class group member: the person who, having established rapport with the class, can function as an integral member of the class group. Experienced language teachers are able to strike a balance between these two roles. They sense when it is appropriate to switch from a more distant to a closer role – and when to switch back again. Their in-built sense of balance alerts language teachers to the danger of overstepping the mark in either direction – remaining too distant and unapproachable on the one hand, or becoming too friendly and familiar on the other.

> 'Followers do like being treated with consideration, do like to have their say, do like a chance to exercise their own initiative – and participation does increase acceptance of decisions. But there are times when followers welcome rather than reject authority, want prompt and clear decisions from the leader, and want to close ranks around the leader. The ablest and most effective leaders do not hold to a single style; they may be highly supportive in personal relations when that is needed, yet capable of a quick, authoritative decision when the situation requires it.'
> Gardner (1990: 26, quoted by Ehrman and Dörnyei, 1998: 165)

In sum, the principle of balance underpins the daily classroom practices of experienced language teachers. Such teachers sense that their classes need to be maintained in a state of dynamic equilibrium, with all the various aspects and elements of the language classroom counterbalancing each other. Can any metaphor be identified that encapsulates this notion of dynamic equilibrium?

The picture on the lid of the jigsaw puzzle

In Chapter 1 I suggested that the process of developing a grounded theory was like doing a jigsaw puzzle without having the picture on the lid to act as a guide. Where do the many thousands of pieces fit: in the top left-hand corner, or the bottom right? Are they part of the central image, or are they part of the background? And what is that central image anyway? Is it just a vague blur without discernible shape or form – or is it something from the real world that can be readily recognised?

In the early days of my research, when I was interviewing language teachers about their definitions of good classes, I became interested in systems theory. A key feature of systems theory is the notion that the whole is equal to more than the sum of the individual parts, and that a whole that functions in a satisfactory manner is not composed of parts that are in themselves perfect. From what the teachers were telling me about how good language classes functioned, it seemed that there were some important ways in which language classes functioned as systems.

Systems theory enabled me to accommodate a fact that I had initially found puzzling: that language classes could function in a highly success-ful manner, even when they contained less-than-perfect elements (in the form of students with poor linguistic levels, tricky behaviour, the occa-sional unsuccessful lesson and so on). Language teachers repeatedly told me that their most successful classes were often those that did not contain well-behaved, conscientious, high-achieving students who never put a foot wrong. On the contrary, the classes that they considered func-tioned most successfully were often a bit rough at the edges, containing certain students who represented something of a challenge and who com-pelled them to interact with their classes in creative and dynamic ways. In contrast, classes that contained 'perfect' students did not necessarily function particularly well. Again, the teachers' view matched systems theory, which explains how the most successful automobile is not the one whose individual parts are necessarily the best: it does not have the best carburettor, the best braking system, the best cooling system and so on. What the 'best' car has is a set of component parts that, while not indi-vidually the best, nevertheless function in combination with one another in a highly effective manner.

Systems theory is a useful way of explaining the functioning of complex systems in both the natural and the man-made world (Owens: 1991). It has been used to describe systems as diverse as agricultural systems, educational systems, or industrial systems such as aircraft manufacturing companies. A key tenet of the systems approach is the notion that there is an interrelationship between the various parts that constitute the whole, and that no part ever oper-ates in isolation (Gharajedaghi and Ackoff: 1985).

Even though I was initially attracted to the idea of defining language classes in terms of systems theory, I eventually rejected this notion. I decided that the word 'system' had a mechanistic ring to it, suggesting that each element within the system had its own designated part to play that was somehow fixed and immutable. Language teachers indicated that this was far from the case. In their minds language classes were flexible, adaptable places that could readily accommodate new members. They also made it clear that the roles and relationships that developed within their classes were in a constant state of adaptation and flux.

Other people have suggested that chaos theory might be a useful way of explaining the complex nature of language classes. There is certainly a sense in which the proverbial image of the butterfly flapping its wings in a far-flung corner of the globe, leading to a chain of processes that affect overall climate systems, can be applied to language classes. A single careless remark made by the teacher, or the classroom behaviour of a single student on one particular occasion, can have a long-lasting effect on the overall tenor of the class. There is also a sense in which language classrooms can sometimes appear to the outside observer to be chaotic places in which little patterned behaviour can be seen. It must also be said that language classes, like classes in any other subject, can occasionally descend into chaos – with the teacher losing control and wishing that a hole would open in the floor and swallow them up. However, by and large, language classrooms are not chaotic places. Even though many disparate events may be occurring simultaneously, experienced language teachers know precisely what these are and how they are contributing to student learning.

Language classes as complex organisms

In 1996, van Lier took systems theory a step further and suggested that language classrooms should be regarded as complex adaptive systems. In his view:

> The educational context, with the classroom as its centre, is viewed as a complex system in which events do not occur in linear causal fashion, but in which a multitude of forces interact in complex, self-organizing ways, and create changes and patterns that are part predictable, part unpredictable. (van Lier, 1996: 148)

The data upon which the present book is based provide ample support for van Lier's statement. However, the ways in which the various elements in language classrooms interact in complex, self-organising ways to create changes that can seldom be predicted make language classes more like biological organisms than systems. In my mind the picture on the lid of the jigsaw puzzle is therefore that of a biological organism.

Biological organisms can exist at any level of complexity – ranging from those composed of a single cell, such as the amoeba shown in Figure 12.1, to those composed of countless numbers of cells, such as the human body. In complex organisms cells cluster together to form organs, each

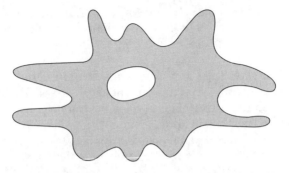

Figure 12.1   The language class as a biological organism

of which performs a specialised function: the heart, the lungs, the liver and so on. A further characteristic of complex organisms is that they maintain themselves in a state of physical equilibrium through an internal regulatory process known as homeostasis. Homeostasis is the process by which organisms constantly adjust their internal functioning in accordance with the negative feedback that they receive – thus maintaining favourable internal conditions that allow them to function in a healthy manner.

The ways in which language classes operate suggest that they have a good deal in common with biological organisms. Although there is always the danger of extending metaphors too far, and although no metaphor provides a perfect 'fit', the analogy of language class as organism seems to be a fruitful one. Language classes are like organisms in a number of ways. First, they are composed of a wide range of students, each of whom has the potential to perform a number of functions that enable the class to maintain its overall state of dynamic equilibrium. Second, language classes adapt to changing circumstances. In line with the negative feedback they receive, language teachers make compensatory classroom decisions whenever things show signs of going wrong. Third, students in language classes can behave in ways that have an adverse effect on the class – just as malfunctioning organs can affect the health of the organism as a whole. Finally, just as the internal balancing mechanisms of organisms can cease to function under extreme conditions, so language classes can sometimes reach a point where they are no longer manageable.

Since both language classes and organisms share a number of features, it seems useful to view language classes as organisms. The process of comparing and contrasting the features of organisms with those of language classes generates additional insights into the kinds of ways in which language classes function. It may even be reasonable to apply the term 'healthy', used to describe organisms in a state of physical equilibrium, to language classes that are functioning in a harmonious manner.

12.2 A teacher-generated theory of classroom practice

In the minds of many people the term 'theory' conjures up the idea of something grand and all-embracing: something that only people such as Sir Isaac Newton or Albert Einstein were able to formulate. However, not all theories function at a grand level. Most are initially developed at a localised level, with some that are relevant to situations other than the ones for which they were formulated being applied more generally. All theories have a similar starting point: someone is puzzled about a particular phenomenon – whether in the natural sciences or the realm of human behaviour – and wishes to come up with a satisfactory explanation. Theories develop as the result of persistently asking 'Why?' questions. Language teachers know that 'Why?' questions invite 'Because' answers: answers that provide explanations for why things are the way they are – in the case of language classes, why people within them behave in such complex and unpredictable ways.

Many leaders in the field of classroom-based research have lamented the lack of overall theoretical frameworks for understanding classroom processes – frameworks that show how the multiple variables involved in classroom second-language learning are interrelated. The advantage of the inductive, grounded theory approach to qualitative research – the approach that I used to gather the data for this book – is that its goal is to develop theory rather than simply to produce detailed description.

Speziale and Carpenter (2003: 108) outline different levels of theory, ranging from substantive theory at the context-bound end of the continuum to grand theory with broader application at the other end – with formal theory occupying the middle ground. According to Freese (2002: 307): 'A grand theory consists of a global conceptual framework that defines broader perspectives for practice and includes diverse ways of viewing . . . phenomena based on these perspectives.' Speziale and Carpenter (2003: 108) also quote Fawcett (1989), who observes that 'grand theories are broadest in scope, frequently lack operationally defined concepts, and are unsuitable to direct empirical testing.'

Towards a teacher-generated theory of classroom practice

When I completed the first phase of my research I was able to formulate a low-level, substantive theory: that a sample of language teachers working in a particular language school defined the quality of their classes in terms of how successfully they function as groups. Now, ten years and four studies later, I find myself in the position of bing able to formulate a higher-level theory.

The data collection framework

As outlined in Chapter 1, the framework that was selected for the collection of the data – the functional approach to leadership – posits that leadership is the property of the whole group (in this case the whole language class), rather than being the prerogative of one group member alone (the teacher). According to this flexible interpretation of leadership, any group member (the teacher or any student) can play a leadership role – and many different kinds of behaviour can be construed as leadership behaviour. These include any pedagogically driven behaviour that helps the group to progress towards its learning goals, or any socially driven behaviour that helps the group to maintain a spirit of unity and 'togetherness'. Behaviour in the latter category can be anything from a student making an off-the-cuff remark to someone suggesting that the class do something together at the weekend.

The decision to view classroom behaviour through such a wide-angle lens immediately opens up new possibilities. It enables the researcher to include in their field of vision many kinds of classroom behaviour, ranging from whispered asides to bursts of whole-class laughter, that to date have been largely ignored by classroom-based research. It gives them permission to document the kinds of everyday classroom events and behaviours that have traditionally been considered peripheral to the learning process and therefore of minor importance. In fact, once a functional approach to classroom leadership is adopted, it becomes immediately evident that such behaviour is highly significant. Indeed, it may be said to be central to the whole learning process.

The traditional, linear view of teaching and learning suggests that there is a direct, one-way relationship between the behaviour of the teacher (including the quality of their program, their teaching skills and the quality of the learning tasks they set up) and student learning. This view is depicted in Figure 12.2 below.

Teacher behaviour ⟶ Student learning

Figure 12.2   The traditional view of the teaching–learning relationship

In contrast, from a class-centred perspective, the quality of the class group is central to the learning process. Both teacher and student behaviour contributes to the quality of the class group, and the quality of the class group is related to the quality of the learning that occurs within it. Figure 12.3 represents a class-centred perspective.

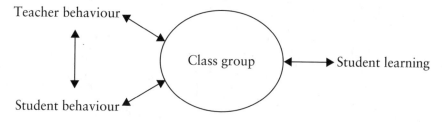

Figure 12.3   A class-centred perspective of teaching and learning

From a class-centred perspective, there is a relationship between the quality of the class group and the quality of the learning that occurs within it. A good class group enables students to learn effectively, while the experience of learning effectively and making good progress creates a feeling of unity within the class. The converse is also true: a class that functions poorly as a group makes learning more difficult to achieve, while minimal learning progress makes it more difficult for language classes to hang together and maintain a spirit of unity.

A socio-pedagogic theory of classroom practice

Classroom language learning is a group experience. It is something that students do in the company of others, in an open and public manner, rather than independently in the privacy of their own homes. The twin processes

> At a conference in 1989, whose proceedings were published in 1992, Allwright drew attention to the fact that teachers have both pedagogic and social priorities in their classrooms. He pointed out that they often appear to be pulled in opposite directions by these apparently conflicting demands. In 1996 he modified this view, observing that, 'Classroom behaviour . . . is not a simple binary matter of a set of straightforward either/or decisions. It is perhaps much better represented as some sort of balancing act between opposing forces, a tightrope walk for the most conscientious of teachers and learners, a continually reinvented compromise between competing social and pedagogic demands.' (1996: 223)

of teaching and learning in language classrooms cannot be understood without reference to the social context within which they occur. Classroom language learning is not only a learning but also a social experience.

A visual representation of the notion of classroom behaviour sometimes drawing classes together, sometimes drawing them along, and sometimes performing the two functions at the same time, is represented in the figures below:

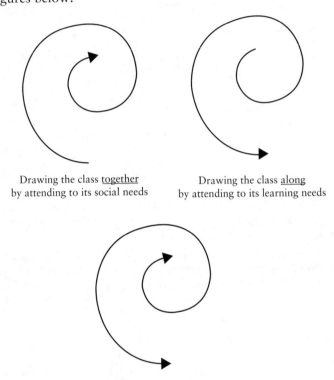

Drawing the class <u>together</u>
by attending to its social needs

Drawing the class <u>along</u>
by attending to its learning needs

Drawing the class both
together and along

Figure 12.4   Drawing the class both together and along

Within the context of any single lesson in any language classroom, the widest possible range of pedagogic and social processes occur. These processes are intermingled and intertwined and cannot be teased apart. Sometimes classroom behaviour is pedagogically driven, at other times it is socially driven. On most occasions it is a subtle combination of both. The 'truth' (if such a thing exists) is always a matter of conjecture: our own interpretations of classroom behaviours and events are personal ones – as are those of teachers and learners, the co-players in the constantly evolving drama of the language classroom.

A second biological image may be used to represent the inextricably linked nature of social and pedagogic processes in language classrooms: that of the double helix.

Figure 12.5   Social and pedagogic processes in language classrooms

Here the double-stranded DNA molecule twisted into a helix represent the pedagogically and socially oriented 'strands' of classroom behaviour. The encoded message of each strand can only be decoded in conjunction with the encoded message of the other: like the combination on a lock, the message on each strand cannot be read in isolation from its other 'half'.

From this biological image a socio-pedagogic theory of classroom practice can be formulated. This theory encompasses the notion that when teachers and learners come together in language classrooms something dynamic happens: the individuals within the class begin to function as a group. Because all language classes function as groups (regardless of the level of cohesion they achieve), both pedagogic and social processes occur concurrently at all times during lessons. This self-evident truth cannot be ignored.

Comment

This theory accords with a social constructivist view of language classrooms. According to Brown (2000: 286): 'The social constructivist perspectives that are associated with more current approaches to both first and second language acquisition emphasize the dynamic nature of the interplay between learners and their peers and their teachers and others with whom they interact. The interpersonal context in which a learner operates takes on great significance, and therefore, the interaction between learners and others is the focus of observation and explanation.'

Kumaravadivelu (2001: 541) defines as a pedagogy of practicality one that aims for a teacher-generated theory of practice. He explains that this assertion is premised on the proposition that no theory of practice can be useful and usable unless it is generated through practice.

The socio-pedagogic theory of classroom practice provides an explanation of why language teachers behave in such a wide range of unanticipated and at times seemingly fickle ways in their classrooms. Because experienced language teachers are driven by a desire to keep their classes functioning as groups, they engage in pedagogically oriented behaviour one moment and socially oriented behaviour the next. They find themselves constantly adjusting their behaviour to the learning and/or social needs of individuals and/or the class group because they want to keep their class in a state of dynamic equilibrium. Because they are alert to the social and learning needs of their class groups they find themselves continually making impromptu classroom decisions from moment to moment – often without prior deliberation or conscious thought. If they receive negative feedback they may take further action of a similar or different kind. They may behave in ways in which they have behaved in the past, or they may make subtle adaptations to their tried-and-tested routines in response to new situations never previously encountered. The relationship between language teachers and their classes is a constant process of adaptation and change. It is not surprising that the classroom behaviour of experienced language teachers is virtually impossible to predict.

This socio-pedagogic theory of classroom learning has emerged from what more than a hundred practising teachers have said about how their classes function and about why they behave in the ways that they do in their classrooms. It is grounded in their personal experiences of being language teachers in communicative classrooms today. In a sense, the 'ownership' of the theory belongs to teachers themselves, since it is they who have provided the data and insights upon which the theory is based. I have simply tried to make sense of the information provided by them by repeatedly analysing and re-analysing it until common patterns could be seen. The socio-pedagogic theory of classroom practice that has emerged appears the most concise way of encompassing everything that the teachers have collectively been saying.

Hopefully the explanatory theory of classroom practice presented here has gone some way to explaining why language teachers who teach communicatively in western educational contexts behave in the ways they do in their classrooms. The following section discusses the applicability of the theory to alternative educational contexts.

The applicability of the theory to alternative educational contexts

In qualitative research it is not the researcher's prerogative to claim that their findings and insights are applicable to other contexts. It is for the reader to decide whether or not the findings reflect their own experience in any meaningful and useful way. If the reader finds that the findings resonate or 'ring true', then they are free to accept them. If, on the other hand, the findings do not reflect the reality of the language teaching situation as they know it to be, they will be likely to reject them.

I am confident that the picture of the experience of language teaching that I have presented in this book is a fair representation of the current situation in Australia and the UK. It may be recalled from the Introduction that the majority of the teachers who provided data for the book, while currently teaching in Western Australia, had previously taught in a number of countries around the world. The teachers who were interviewed in the UK were in a similar situation: they too had taught in several different countries and contexts prior to their present jobs. The collective wisdom of the teachers is therefore based on a broader experiential database than the geographical location of Perth might suggest. However, the sample is limited by the fact that all the teacher informants were native English speakers who were either CELTA or DELTA trained, or who had to some degree been introduced to what might be termed the Cambridge ESOL style of communicative language teaching.

Further research will need to be conducted to establish whether or not the socio-pedagogic theory of classroom practice proposed in the present chapter can be applied to a wider range of educational contexts. Preliminary research suggests that students learning English in teacher-fronted lessons in China perceive that the nature of the overall class group is related to the quality of their learning (Xu: 2001). However, the ways in which group processes operate in large teacher-fronted classes are likely to be different from the ways in which they function in intimate and informal language classrooms such as those described in the present book.

Classroom control in the post-authoritarian era

Traditionally the classroom relationship between teacher and students has been one of imbalance. The teacher is the person who implements the syllabus, selects the learning tasks and manages the classroom environment – while the students have relatively few choices. Indeed, it could be said that in traditional classrooms the teacher wields virtually all of the power, while the students wield virtually none. The structure of educational institutions over the centuries has been based on the premise that the teacher is a figure of authority who must be obeyed – and who can behave in authoritarian ways if they so wish.

Although this model is still widely accepted as being an effective way of educating young people, its limitations are becoming increasingly recognised. Teachers of young people in language classrooms in many countries are increasingly finding that the students they are teaching are not as malleable as they would like. Students may regard the relative freedom they enjoy while engaging in communicative tasks as a golden opportunity to pursue their own agendas – rather than focusing solely on language learning. This can make teaching a frustrating and stressful endeavour. In the interests of self-preservation some teachers resort to behaving in ways that they later regret: glowering, raising their voices, separating students from their friends, banishing them from the room, and so on. Teachers find that such behaviour seldom leads to the desired outcome of more responsive and better-behaved students.

Teachers who transfer into the area of adult language teaching often do so because they do not wish to behave in authoritarian ways. They assume that, when teaching adult language learners, classroom discipline will be less of an issue than it is in schools: they will be able to spend more time engaged in the business of teaching, and less time struggling to keep control of their classes. To a large extent they are right. However, in order to teach anything at all a teacher must remain in control of their class: failure to do so will mean that they lose the respect of their class. Learning will then be compromised.

How do teachers in a post-authoritarian era – particularly those who wish the students in their classes to behave naturally and spontaneously – exercise control over their classes? If we accept the evidence from the accounts of the teachers in the present book, the answer seems clear. By behaving in flexible and approachable ways, and positioning themselves inside rather than outside their class groups for much of the time, language teachers are providing classroom environments within which a range of group processes can readily occur. By shifting the locus of control from themselves to their class groups, they play a less obviously dominant role in their classes. In class-centred classroom environments, a higher proportion of students find themselves playing leadership roles that enhance a positive group feeling within the class as a whole. On finding themselves viewed as valuable and valued members of their class communities, rather than as sources of irritation to their teachers, even students who might under other circumstances be difficult to manage can find themselves working with rather than against their teachers.

Once group processes involving both teacher and students functioning in a collaborative manner have been set in motion, the class itself has a strong moderating influence on the behaviour of individuals. Although there are always strong-minded students who are able to resist the power of the group, dissident voices are less readily heard in classes in which there is a strong group feeling. Most students find themselves compelled to join with the group rather than to remain as outsiders, particularly in classes in which there is a strong feeling of camaraderie, friendliness and fun – and where the teacher is popular, friendly and approachable. It takes considerable determination for an individual to question the teaching approach or the quality of the teaching program when there is a strong group feeling within the class as a whole. Under such circumstances students tend to hold their counsel.

> Research in the area of group dynamics demonstrates that group norms influence the behaviour of group members. According to Shaw (1981: 218): 'Groups characterised by friendliness, cooperation, interpersonal attraction, and similar indications of group cohesiveness exert strong influences upon members to behave in accordance with group expectations.'

It seems, then, that by behaving in non-authoritarian ways, language teachers are not relinquishing control over their classes. On the contrary, by setting in train social processes that in turn regulate the behaviour of individuals, they are exerting a more subtle, indirect form of control over their classes.

In conclusion, the teachers whose experiences have been described in this book have indicated that they favour a class-centred approach to classroom leadership. By so doing they have drawn attention to the relationship between the leadership style of language teachers and the development of classroom environments that appear to facilitate learning. Might it not be that the success of any teaching approach depends to a significant extent on the leadership style of the teacher? If the teacher plays a traditional role in their classroom, it is likely that learning activities, and particularly communicative tasks, will be less successful than they would be were the teacher to adopt a more class-centred approach.

12.3 Conclusion

This chapter has presented a socio-pedagogic theory of classroom practice that was generated by analysing in detail the classroom experiences and practices of more than a hundred language teachers. The chapter began by suggesting that a key principle that governs the classroom decision-making of experienced language teachers is that of balance: keeping all the various elements in their classes in a state of dynamic equilibrium. A biological metaphor was suggested as a way of encapsulating the notion that language teachers and their students routinely adjust to one another and to constantly changing circumstances during the course of each and every lesson.

The second part of the chapter referred back to the framework that was used to guide the collection and analysis of disparate kinds of classroom behaviour: that of the functional approach to leadership. This framework, with its metaphorical wide-angle lens, enabled a wide range of both pedagogically and socially oriented classroom behaviour to be documented. A class-centred perspective was then suggested as a way of drawing attention to the relationship between the level of cohesiveness of any class group and the quality of the learning that occurs within it.

Having demonstrated that pedagogically and socially driven classroom behaviours are inextricably linked, a teacher-generated theory of classroom practice was then proposed. The socio-pedagogic theory of classroom practice explains why classrom lanugage teachers behave in such flexible ways. After drawing attention to the potential applicability of the theory to alternative educational contexts, the section ended by suggesting that class-centred teaching, in which teachers are constantly mindful of group processes and constantly seeking to maintain a positive group feeling within their classes, represents a post-authoritarian approach to class management.

Summary

- The classroom decisions of experienced language teachers are guided by a desire to keep the various elements in their classrooms in a state of dynamic equilibrium: the teaching processes, the social processes and the different roles that they themselves play.
- The metaphor of the language class as a complex organism encapsulates the notion of constant adaptation and change – with the concept of homeostasis (the internal regulatory system of biological organisms) reflecting the efforts of experienced language teachers to maintain a state of harmony and balance in their classes.
- From a class-centred perspective, the quality of the class group is central to the learning process. Classes that function in a cohesive manner provide increased opportunities for interaction and are therefore likely to enhance learning.
- The socio-pedagogic theory of classroom behaviour articulates the relationship between pedagogically and socially driven teacher and student behaviour.
- The socio-pedagogic theory of classroom practice represents a social constructivist view of language classrooms.
- The intertwined nature of pedagogically and socially driven classroom behaviour can be represented schematically by the image of a double helix.
- Further research needs to be conducted to establish whether the socio-pedagogic theory of classroom practice might be a useful way of understanding the relationship between teachers and students in alternative educational contexts.
- In this post-authoritarian era it is often neither possible nor desirable for the teacher to exert control over classes by repressive means.
- Adopting a class-centred approach allows students to participate in the class management process. This means that the responsibility for classroom behaviour is a shared endeavour, rather than being the sole prerogative of the teacher.

References

Adler, R. S. 1987. Culture shock and the cross-cultural learning experience. In Luce, L. F. and Smith, E. C. (eds.) *Towards internationalism: Readings in cross-cultural communication*. (2nd edition). New York: Newbury House.

Allwright, D. 1992. *Interaction in the language classroom: Social problems and pedagogic possibilities*. Language Teaching in Today's World. Proceedings of the International Symposium on Language Teaching and Learning (Les États Généraux des Langues), 1989, 32–53.

Allwright, D. 1996. Social and pedagogic pressures in the language classroom: The role of socialisation. In Coleman, H. (ed.) *Society and the language classroom*. Cambridge: Cambridge University Press, 209–28.

Allwright, R. L. and Bailey, K. M. 1991. *Focus on the language classroom*. Cambridge: Cambridge University Press.

Appel, J. 1995. *Diary of a language teacher*. Oxford: Heinemann.

Archer, C. M. 1986. Culture bump and beyond. In Valdes, J. M. (ed.) *Culture bound: Bridging the cultural gap in language teaching*. Cambridge: Cambridge University Press, 170–78.

Arends, R. 2004. *Learning to teach*. (6th edition). Boston: McGraw Hill.

Arnold, J. (ed.) 1999. *Affect in language learning*. Cambridge: Cambridge University Press.

Arthur, M., Gordon, C. and Butterfield, N. 2003. *Classroom management: Creating positive learning environments*. Melbourne: Thomson.

Atkinson, D. 1989. 'Humanistic' approaches in the adult classroom: An affective reaction. *ELT Journal* 43(4): 268–73.

Atkinson, T. and Claxton, G. (eds.) 2000. *The intuitive practitioner: On the value of not always knowing what one is doing*. Buckingham: Open University Press.

Bailey, K. M., *et al.* 1996. The language learner's autobiography: Examining the 'apprenticeship of observation'. In Freeman, D. and Richards, J. C. (eds.) *Teacher learning in language teaching*. Cambridge: Cambridge University Press.

Bailey, K. M. and Nunan, D. (eds.) 1996. *Voices from the language classroom: Qualitative research in second language education*. Cambridge: Cambridge University Press.

Barnes, D. 1976. *From communication to curriculum*. London: Penguin.

Bax, S. 2003. The end of CLT: A context approach to language teaching. *ELT Journal* 57(3): 278–87.

Benne, K. and Sheats, P. 1978. Functional roles of group members. In Bradford, L. (ed.) *Group development*. La Jolla, CA: University Associates, 52–61.

288

Bereiter, C. and Scardamalia, M. 1993. *Surpassing ourselves – an inquiry into the nature and implications of expertise.* Chicago: Open Court.

Borg, S. 2003. Teacher cognition in language teaching: A review of research on what language teachers think, know, believe and do. *Language Teaching* 36: 81–109.

Breen, M. P. 1986. The social context for language learning – a neglected situation? *Studies in Second Language Acquisition* 7: 135–58.

Breen, M. P. and Littlejohn, A. (eds.) 2000. *Classroom decision-making: Negotiation and process syllabuses in action.* Cambridge: Cambridge University Press.

Brown, H. D. 2000. *Principles of language learning and teaching.* (4th edition). White Plains, NY: Pearson Education.

Candy, P. C. 1991. *Self-direction for lifelong learning.* San Francisco: Jossey Bass.

Carter, R. and Nunan, D. (eds.) 2001. *The Cambridge guide to teaching English to speakers of other languages.* Cambridge: Cambridge University Press.

Chenitz, C. and Swanson, J. M. (eds.) 1986. *From practice to grounded theory: Qualitative research in nursing.* Menlo Park, CA: Addison Wesley.

Chi, M. T. H., Glaser, R. and Farr, M. (eds.) 1988. *The nature of expertise.* Hillsdale, NJ: Erlbaum.

Clandfield, L. and Kerr, P. 2004. Professionalism in ELT: An obscure object of desire. *IATEFL: The Teacher Trainers and Educators SIG Newsletter* (3): 25–8.

Clark, J. D. 1969. The Pennsylvania Project and the 'Audio-Lingual vs. Traditional' question. *The Modern Language Journal* 53(6): 388–96.

Claxton, G. 2000. The anatomy of intuition. In Atkinson, T. and Claxton, G. (eds.) *The intuitive practitioner: On the value of not always knowing what one is doing.* Buckingham: Open University Press, 32–52.

Cortazzi, M. 1990. Cultural and educational expectations in the language classroom. In Harrison, B. (ed.) *Culture in the language classroom (ELT Documents: 132).* London: Modern English Publications.

Covington, M. 1992. *Making the grade: A self-worth perspective on motivation in school reform.* Cambridge: Cambridge University Press.

Cresswell-Turner, S. 2004. The slavery of teaching English. *Daily Telegraph*, 17 January 2004.

Creswell, J. W. 1998. *Qualitative inquiry and research design: Choosing among five traditions.* Thousand Oaks, CA: Sage.

Csikszentmihalyi, M. 1997. *Finding flow.* New York: Basic Books.

Davis, J. A. 1961. Compositional effects, role systems, and the survival of small discussion groups. *Public Relations Quarterly* 25: 575–84.

Denzin, N. K. and Lincoln, Y. S. (eds.) 1994. *Handbook of qualitative research.* Thousand Oaks, CA: Sage.

Denzin, N. K. and Lincoln, Y. S. (eds.) 2003. *Strategies of qualitative inquiry.* Thousand Oaks, CA: Sage.

Dey, I. 1999. *Grounding grounded theory: Guidelines for qualitative inquiry.* London: Academic Press.

Dörnyei, Z. 2001. *Motivational strategies in the language classroom.* Cambridge: Cambridge University Press.

References

Dörnyei, Z. and Malderez, A. 1999. The role of group dynamics in foreign language learning and teaching. In Arnold, J. (ed.) *Affect in language learning*. Cambridge: Cambridge University Press, 155–69.

Dörnyei, Z. and Murphey, T. 2003. *Group dynamics in the language classroom*. Cambridge: Cambridge University Press.

Doyle, W. 1986. Classroom organization and management. In Wittrock, M. C. (ed.) *Handbook of research on teaching*. New York: MacMillan, 392–431.

Dreyfus, H. L. and Dreyfus, S. E. 1986. *Mind over machine*. New York: Free Press.

Duff, P. and Uchida, Y. 1997. The negotiation of teachers' sociocultural identities and practices in postsecondary EFL classrooms. *TESOL Quarterly* 31: 451–86.

Ehrman, M. 1996. *Understanding second language learning difficulties*. Thousand Oaks, CA: Sage.

Ehrman, M. E. and Dörnyei, Z. 1998. *Interpersonal dynamics in second language education: The visible and invisible classroom*. Thousand Oaks, CA: Sage.

Fawcett, J. 1989. *Analysis and evaluation of conceptual models of nursing*. Philadelphia: F. A. Davis.

Feiman-Nemser, S. and Floden, R. 1986. The cultures of teaching. In Wittrock, M. C. (ed.) *Handbook of research on teaching*. (3rd edition). New York: MacMillan, 505–26.

Ferguson, G. and Donno, S. 2003. One-month teacher training courses: Time for a change? *ELT Journal* 57(1): 26–33.

Foot, H. C. 1997. Humour and laughter. In Hargie, O. D. W. (ed.) *The handbook of communication skills*. 2nd edition. London: Routledge, 259–85.

Freese, B.T. (2002). Betty Neuman: Systems model. In Tomey, A.M. and Alligood, M.R. (eds.) *Nursing theorists and their work*. St Louis, MO: Mosby, 299–335.

Furnham, A. and Bochner, S. 1986. *Culture shock: Psychological reactions to unfamiliar environments*. London: Methuen.

Gardner, J. W. 1990. *On leadership*. New York: Free Press.

Gharajedaghi, J. and Ackoff, R. 1985. Towards systemic education of system scientists. *Systems Research* 2: 21–7.

Graf, J. 2003. Part-time employment in TESOL: A sociopolitical concern? *TESOL Matters*. Waldorf, MD, March–April–May Issue.

Guiora, A. Z., Beit-Hallahmi, B., Brannon, R. C. L., Dull, C. Y. and Scovel, T. 1972. The effects of experimentally induced changes in ego states on pronunciation ability in second language: An exploratory study. *Comprehensive Psychiatry* 13(5): 421–8.

Hadfield, J. 1992. *Classroom dynamics*. Oxford: Oxford University Press.

Harmer, J. 2001. *The practice of English language teaching* (3rd edition). Harlow: Longman.

Harmer, J. 2003. Popular culture, methods, and context. *ELT Journal* 57(3): 288–94.

Helms, R. 1999. An exploration of professional development within the field of teaching English as a foreign language. Unpublished MSc dissertation, Graduate School of Social and Political Studies, University of Edinburgh.

Henesey-Smith, V. 1997. *The special learning needs of people suffering from their experiences of torture and trauma.* Adelaide: AMES, Adelaide Institute of TAFE.

Highet, G. 1963. *The art of teaching.* London: Methuen.

Hook, P. and Vass, A. 2000. *Confident classroom leadership.* London: David Fulton.

Jiang, W. 2001. Handling 'culture bumps'. *ELT Journal* 55(4): 382–90.

Johnson, K. E. 1996. The vision versus the reality: The tensions of the TESOL practicum. In Freeman, D. and Richards, J. C. (eds.) *Teacher learning in language teaching.* Cambridge: Cambridge University Press 30–49.

Karavas-Doukas, E. 1996. Using attitude scales to investigate teachers' attitudes to the communicative approach. *ELT Journal* 50(3): 187–98.

Knowles, M. S. 1984. *The adult learner: A neglected species.* Houston, TX: Gulf Publishing.

Korobkin, D. 1988. Humor in the classroom: Considerations and strategies. *College Teaching* 36(4): 154–8.

Kounin, J. 1970. *Discipline and group management in classrooms.* New York: Holt, Rinehart & Winston.

Kumaravadivelu, B. 2001. Towards a postmodern pedagogy. *TESOL Quarterly*, 35(4): 537–60.

LaGaipa, J. J. 1977. The effects of humour on the flow of social conversation. In Chapman, A. J. and Foot, H. C. (eds.) *It's a funny thing, humour.* Oxford: Pergamon.

Lave, J. and Wenger, E. 1991. *Situated learning: Legitimate peripheral participation.* Cambridge: Cambridge University Press.

Lightbown, P. M. and Spada, N. 1999. *How languages are learned.* Oxford: Oxford University Press.

Littlewood, W. 2000. Do Asian students really want to listen and obey? *ELT Journal* 54(1): 31–6.

Littlewood, W. 2004. The task-based approach: Some questions and suggestions. *ELT Journal* 58(4): 319–26.

Livingston, C. and Borko, H. 1989. Expert–novice differences in teaching: A cognitive analysis and implications for teacher education. *Journal of Teacher Education* 40(4): 36–42.

Lortie, D. 1975. *School teacher.* Chicago: University of Chicago Press.

Luft, J. 1984. *Group processes: An introduction to group dynamics.* Palo Alto, CA: Mayfield.

Martineau, W. H. 1972. A model of the social functions of humor. In Goldstein, J. H. and McGhee, P. E. (eds.) *The psychology of humor: Theoretical perspectives and empirical issues.* New York: Academic Press, 101–25.

Martinez, A. 1997. *Teaching survivors of torture and trauma: A handbook for teachers.* Sydney: TAFE Multicultural Education Unit, NSW TAFE Commission.

Meddings, L. 2004. Running after the gravy train. *Education Guardian*, 29 Jan 2004.

Medin, D. L. and Ross, B. H. 1992. *Cognitive psychology.* Fort Worth, TX: Harcourt Brace Jovanovich.

References

Meyer, J. E. L. 2003. PRC students and group work: Their actions and reactions. In Lee, G. L., Meyer, J. E. L., Varaprasad, C. and Young, C. (eds.) *Teaching English to students from China*. Singapore: Singapore University Press, 73–93.

Miles, M. B. and Huberman, A. M. 1984. *Qualitative data analysis: A sourcebook of new methods*. Newbury Park, CA: Sage.

Nixon, U. 1993. Coping in Australia: Problems faced by overseas students. *Prospect* 8(3): 42–51.

Noddings, N. 2001. The caring teacher. In Richardson, V. (ed.) *Handbook of research on teaching*. 4th edition. Washington: American Educational Research Association, 99–105.

Nuffield Languages Inquiry. 2000. *Languages: The next generation*. London: Nuffield.

Nunan, D. 1996. Hidden voices: Insiders' perspectives on classroom interaction. In Bailey, K. M. and Nunan, D. *Voices from the language classroom: Qualitative research in second language education*. Cambridge: Cambridge University Press, 41–56.

Ormrod, J. E. 2000. *Educational psychology* (3rd edition). Upper Saddle River, NJ: Prentice-Hall.

Owens, R. 1991. *Organizational behavior in education*. Boston: Allyn & Bacon.

Oxford, R. L. 1999. Anxiety and the language learner: New insights. In Arnold, J. (ed.) *Affect in language learning*. Cambridge: Cambridge University Press, 58–67.

Pajares, M. F. 1992. Teachers' beliefs and educational research: Cleaning up a messy construct. *Review of Educational Research* 62/3: 307–32.

Qualifications and Curriculum Authority. 2004. *Modern Foreign Languages in the Key Stage 4 Curriculum*. London: Qualifications and Curriculum Authority.

Richards, J. C. 1998. *Beyond training: Perspectives on language teacher education*. Cambridge: Cambridge University Press.

Richards, J. C. and Rodgers, T. S. 2001. *Approaches and methods in language teaching*. (2nd edition). Cambridge: Cambridge University Press.

Roberts, J. 1998. *Language teacher education*. London: Arnold.

Rogers, C. R. 1961. *On becoming a person*. Boston: Houghton Mifflin.

Rubin, L. J. 1985. *Artistry in teaching*. New York: Random House.

Salmon, P. 1988. *Psychology for teachers: An alternative approach*. London: Hutchinson.

Sato, K. 2002. Practical understandings of communicative language teaching and teacher development. In Savignon, S. J. (ed.) *Interpreting language teaching: Contexts and concerns in teacher education*. Newhaven, CT: Yale University Press.

Sato, K. and Kleinsasser, R. C. 1999. Communicative language teaching (CLT): Practical understandings. *Modern Language Journal* 83(4): 494–517.

Schmuck, R. A. and Schmuck, P. A. 2001. *Group processes in the classroom*. (8th edition). Madison, WI: Brown & Benchmark.

Schön, D. A. 1987. *Educating the reflective practitioner: Towards a new design for teaching and learning in the professions*. San Francisco: Jossey Bass.

Scrivener, J. 1994. *Learning teaching*. Oxford: Heinemann.

Seifert, C. M., Patalano, A. L., Hammond, K. L. and Converse, T. M. 1997. Experience and expertise: The role of memory in planning for opportunities. In Feltovich, P. J., Ford, K. M. and Hoffman, R. R. (eds.) *Expertise in context*. Menlo Park, CA: AAAI Press/The MIT Press, 101–23.

Selleck, D. F. 1991. *The use of humor in the English as a second language classroom*. San Francisco: San Francisco State University.

Senior, R. 1999. *The good language class: Teacher perceptions*. Unpublished doctoral dissertation. Perth, Western Australia: Edith Cowan University.

Senior, R. 2001. The role of humour in the development and maintenance of class cohesion. *Prospect* 16(2): 45–54.

Senior, R. 2002. A class-centred approach to language teaching. *ELT Journal* 56(4): 397–403.

Senior, R. 2004. A spirit of cohesion. *English Teaching Professional*. November 2004(35): 48–50.

Senior, R. 2005. The benefits of brainstorming. *English Teaching Professional*. 2005(41): 26–7.

Shaw, M. E. 1981. *Group dynamics: The psychology of small group behavior*. New York: McGraw-Hill.

Smith, D. 1996. Teacher decision making in the adult ESL classroom. In Freeman, D. and Richards, J. (eds.) *Teacher learning in language teaching*. Cambridge: Cambridge University Press, 197–216.

Speziale, H. S. and Carpenter, D. R. 2003. *Qualitative research in nursing: Advancing the humanistic imperative*. 3rd edition. Philadelphia: Lippincott, Williams & Wilkins.

Stein, E. W. 1997. A look at expertise from a social perspective. In Feltovich, P. J., Ford, K. M. and Hoffman, R. R. (eds.) *Expertise in context*. Menlo Park, CA: AAAI Press/the MIT Press, 181–94.

Stevick, E. 1976. *Memory, meaning and method*. Rowley, MA: Newbury House.

Stevick, E. 1980. *Teaching languages: A way and ways*. Cambridge, MA: Newbury House.

Strauss, A. and Corbin, J. 1998. *Basics of qualitative research: Techniques and procedures for developing grounded theory*. (2nd edition). Thousand Oaks, CA: Sage.

Szesztay, M. 2004. Teachers' ways of knowing. *ELT Journal* 58(2): 129–36.

Tardy, C. M. and Snyder, B. 2004. 'That's why I do it': 'Flow' and EFL teachers' practices. *ELT Journal* 58(2): 118–26.

Thompson, G. 1996. Some misconceptions about communicative language teaching. *ELT Journal* 50(1): 9–15.

Thornbury, S. and Meddings, L. 2002. Using a coursebook the Dogme way. *Modern English Teacher* 11(1): 36–40.

Thorp, D. 1991. 'Confused encounters': Differing expectations in the EAP classroom. *ELT Journal* 45(2): 108–18.

Tsui, A. B. M. 1996. Learning how to teach ESL writing. In Freeman, D. and

Richards, J. C. (eds.) *Teacher learning in language teaching*. Cambridge: Cambridge University Press, 97–119.

Tsui, A. B. M. 2003. *Understanding expertise in teaching: Case studies of ESL teachers*. Cambridge: Cambridge University Press.

van Lier, L. 1988. *The classroom and the language learner*. Harlow: Longman.

van Lier, L. 1996. *Interaction in the language curriculum*. Harlow: Addison Wesley Longman.

Vaughan, G. and Hogg, M. 1995. *Introduction to social psychology*. Sydney: Prentice-Hall.

Wajnryb, R. 1988. V is for vulnerability: Some reflections on learning and the learner. *Prospect* 3(3): 339–51.

Ward, H. 2005. Little England expects . . . everyone to speak English. *Times Educational Supplement*, 1 July 2005.

Watts, C. 2004. Some reasons for the decline in numbers of MFL students at degree level. *Language Learning Journal* 29: 59–67.

Watts, R. and Horne, D. J. de L. (eds.) 1994. *Coping with trauma: The victim and the helper*. Brisbane: Australian Academic Press.

Widdowson, H. G. 1990. *Aspects of language teaching*. Oxford: Oxford University Press.

Williams, M. and Burden, R. L. 1997. *Psychology for language teachers*. Cambridge: Cambridge University Press.

Willis, J. 1996. *A framework for task-based learning*. Harlow: Pearson Education.

Wilson, G. L. 2002. *Groups in context: Leadership and participation in small groups*. 6th edition. Boston: McGraw-Hill.

Xu, Z. 2001. Problems and strategies of teaching English in large classes in the People's Republic of China. Proceedings of the 2001 Teaching and Learning Forum, Curtin University, Perth, Western Australia, available at http://lsn.curtin.edu.au/tlf/tlf2001/xu.html

Ziv, A. 1976. Facilitating effects of humor on creativity. *Journal of Educational Psychology* 68: 318–22.

Ziv, A. 1983. The influence of humorous atmosphere on divergent thinking. *Contemporary Educational Psychology* 8: 68–75.

Index

Index

Index